Edwin Abbott Abbott

The kernel and the husk

Letters on spiritual Christianity

Edwin Abbott Abbott

The kernel and the husk
Letters on spiritual Christianity

ISBN/EAN: 9783337334215

Printed in Europe, USA, Canada, Australia, Japan

Cover: Foto ©Lupo / pixelio.de

More available books at **www.hansebooks.com**

AND

THE HUSK

Letters on Spiritual Christianity

BY THE AUTHOR OF
"PHILOCHRISTUS" AND "ONESIMUS"

BOSTON
ROBERTS BROTHERS
1887

TO

THE DOUBTERS OF THIS GENERATION

AND

THE BELIEVERS OF THE NEXT

TO THE READER

THE time is not perhaps far distant when few will believe in miracles who do not also believe in an infallible Church; and then, such books as the present will appeal to a larger circle. But, as things are, the author would beg all those who worship a miraculous Christ without doubt and difficulty to pause here and read no further. The book is not intended for them; it is intended for those alone to whom it is dedicated, "the doubters of this generation."

For there are some who feel drawn towards the worship of Christ by love and reverence, yet repelled by an apparently inextricable connection of the story of Christ with a miraculous element which, in their minds, throws a doubt over the whole of His acts, His doctrine, His character, and even His existence. Others, who worship Christ, worship Him insecurely and tremulously. They assume that their faith must rest on the basis of the Bible miracles; and at times they cannot quite suppress a thrill of doubt and terror lest some horrible discovery of fresh truth, resulting in the destruction of the miraculous element of the Bible, may impair their right to regard Christ as "anything better than a mere man." It is to these two classes—the would-be worshippers and the doubtful worshippers of Christ—that the following Letters are addressed by one who has for many years found peace and salvation in the worship of a non-miraculous Christ.

Not very long ago, but some years after the publication of a work called *Philochristus*, the author received a letter from a stranger and fellow-clergyman, asking him whether he could spare half an hour to visit him on his death-bed, "dying of a disease"—so ran the letter—"which will be fatal within some uncertain weeks (possibly however days, possibly months). No pains just now, head clear, voice sound. And mind at peace, but the peace of reverent agnosticism. . . . . . Now I have read and appreciated *Philochristus*. It would comfort my short remainder of life if you would come and look me dying in the face and say, 'This theology and Christology of mine is not merely literary: I feel with joy of heart that God is not unknown to man: try even now to feel with me.'"

Of what passed at the subsequent interview nothing must be said except that the dying man (whose anticipations of death were speedily verified) expressed the conviction that one reason why he had fallen into that abyss of agnosticism—for an abyss he then felt it to be—was that he had been "taught to believe too much when young;" and he urged and almost besought that something might be done soon to "give young men a religion that would wear." These words were not to be forgotten; they recurred again and again to the author with the force of a command. The present work is an attempt to carry them into effect, an attempt, by one who has passed through doubts into conviction, to look the doubting reader in the face and say, "This theology and Christology of mine is not merely literary. I feel with joy of heart that God is not unknown to man. Try even now to feel with me."

The author does not profess to clear Christianity from all "difficulties." If a revelation is to enlarge our conceptions of God, it must involve some spiritual effort on our part to receive the larger truth; if it claims to be historical, it may well impose on some of its adherents the labour needed for the judgment of historical evidence; if it prompts, without enforcing, obedience, it must excite in all some questionings as to the causes which led the Revealer not to make His revelation irresistibly convincing. Even the explanations of the mysterious phenomena of motion, light, and chemistry, involve "difficulties" in the acceptance of still more mysterious Laws which we cannot at present explain. Nevertheless we all feel that we understand astronomy better in the light of the Law of gravitation: and in the same way some may feel that Christianity becomes more spiritual, as well as more clear, when it becomes more natural; and that many of its so-called "difficulties" fade or vanish, when what may be called its celestial and its terrestrial phenomena are found to rest upon similar principles.

TABLE OF CONTENTS

Letter		Page
1	Introductory	1
2	Personal	5
3	Knowledge	20
4	Ideals	29
5	Ideals and Tests	40
6	Imagination and Reason	47
7	The Culture of Faith	59
8	Faith and Demonstration	72
9	Satan and Evolution	80
10	Illusions	97
11	What is Worship?	111
12	The Worship of Christ	125
13	What is "Nature"?	134
14	The Miracles of the Old Testament	142
15	The Miracles of the New Testament	158
16	The Growth of the Gospels	170
17	Christian Illusions	185
18	Are the Miracles inseparable from the Life of Christ?	201
19	The Feeding of the Four Thousand and the Five Thousand	212
20	The Manifestation of Christ to St. Paul	225
21	The Development of Imagination and its bearing on the Revelation of Christ's Resurrection	233
22	Christ's Resurrection regarded naturally	240
23	Faith in the spiritual Resurrection is better than so-called knowledge of the material Resurrection	246
24	What is a Spirit?	258
25	The Incarnation	267
26	Prayer, Heaven, Hell	281
27	Pauline Theology	298
28	Objections	310
29	Can Natural Christianity commend itself to the masses?	320

APPENDIX

30	Can a believer in Natural Christianity be a Minister in the Church of England?	339
31	What the Bishops might do	354
	DEFINITIONS	369

THE KERNEL

AND

THE HUSK.

INTRODUCTORY

I

My dear ——,

I am more pained than surprised to infer from your last letter that your faith has received a severe shock. A single term at the University has sufficed to make you doubt whether you retain a belief in miracles; and "If miracles fall, the Bible falls; and with the fall of the Bible I lose Christ; and if I must regard Christ as a fanatic, I do not see how I can believe in a God who suffered such a one as Christ thus to be deceived and to deceive others." Such appear to be the thoughts that are passing through your mind, as I infer them from incidental and indirect expressions rather than from any definite statement.

Unfortunately I understand all this too well not to be able to follow with ease such phases of disbelief even when conveyed in hints. Many young men begin by being taught to believe too much, a great deal too much. Then, when they find they must give up something, (the husk of the kernel) their teachers too often bid them swallow husk and all, on pain of swallowing nothing: and they prefer to swallow nothing. An instance of this at once occurs to me. Many years ago, a young man who wished to be ordained, asked me to read the Old Testament with him. We set to work at once and read some miraculous history—I forget precisely what—in which I thought my young friend must needs see a difficulty. So I began to point out how the difficulty might be at least diminished by critical considerations. I say " I began : " for I stopped as soon as I had begun, finding that my friend saw no difficulty at all. He accepted every miracle on every page of the Old and New Testament on the authority of the Bible; just as a Roman Catholic accepts every ecclesiastical doctrine on the authority of the Church. This seemed to me not a state of mind that I ought to interfere with : I might do more harm than good. So I stopped. But I have since regretted it. Circumstances prevented me from meeting my friend for some weeks. During that time he had fallen in with companions of negative views, against which he had no power to maintain his position: and he had passed from believing everything to believing nothing. That is only too easy a transition ; but I hope you will never experience it. Surely there is a medium between swallowing the husk, and throwing the nut away. Is it not possible to throw away the husk and keep the kernel?

Now I have no right (and therefore I try to feel no wish) to extract from you a confidence that you do not care to repose in me. I have never tried to shake any one's faith in miracles. There may come—I think there will soon come—a time when a belief in miracles will be found so incompatible with the reverence which we ought to feel for the Supreme Order as almost to necessitate superstition, and to encourage immorality in the holder of the belief: and then it might be necessary to express one's condemnation of miracles plainly and even aggressively. But that time has not come yet: and for most people, at present, an acceptance of miracles seems, and perhaps is, a necessary basis for their acceptance of Christ. In such minds I would no more wish to disturb the belief in miracles than I would shake a little child's faith that his father is perfectly good and wise. But when a man says, "the miracles of Christ are inextricably connected with the life of Christ; I am forced to reject the former, and therefore I must also reject the latter"—then I feel moved to shew him that there is no such inextricable connection, and that Christ will remain for us a necessary object of worship, even if we detach the miracles from the Gospels. Now I cannot do this without shewing that the miraculous accounts stand on a lower level than the rest of the Gospel narrative, and that they may have been easily introduced into the Gospels without any sufficient basis of fact, and yet without any intention to deceive; so that the discrediting of the miracles will not discredit their non-miraculous context. In doing this, I might possibly destroy any lingering vestige of belief which you may still have in the miraculous; and this I am most unwilling to do, if you find miracles a necessary foundation of Christian faith.

I do not therefore quite know as yet how I ought to try to help you, except by saying that I have myself passed through the same valley of doubt through which you are passing now, and that I have reached a faith in Christ which is quite independent of any belief in the miraculous, and which enables me not only to trust in Him, but also to worship Him. This new faith appears to me purer, nobler, and happier, as well as safer, than the old: but I do not feel sure that it is attainable (in the present condition of thought) without more unprejudiced reflection and study than most people are willing to devote to subjects of this kind. And to give up the old faith, without attaining the new, would be a terrible disaster. Hence I am in doubt, not about what is best, but about what may be *best for you*. Do not at all events assume —so much I can safely say—that you must give up your faith in Christ, if you are obliged to give up your belief in miracles. At the very least, wait a while; stand on the old paths; keep up the old habits, above all, the habit of prayer; pause and look round you a little before taking the next step. I do not say, though I am inclined to say, "avoid for the present all discussions with people of negative views," because I fear my advice, though really prudent, would seem to you cowardly: but I do unhesitatingly say, "avoid all frivolous talk, and light, airy, epigrammatic conversations on religious subjects." You cannot hope to retain or regain faith if you throw away the habit of reverence. With this advice, farewell for the present.

II

My dear ——,

You tell me that you fear your faith is far too roughly shaken to suffer now from anything that may be said against miracles: you are utterly convinced that they are false. As for the possibility of worshipping a non-miraculous Christ, "the very notion of it," you say, " is inconceivable: it seems like a new religion, and must surely be no more than a very transient phase of thought." But you would "very much like to know what processes of reasoning led to such a state of mind," and how long I have retained it.

I think I am hardly doing you an injustice in inferring from some other expressions in your letter, about "the difficulty which clergymen must necessarily feel in putting themselves into the mental position of the laity," that you entertain some degree of prejudice against my views, not only because they appear to you novel, but because—although you hardly like to say so—they come from a clerical source, and are likely to savour of clericalism. Let me see if I can put your thoughts into the plain words from which your own modesty and sense of propriety have caused you to refrain. " A clergyman," you say to yourself, " has enlisted; he has deliberately taken a side and is bound to fight for it. After twenty years of seeing one side of a question, or only so much of the other side as is convenient to see, how can even a candid, middle-aged cleric see two sides impartially? All his interests combine with all his sympathies to make him at least in some sense orthodox. The desire of social esteem, the hope of preferment, loyalty to the Church, loyalty to Christ Himself, make him falsely true to that narrow form of truth which he has bound himself to serve. Even if truth and irresistible conviction force him to deviate a little from the beaten road of orthodoxy, he will find his way back by some circuitous by-path; and of this kind of self-persuasion I have a remarkable instance in the person of my old friend, who rejects miracles and yet persuades himself that he worships Christ. He has cut away his foundations and now proceeds to substitute an aerial basis upon which the old superstructure is to remain as before. Such a novel condition of mind as this can only be a very transient phase."

I do not complain of this prejudice against novelty, although it comes ungraciously from one who is himself verging on advanced and novel views. It is good that new opinions should be suspiciously scrutinized and passed through the quarantine of prejudice. And when a man feels (as I do) that he has at last attained a profound spiritual truth which will, in all probability, be generally accepted by educated Christians who are not Roman Catholics, before the twentieth century is far advanced, he can well afford to be patient of prejudice. Even though the truth be not accepted now, it is pretty sure to be restated by others with more skill and cogency, and perhaps at a fitter season, and to gain acceptance in due time. But when you speak of my opinions as a "transient phase," which I am likely soon to give up, and when you shew a manifest suspicion that any modicum of orthodoxy in me must needs be the result of a clerical bias, then I hardly see how to reply except by giving you a detailed answer to your question about "the processes" by which I was led to "such a novel condition of mind." Yet how to do this without being somewhat egotistically autobiographical I do not know. Some good may come of egotism perhaps, if it leads you to see that even a clergyman may think for himself, and work out a religious problem without regard to consequences. So on the whole I think I will risk egotism for your sake. A few paragraphs of autobiography may serve as a summary of the argument which I might draw out more fully in future letters. If I am tedious, lay the blame on yourself and on your insinuation that my views must be "a transient phase." A man who is getting on towards his fiftieth year and has retained a form—a novel form if you please—of religious conviction for a full third of his life may surely claim that his views—so far at least as he himself is concerned—are not to be called "transient." Prepare then for my *Apologia*.

During my childhood I was very much left to myself in the matter of religion, and may be almost said to have picked it up in a library. I was never made to learn the Creed by heart, nor the Catechism, nor even the Ten Commandments; and to this day I can recollect being reproached by a class-master when I was nearly fourteen years old, for not knowing which was the Fifth Commandment. All that I could plead in answer was, that if he would tell me what it was about, I could give him the substance of the precept. Having read through nearly the whole of Adam Clarke's commentary as a boy of ten or eleven, and having subsequently imbued myself with books of Evangelical doctrine, I was perfectly "up," or thought I was, in the Pauline scheme of salvation, and felt a most lively interest—on Sundays, and in dull moments on week days, and especially in times of illness, of which I had plenty—in the salvation of my own soul. My religion served largely to intensify my natural selfishness. In better and healthier moments, my conscience revolted against it; and at times I felt that the morality of Plutarch's Lives was better than that of St. Paul's Epistles—as I interpreted them. Only to one point in the theology of my youthful days can I now look back with pleasure; and that is to my treatment of the doctrine of Predestinarianism and necessity. On this matter I argued as follows: "If God knows all things beforehand, God has them, or may have them, written down in a book; and if all things that are going to happen are already written down in a book, it's of no use our trying to alter them. So, if it's predestined that I shall have my dinner to-day, I shall certainly have it, even if I don't come home in time, or even though I lock myself up in my bedroom. But *practically, if I don't come home in time, I know I shall not have my dinner. Therefore it's no use talking about these things in this sort of way, because it doesn't answer; and I shall not bother myself any more about Predestination, but act as though it did not exist.*"[1] This argument, if it can be called an argument, I afterwards found sheltering itself under the high authority of Butler's *Analogy*; and I still adhere to it, after an experience of more than five and thirty years. To some, this "Short Way with Predestinarians" may seem highly illogical; but it *works*.

Up to this time I had been little, if at all, impressed by preaching. Our old Rector was a good Greek scholar and a gentleman; but he had a difficulty in making his thoughts intelligible to any but a refined minority among the congregation; and even that select few was made fewer, partly by an awkwardness of gesture which reminded one of Dominie Sampson, and partly by a grievous impedi-

---

[1] That children, even at a much younger age than ten, do sometimes exercise their young minds to very ill purpose about these subtle metaphysical questions is probably within the experience of all who know anything about children, and it is amusingly illustrated by the following answer (which I have on the authority of an intimate friend) from a seven-years-old to his mother when blaming him for some misconduct: "Why did you born me then? I didn't want to be borned. You should have asked me before you borned me."

ment in his speech. Consequently I had been permitted, and indeed encouraged, never to listen, nor even to appear to listen, to the weekly sermon; and as soon as the Rector gave out his text, I used to take up my Bible and read steadily away till the sermon was over. This sort of thing went on till I was about sixteen years old; when a new Rector came to preach his first sermon. That was a remarkable Sunday for me. To my surprise, when he read out his text, and I, in accordance with unbroken precedent, reached out my hand for the invariable Bible, my father, somewhat abruptly, took it out of my hand, bidding me "for once shut up that book and listen to a sermon." I can still remember the resentment I felt at this infringement on my theological and constitutional rights, and how I stiffened my neck and hardened my heart and determined "hearing to hear, but not to understand." But I was compelled to understand. For here, to my astonishment, was an entirely new religion. This man's Christianity was not a "scheme of salvation;" it was a faith in a great Leader, human yet divine, who was leading the armies of God against the armies of Evil; "Each for himself is the Devil's own watchword: but with us it must be each for Christ, and each for all." The scales fell from my eyes. After all, then, Christianity was not less noble than Plutarch's lives; it was more noble. There was to be a contest; yet not each man contending for his own soul, but for good against evil. A Christian was not a mercenary fighting for reward, nor a slave fighting for fear of stripes, but a free soldier fighting out of loyalty to Christ and to humanity.

But what about the doctrine of the Atonement, Justification by Faith, and the other Pauline doctrines? About these our new Rector did not say much that I could understand. He was a foremost pupil of Mr. Maurice, and in Mr. Maurice's books (which now began to be read freely in my home) I began to search for light on these questions. But help I found none or very little, except in one book. Mr. Maurice seemed to me, and still seems, a very obscure writer. Partly owing to a habit of taking things for granted and "thinking underground," partly (and much more) owing to a confusing use of pronouns for nouns and other mere mechanical defects of style, he requires very careful reading. But his book on Sacrifice, after I had three times read it through, gave me more intellectual help than perhaps any other book on Christian doctrine; for here first I learned to look below the surface of a rite at its inner meaning, and also to discern the possibility of illustrating that inner meaning by the phenomena of daily life. It was certainly a revelation to me to know that the sacrifice of a lamb by a human offerer was nothing, except so far as it meant the sacrifice of a human life, and that the sacrifice of a life meant no more (but also no less) than conforming one's life to God's will, doing (and not saying merely) "Thy will, not mine, be done." If one theological process could be illustrated in this way, why not another? If "sacrifice" was going on before my eyes every day, why might there not be also justification by faith, imputation of righteousness, remission of sins, yes, even atonement itself? Thus there was sown in my mind the seed of the notion that all the Pauline doctrines might be natural, and that Redemption through Christ was only a colossal form of that kind of redemption which was going on around me, Redemption through Nature. This thought was greatly stimulated by the study of *In Memoriam*, which was given to me by a college friend about the time when I lost a brother and a sister, both dying within a few weeks of one another. I read the poem again and again, and committed much of it to memory; and it exerted an "epoch-making" influence on my life. However, for a long time this notion of the naturalness of Redemption existed for me merely in the germ.

Meantime, as to the miracles I had no doubts at all, or only such transient doubts as were suggested by pictures of Holy Families and other sacred subjects, which exhibited Christ as essentially non-human, with a halo around his head, or as an infant with three outstretched fingers blessing his kneeling mother. As a youth, I took it for granted that God could not become man save by a miracle, and therefore that the God-man must work miracles. Further, I assumed that Moses and some of the prophets had worked miracles, and if so, how could it be that the Servants should work miracles and the Son should not? As I grew towards manhood, such rising qualms of doubt as I felt on this point were stilled by the suggestion (which I found in Trench's book on miracles) that the miracles of Christ must be in accordance with some latent law of spiritual nature. It was a little strange certainly that these latent laws should be utilised only for the children of Abraham, and it was inconvenient that the miracles of Moses should be, materially speaking, so stupendously superior to those of Christ; but I took refuge in the greater beauty and emblematic meaning of the latter. Even at the time when I signed the Thirty-nine Articles I had no suspicion that the miracles were not historical. Partly, I had never critically and systematically studied the Gospels as one studies Thucydides or Æschylus; partly the miracles had always been kept in the background by my Rector and the books of the Broad Church School, and I had been accustomed to rest my faith on Christ Himself and not on the miracles; and so it came to pass that, for some time after I was ordained, I was quite content to accept all the miracles of the Old and New Testaments, and to be content with the explanation suggested by "latent laws."

But now that I was ordained, I set to work in earnest (the stress of working for a degree and the need of earning one's living had left no time for it before) at the study of the New Testament. Of course I had "got it up" before, often enough, for the purpose of passing examinations; but now I began to study it for its own sake and at leisure. While reading for the Theological Tripos I had been struck by the inadequacy of many of the theological books that I had had to "get up." Especially on the first three Gospels—looking at them critically, as I had been accustomed to look at Greek and Latin books—I was amazed to find that little or nothing had been done by English scholars to compare the different styles and analyse the narratives into their component parts. For such a task I had myself received some little preparation. I had picked up my classics without very much assistance from the ordinary means, mainly by voluntarily committing to memory whole books or long continuous passages of the best authors, and so imbuing myself with them as to "get into the swing of the author." I had early begun to tabulate these differences of style; and in my final and most important University examination I remember sending up more than one piece of composition rendered in two styles. Though I was never a first-rate composer, owing to my want of practice at school, this method had succeeded in bringing me to the front in "my year;" and I now desired to apply my classical studies to the criticism of the first three Gospels. It seemed to me a monstrous thing that we should have three accounts of the same life, accounts closely agreeing in certain parts, but widely varying in others, and yet that, with all the aids of modern criticism, we should not be able to determine which accounts, or which parts of the three accounts, were the earliest. At the same time I began to apply the same method, though without the same attempt at exactness, to the study of the text of Shakespeare; in which I perceived some differences of style that implied difference of date, and some that appeared to imply difference of authorship.

About this time people began to talk in popular circles concerning Evolution, and alarm began to be felt in some quarters at the difficulty of harmonizing its theories with theology. With these fears I never could in the least degree sympathize. I welcomed Evolution as a luminous commentary on the divine scheme of the Redemption of mankind. That most stimulating of books, the *Advancement of Learning*, had taught me to be prepared to find that in very many cases "while Nature or man intendeth one thing, God worketh another;" and it was a joy to me to find new light thrown by Evolution on the unfathomable problems of waste, death, and conflict. Death and conflict could never be thus explained—I knew that—but one was enabled to wait more patiently for that explanation which will never come to us till we are behind the veil, when one found that death and conflict had at least been subordinated to progress and development. So I thought; and so I said from the pulpit of one of the Universities in times when the clergy had not yet learned to call Darwin "a man of God." My doctrine was thought "advanced" in those days; but time has gone on and left me, in some respects, behind it. I should never have thought, and should not think now, of calling Darwin "a man of God," except so far as all patient seekers after truth are men of God: but I still adhere to the belief that Evolution has made it more easy to believe in a rational, that is to say a non-miraculous, though supernatural, Christianity.

In this direction, then, my thoughts went forward and, so far, found no stumbling-block. Guided by the poets and analytic novelists, I was also learning to find in the study of the phenomena of daily life fresh illustrations of the Pauline theology, confirming and developing my notion (now of some years' standing) that the Redemption of mankind was natural, nothing more than a colossal representation of the spiritual phenomena that may be seen in ordinary men and women every day of our lives; just as the lightning-flash is no more than (upon a large scale) the crackling of the hair beneath the comb. Good men and women, I perceived, are daily redeeming the bad, bearing their sins, imputing righteousness to them, giving up their lives for them, and imbuing them with a good spirit. This thought, as it gained force, was a great help towards a rational Christianity.

But now my feet began to be entangled in snares and pitfalls. I had begun the study of the Greek Testament, believing that it would bring forth *some* new truth, and assuming that *all* truth must tend to the glory of God and of Christ. "Christ," I said, "is the living Truth, so that I have but, as Plato says, to 'follow the Argument,' and that must lead me to the truth, and therefore to Him." But I was not prepared for the result. After some years of work I found myself gradually led to the conclusion that the miraculous element in the Gospels was not historical. A mere glance at the Old Testament shewed that, if there was not evidence enough for the miracles in the New Testament, much less was there for the miracles in the Old.

Before me rose up day by day fresh facts and inferences, not only demonstrating the insufficiency of the usual evidence to prove that the miracles were true, but also indicating a very strong probability that they were false. Often, as I studied the accounts of a miracle, I could see it as it were in the act of growing up, watch its first entrance into the Gospel narrative, note its modest beginning, its subsequent development: and then I was forced to give it up. Worst of all, that miracle of miracles which was most precious to me, the Resurrection of Christ, began to appear to be supported by the feeblest evidence of all. I had not at that time learned to distinguish between the Resurrection of Christ's material body and the Resurrection of His Spirit or spiritual body. Christ's Resurrection seemed to me therefore in those days to be either a Resurrection of the material and tangible body or no Resurrection at all. Now for the Resurrection of the material body I began to be forced to acknowledge that I could find no basis of satisfying testimony. I had heard an anecdote of the Head of some College of Oxford in old days, how he fell asleep after dinner in the Combination Room, while the Fellows over their wine were discussing theology, and presently made them all start by exclaiming as he awoke, "After all there, is no evidence for the Resurrection of Christ!" I realized that now, not with a start, but gradually, and with a growing feeling of deep and wearing anxiety. If the Resurrection of Christ fell, what was to become of my faith in Christ?

Amid this impending ruin of my old belief I saw one tower standing firm. It was clear that *something* had happened after the death of Christ to make new men of His disciples. It was clear also that St. Paul had seen *something* that had induced him to believe that Christ had risen from the dead. That which had convinced St. Paul, an enemy, might very well convince the Apostles, the devoted followers of Christ. What was this *something?* It seemed to me that I ought to try to find out. Meantime, I determined to adopt the advice I gave you in my last letter—to stand upon the old ways and look around me and consider my path before taking another step. Circumstances had placed me in such a position that I was not called on to decide whether a clergyman could entertain such views as were looming on me, and remain a clergyman. I was not engaged in any work directly or indirectly requiring clerical qualifications; and as far as my affections and sentiments were concerned, I went heartily with the services of the Church of England.

So I resolved to put aside all theology for two or three years and to devote myself, during that time, to literary work of another kind. Meantime, I would retain, as far as possible, the old religious ways of thought, and, at all events, the old habits. None the less, I would not give up the intention of investigating the whole truth about the Resurrection. That there was some nucleus of truth I felt quite certain; and even if that truth had been embedded in some admixture of illusion, what then? Were there no illusions in the history of science? Were there no illusions in the history of God's Revelation of Himself through the Old and New Testaments? Might it not be God's method of Revelation that men should pass through error to the truth? This line of thought seemed promising, but I would not at once follow it. I would wait three years and then work out the question of the influence of illusion on religious truth.

An old college acquaintance, an agnostic, whom I met about this time, was not a little startled when I told him my thoughts. He frankly informed me that, though I was "placed in a painful position," I was "bound to speak out." I also thought that I was "bound to speak out;" but I did not feel bound to obtrude immature views upon the world, with the result perhaps of afterwards altering or recanting them. So I took time, plenty of time; I looked about me, on life as well as on books; I formed a habit of testing assumptions and asking the meaning of common words, especially such words as knowledge, faith, certainty, belief, proof, and the like. Believing that theology was made for man and not man for theology, I began to test theological as well as other propositions by the question "How do they *work?*" Meantime I tried my utmost to do the duties of my daily life without distraction and with the same energy as before, hoping that life itself, and the needs of life, would throw some light upon the question, "What knowledge about God is necessary for men who are to do their duty? And how can that knowledge be obtained?"

By these means I was led to see that a great part of what we call knowledge does not come to us, as we falsely suppose it does, through mere logic or Reason, nor through unaided experience, but through the emotions and the Imagination, tested by Reason and experience. Even in the world of science, I found that the so-called "laws and properties of matter," nay, the very existence of matter, were nothing more than suggestions of the scientific Imagination aided by experience. A great part of the environment and development of mankind appeared to have been directed towards the building up of the imaginative faculty, without which, it seemed that religion, as well as poetry, would have been non-existent. So by degrees, it occurred to me that perhaps I had been on the wrong track in my search after religious truth. I had been craving a purely historical and logical proof of Christ's divinity, and had felt miserable that I could not obtain it. But now I perceived that I was not intended to obtain it. Not thus was Christ to be embraced. There must indeed be a basis of fact: but after all it was to that imaginative faculty which we call "faith," that I must look, at least in part, for the right interpretation of fact. That Christ could be apprehended only by faith was a Pauline common-place; but that Christ's Resurrection could be grasped only by faith, and not by the acceptance of evidence, was, to me, a new proposition. But I gradually perceived that it was true. I might be doubtful whether Thomas touched the side of the risen Saviour, yet sure that Christ had risen from the dead in the Spirit, and had manifested Himself after death to His disciples. My standard of certainty being thus shifted, many things of which I had formerly felt certain became uncertain; but, by way of compensation, other things—and these the most necessary and vital—became more certain than ever. I felt less inclined to dogmatize about the existence of matter; but my soul was imbued with a fuller conviction of the existence of a God; and deeper still became the feeling that, so far as things are known to me, there is nothing in heaven or earth more divine than Christ.

Thus at last light dawned upon my darkness; and when the sun rose once more upon me, it was the same sun as before, only more clearly seen above the mists of illusion which had before obscured it. The old beliefs of my youth and childhood remained or came back to me, exhibiting Jesus of Nazareth as the Incarnate Son of God, the Eternal Word triumphant over death, seated at the right hand of the Father in heaven, the source of life and light to all mankind. Like Christian in *Pilgrim's Progress*, I found myself suddenly freed from a great burden —a burden of doubts, and provisos, and conditions which, in old days, had seemed to forbid me from accepting Jesus as the Lord and Saviour of mankind unless I could strain my conscience to accept as true a number of stories many of which I almost certainly knew to be false. In order to believe in Christ, it was now no longer needful to believe in suspensions of the laws of Nature: on the contrary, all Nature seemed to combine to prepare the way to conform humanity to that image of God which was set forth in the Incarnation. I did not, as some Christians do, ignore the existence of Satan (and almost of sin) which Christ Himself most clearly recognized; but I seemed to see that evil was being gradually subordinated to good, and falsehood made the stepping-stone to truth.

Through evil to good; through sin to a righteousness higher than could have been attained save through sin; through falsehood to the truth; through superstition to religion—this seemed to me the divine evolution discernible in the light that was shed from the cross of Christ. No longer now did it seem impossible or absurd that the Gospel of the Truth might have been temporarily obscured by illusions or superstitions even in the earliest times.

I think it must be now some ten years since I settled down to the belief that the history of Christianity had been the history of profound religious truth, contained in, and preserved by, illusions; an ascent of worship through illusion to the truth. A belief that has been fifteen years in making, and for ten years more has been reviewed, criticized, and finally retained as being historically true and spiritually healthful, you must not call, I think, "a transient phase." But I forgive you the expression. A dozen pages of autobiography are a sufficient penalty for three offending words.

III

My dear ——,

You ask me to explain, in detail, what I mean by asserting that the Imagination is the basis of knowledge. "Apparently," you say, "our knowledge of the world external to ourselves seems to you to spring, not from the sensations as interpreted by the Reason, but (at all events to a large extent) from the sensations as interpreted by the Imagination. If you mean this, I wish you would show how the Imagination thus builds up our knowledge of the world. But I think I must have misunderstood you."

You have not misunderstood me. I would go even further than the limits of your statement: for I believe that we are largely indebted to the Imagination for our knowledge, not only of the external world, but also of ourselves. However, suppose we first take a simple instance of the knowledge of external things: "This inkstand is hard. How did I come to know that it was hard? How do I know that it is hard now?"

Let us begin from the beginning. I am an infant scrambling on the floor where the said inkstand is casually lying. Having a congenital impulse (commonly called "instinct") to touch and suck anything that comes in my way, and especially anything bright, I greedily and rapidly approximate my lips to the corner of this polished object. I recoil with a sharp shock of pain. The pain abates. The instinctive recoil from the inkstand has left in me an instinctive aversion to the pain-causing object: but my touching and sucking instinct again revives, and as soon as it prevails over the recoiling instinct, I am impelled again towards the inkstand, not so rapidly as before, but still too rapidly. I recoil again, with pain lessened but still acute. I am acquiring "knowledge:" I "know," though I cannot put it into words, that I have twice found the inkstand not-to-be-rapidly-approached-under-penalty-of-a-certain-kind-of-pain, in other words, "hard." But I try again; I try four, five, six times: I find that when I approach with less velocity my pain is less, and when with sufficiently diminished velocity, there is no pain at all; I touch and suck in peace: but when I forget my experience and suppose that the inkstand—even though I dash wildly at it after my old fashion—will "behave differently this time," I find that I am mistaken: the inkstand will not "behave differently;" it always behaves in the same way. By this time then I know something very important indeed.

But pause now, my friend, and ask yourself how much this infant has a right to say he "knows," so far as the evidence of the senses guides him. All that the senses have told him is that on five, six, seven, say even seventy, occasions, he found the inkstand hard. But is this all that he "knows"? You know perfectly well that he knows infinitely more: he has made a leap from the past into the future and knows that the inkstand *will* be found hard whenever he touches it. When he grows up and attains the power of speech he will generally express his knowledge in the Present Tense: "I must not strike the inkstand with my mouth for it *is* hard:" but in reality this "is" implies "will be;" "I must not strike the inkstand with my mouth for I *shall find* it hard." Now what is it that has produced in him this conviction which no philosopher can justify by mere logic, but which every baby acts on? It seems to have arisen thus. The baby has received in rapid succession two sensations, first, that of a violent approximation to the inkstand, secondly, a sudden shock of pain. Having received this pair of sensations very frequently, he cannot help associating them together in his thoughts; so that now the thought of a violent approximation to the inkstand necessarily suggests to him the thought that it is not-to-be-approached-violently, or " hard." He began by learning to expect that perhaps, or probably, the first sensation would be followed by the second; but having found, after constant experiments, that the second sensation, so far as his experience goes, always follows the first, he gradually passes from belief into certainty, or knowledge, that the second always will, or must, follow the first.

A similar transition is going on at the same time in the infant's mind—I mean the transition from belief to certainty —-in regard to thousands of other propositions besides the one we have selected, "this inkstand is hard." Every single case of such transition facilitates the transition in other cases, by making the child feel that, if he is to get on in the world and make his way through it without incurring the constant pains and penalties of Nature, he must not disregard these juxtapositions, or pairs of sensations, (which, when he grows older, he will, if ever he becomes an educated man, call " cause " and " effect "), but must take them to heart and remember them ; when the first of a familiar pair comes, he must be prepared to find the second immediately following. Not unfrequently the child's limited experience associates together in his mind sensations that Nature has not associated; as, for example, when he infers that a clock must tick because he has never yet in his life seen a clock that has stopped. In this and other cases the child has afterwards to dissociate what he had too hastily joined together, and to correct his conclusions by wider experience. But, on the whole, the transition from belief to certainty, in any one case, is facilitated by the great majority of similar cases in which the same transition is going on with results that are confirmed by his own experience and by that of his elders. What helps the transition, in each case, is its general success; it *works*: it helps the child to move more and more confidently in the world without subjecting himself to the punishments which Nature has attached to ignorance.

Now therefore, reviewing the stages of the progress upwards, we see that the knowledge of which we are speaking is based upon an inherent and fundamental belief of which we can give no logical justification whatever. Why should an inkstand always be hard? The child can allege no reason for this except that, having found the inkstand to be hard in a great number of past instances, he is compelled to believe that it will be always hard, with such a force of conviction that he cannot but feel and say he "knows" it. But of course there is no logical justification for this assertion. He might argue for some months or even years, in precisely the same way about a clock, and say that "a clock always ticks," because he has seen the clock tick times innumerable and never known it not to tick. Why should not a larger experience confute his so-called knowledge in the case of the inkstand as in the case of the clock? As the clock collapses, why should not the nature of the inkstand collapse—become unwound, so to speak, or altogether transmuted? There is no possible answer to this question for the child, at present, except the following:—" It never has done so, and therefore I believe that it never will. I believe in the uniformity of Nature. The sequences of observed cause and effect are Nature's promises, and if she does not keep them, life will break down. I am compelled to believe, and to act on the belief, that life will not break down. I believe that this inkstand is hard, because this belief *works.'*"

I conclude therefore that all knowledge of the kind we are now describing is based on belief (viz. the belief that what has been will be) tested by experience. I think it must also be admitted that Imagination contributed to the result: for the child not only remembers his two past consecutive sensations but gradually *images* in his mind a kind of bond between them, which memory pure and simple could not have contributed. Memory reproduces "Inkstand and *then* hardness;" Imagination paints, or begins to paint, a new idea, "Inkstand and *therefore* hardness." Again, Memory reproduces vaguely numerous instances, "The inkstand was hard ten, eleven, twenty, many times;" then comes Imagination and at a leap sets before the mind an entirely new notion, and invents for it the word "always."

Concerning other and more complex kinds of knowledge what need is there to say a word? For if such simple propositions as "a stone is hard," are shown to depend upon Imagination for suggesting, and Faith for retaining, a conviction of the uniformity of Nature, much more must these influences be presupposed if the child is to attain knowledge about matters avowedly future, *e.g.* "the sun will rise to-morrow." In reality all knowledge of any practical value has to do with a future, immediate or remote; and therefore I do not think I shall be exaggerating in saying that for all knowledge about things outside us we depend largely upon Imagination and Faith.

But I pass now to consider a child's knowledge about himself. Take for example such a proposition as this, "I like sugar." Is Faith or Imagination required to enable a child to arrive at the knowledge of this proposition about himself? I think so. The very use of the word "I," if used intelligently, appears to need some imaginative effort. Of course I do not deny that this subtle metaphysical idea may have been suggested to us originally by our faculty of touch, and especially the faculty of self-pinching or self-touching. I dare say you have read how men have sometimes caught hold of their own benumbed hand by night, and awakened a household by shouting that they had caught a robber: has it ever occurred to you that, if you never had the power of distinguishing your own hand from anybody else's hand by the sense of touch, you might have gone through life with no sense, or with a very tardily acquired sense, of your own identity? If the monkey who boiled his own tail in the caldron had felt no pain, might he not have been excused for doubting sometimes whether the tail belonged to him? And if his head were equally painless or joyless when he thumped it or scratched it, ought he to be condemned for disowning his own head? And if a monkey, or even a child, could not lay claim to its own head, it seems to me doubtful whether he could ever claim such a separation from the outside world as would necessitate his using the word "I." But, as it is, having this self-pinching faculty, the child soon finds that to pinch a ball, or a bladder, or a sister, is an entirely different thing from pinching himself: and this self-touching faculty confirms the evidence suggested by the bumps and thumps of the external world; all of which lead him to the belief that he has a bodily frame of his own, liable to pain and to pleasure, and largely dependent for pain and pleasure on his own motions, which motions he dimly perceives dependent upon something that appears to be inside himself.

But neither this nor any other explanation of the manner in which the sensations prepare the way for the construction of the idea of the "I," ought to prevent us from recognizing that the idea itself is the work of the

Imagination, and not of the unaided sensations, nor of the unaided reason. Self-pinching and contact with the rough external world might convince the child that he was different from his environment at the time when he made his last experiments and underwent his last experiences; but they could not convince him that he *is* different *now*, or that he *will be* different in the next instant; and for this conviction he depends upon faith. Again, the imagination of the " I " seems closely bound up with two other nearly simultaneous imaginations, those of Force and Cause. First he feels a desire to touch the inkstand, then he feels himself moving towards the inkstand, then he feels the inkstand touched. These sequences of desire, action, result, he can repeat as often as he likes. By their frequency therefore, as well as by their vividness, they impress him more powerfully than sequences of phenomena not dependent on himself; and it is from these probably that he first imagines the idea of "must," or "necessity," or "cause and effect." If he feels a desire to move a limb, the motion of the limb immediately follows; it always obeys him; it *must* obey him. He pushes a brick; what caused the brick to fall? He feels that it was his own force that caused it; he no longer looks upon the push and the fall as if the former merely preceded the latter; he imagines a connection of necessity between the push and the fall, the cause and the effect, and gradually comes to imagine himself as the causer of the cause. But all these imaginations are mere imaginations, not proofs. To gather together all the sensations of which he retains the memory, the sensations of which he is at present conscious, and the sensations to which he looks forward, and to put an " I " behind or below all these, as the foundation of them all, and partial causer of them all —what an audacious assumption is this! Not Plato and Aristotle combined could prove to a child, or to the most consummate of philosophers, that he has a right to call himself " I," or that he is any other than a machine and a part of the universal machinery. How can I prove and vindicate my independence, my right to an " I "? By saying that I will do, or not do, and by then doing, or not doing, any conceivable thing at any conceivable time? Such an attempt is futile. The retort is unanswerable: " In the great machine which you call the universe, that small part which you call 'I' was so constructed and wound up that it could no more help saying and doing what it did and said, than a clock could help pointing and striking."

What then is the real proof that we are right in using the word " I " and in distinguishing ourselves from other objects which we call external? There is no proof at all except that, first, we are led to this way of looking at things by Nature and Imagination, and secondly, this way of looking at things *works* best. The " I-view " is better fitted than the " machine-view " to develop in us the faculties of judgment and self-control, to give us a sense of responsibility and a capability of amendment, and to make us ultimately more hopeful and more active. So too, the belief in " cause and effect " *works* better than a mere mental record of past antecedents and sequences, accompanied by a blank and strictly logical neutrality of mind as to what will happen in the future. Faith in "cause and effect" is the foundation of all stable life and all regular progress alike in the individual and in the state. The unfaithful unbeliever in causality is the Esau, both in the moral and in the intellectual world, the happy-go-lucky hunter who depends on stray venison and refuses to resort to system in order to make a sure provision for the needs of the future; the believer is the quiet plodding Jacob who has his goats in the fold where he knows he can find them when wanted. The unbeliever is the unimaginative savage who has not faith enough to see the harvest in the seed ; the believer is the man of civilisation who can trust Nature through six long months of waiting and can say to her, not in the language of hope, "*do ut des,*" but in the language of conviction, "*do daturae.*" Nevertheless, convenient as these ideas may be for our comfort, nay, though they may be even necessary for our existence, we are bound to recollect that they are merely ideas. Like the ideas of force, cause, effect, necessity, so the idea of " I,"—though produced with the aid of experience and tested by appeal to experience and reason —appears to be nothing but a child of the Imagination, and a foster-child of Faith.

Perhaps your conclusion from all this is that I am proving that we can know nothing? Not in the least. What I am saying does not prove that we know less or more than we profess to know at present. I am merely showing that our knowledge comes to us from sources other than those which are ordinarily assumed.

IV

MY DEAR ——,

You ask me to pass to the consideration of knowledge of a new kind, knowledge of mathematical truth. "Here at least," you say, "severe reasoning dominates supreme, and Imagination has no place." "Two and one make there," "The angles at the base of an isosceles triangle are equal : " "surely we may assume that Imagination has nothing to do with these propositions. They must be decided by pure Reason." Never was assumption more grotesque. Excuse me ; but by what other adjective can I characterize the statement that the Imagination has "nothing to do with" propositions for the very terms of which we are indebted to the Imagination ? I maintain without fear of contradiction that the knowledge of these propositions requires an effort of the Imagination so severe that the very young and the completely untrained cannot attain to it.

For, in the first place, what do you mean by "one," "two," and "three " ? I have never had any experience of such things ; nor have you ; nor can you. " Two " oranges, "two" apples, and the like, we have had experience of, and can realize ; but to think of " one " or " two " by themselves (" one " or " two " with " anythings, or with "nothings " after them), "one " or "two " as " abstract ideas "—this really is a most difficult or rather (I am inclined to say) an impossible task. When I say "one" and "two," I think I see before me dimly "one" or "two" dots or small strokes, and I perceive that two and one of these dots or strokes make up three dots or strokes. When I speak of "twenty" and "thirty," I do not see any images of these existences; and when I say that "twenty" and "thirty" make "fifty," I do not realize the process of addition at all visibly; I merely repeat the statement on the authority of previous observations and reasonings mostly made by others and not by myself. But so far as I approximate to the realization of an abstract number, I do it by a kind of negative imagination. And in any case we can hardly deny that all arithmetical propositions, since they employ terms that denote mere imaginary ideas, must be regarded as based on the imagination.

It is the same with Geometry. The whole of what we call "Euclid" is based upon a most aerial effort of the Imagination. We have to imagine lines without thickness, straightness that does not deviate the billionth part of an inch from perfect evenness, perfectly symmetrical circles, and—climax of audacity!—points that have "no parts and no magnitude!" Obviously these things have no existence except in the dreams of Imagination; yet Euclid's severe reasoning applies to none but these things. If you step from your ideal triangle in Dreamland into your material triangle in chalk-land, you step from absolute truth into statements that are not absolutely true. The angles at the base of your chalk isosceles triangle are not exactly equal, if you measure them with sufficient accuracy. In a word the whole of Geometry is an appeal to the Imagination in which the geometer says to us, "I know that my propositions are not exactly true except with respect to invisible, ideal, and imaginary figures, planes, and solids. These ideas, therefore, you must endeavour to imagine. In order to relieve the strain on your imagination, I will place before you material and visible figures about which my reasoning will be approximately true. From these I must ask you to try to rise upward to the imagination of their archetypes, the immaterial realities."

What shall we reply to our overbearing mathematician who in this abrupt and audacious manner introduces the non-existent and imaginary creatures of his brain as being "realities"? Shall we deride him, and the arithmetician likewise? Shall we bid the latter exchange his calculations in abstract numbers for manifestly useful sums about sacks of wheat and casks of beer? Shall we bid the mathematician descend from his high geometrical theories to the practical measurements of agriculture? Pouring scorn on his avowal that the objects of his reasoning are "invisible, ideal, and imaginary," shall we decline to study a science that is confessedly—so we can word it—visionary and illusive? If we do, he will not be without a reply, somewhat after this fashion: "My practical friends, it will be the worse for you if you despise these invisible, ideal and imaginary objects. I say nothing about the mental training and development to be derived from the study of these things; for to this argument you do not appear to me to be at present accessible: but I will take your own line—the practical. Do you then want to measure your fields with ease and to make accurate maps and charts; to construct houses that shall stand longer, ships that shall sail faster, cannon that shall shoot further, engines that shall pull harder, than any known before; do you want to utilize electricity for lighting, gas for motion, water for pressure; in a word do you wish to make yourselves lords over the material world and to have all the forces of Nature at your beck and call? If you do, you must not despise the non-existent numbers of my arithmetical brother, nor my immaterial and imaginary lines. Give me leave to repeat, in spite of your indignation, that though they are (in this present visible world of ours) non-existent, yet these lines and numbers are 'realities.' That they are realities, and that our conclusions about them are real and true, is proved by the one test of truth : our conclusions *work*. Our discoveries are in harmony with the universe. A perfect circle you never saw and never will see : yet it is as real as a beefsteak and a pint of porter. I believe in a perfect circle by Faith ; I accept it with reverence as an impression, if I may so dare to speak, on the Mind of the Universe, which He has communicated to me. What is more, I believe that He intended us to study this and other immaterial realities that our minds might approximate to His. Take a cone, my practical friends. What do you see in it? Nothing, I fear, except a shape that reminds you of an extinguisher or a fool's cap. Yet this little solid contains within itself the suggestions of all the mysteries of motion in heaven and earth. Slice your cone parallel to the base : there you have the perfect circle. Slice it again, parallel to one of the sides: there you have the parabola, the curve of terrestrial motion. Slice it once more, midway between these two sections : there you have the ellipse, the curve of celestial motion for which all the astronomers were seeking in vain through something like a score of centuries. Seriously now, my half-educated friends, in spite of the sense you may for the most part entertain of your own importance, do you not in your more modest moods sometimes feel inclined to say that, 'A circle is, after all, a reality, perhaps more real than I am myself'?"

What do you think of all this? For my part, I am inclined to think the Mathematician has the best of it. A good deal will turn upon the meaning of that dangerous word "reality," about which I will give you my notions, perhaps, hereafter.[1] But even if you dispute his assertions about the reality of his "ideas," you cannot, I am sure, deny the immense practical importance, as well as the universal acceptance, of his conclusions and discoveries ; and you will do well to remember that this immensely important, this undisputed and indisputable knowledge, could never have been attained if we had not called in the Imagination to create for us ideas that never will be, and never can be, realised in this present material world.

Let us pass now from knowledge about things to knowledge about persons, *i.e.* about actions and motives.

Our knowledge about actions depends on (1) personal observation ; (2) testimony ; (3) circumstantial evidence or any combination of these three.

The knowledge that we derive of actions from our own observation is of course independent of Faith, so far as concerns the past ; but it is very limited, and entirely useless and unpractical, except as a basis for knowledge about the present and future ; for which knowledge (as we have seen) Faith in the permanence of Nature is absolutely necessary.

The knowledge of actions that comes to us from evidence, direct and circumstantial, is largely dependent on Faith. "Julius Cæsar invaded Britain "—how certain we all feel of that ! Yet how slight the testimony ! Simply a few pages of narrative, written by the supposed invader himself, and some casual remarks by one or two contemporary letter-writers about Cæsar's doings in Britain and the Senate's reception of the news. Why should we believe on so apparently flimsy a basis ? Why should not Cæsar have sent one of his lieutenants to invade the island, and afterwards have taken the credit of it himself? Or there might have been no invasion at all, nothing but a reconnaissance grossly exaggerated and

[1] See the *Definitions* at the end of the book.

intermixed with facts derived from travellers. Yet we believe in the invasion without the slightest hesitation. Cæsar, we say, would not have told the lie; or, if he had, it would have been quickly exposed by his enemies. In other words, we believe in the truth of the narrative, because a belief in its falsehood does not "work," that is to say, does not suit with what we know (or, more properly, with what others know) of Cæsar's character and Cæsar's times. Of precisely the same kind is almost all our knowledge about history: it is based upon evidence, but it is belief; and the only test of its truth is, does it "work," *i.e.* does it fit in with other knowledge which we regard as established truth?

But you see that, even in dealing with a simple action of Cæsar's, we have already drifted into a reference to Cæsar's motives: and obviously knowledge about "motives" is an important and indeed a paramount element in knowledge about persons. "My father," says the child, "has his brows knit; his face looks dark; he speaks very loud; his eyes look brighter than usual:"—this is knowledge about actions derived from personal observation, but, so far, perfectly useless, until something is added to it. "Whenever my father has looked and spoken like this before, he has been angry and has punished somebody: therefore he is angry and will punish somebody now"— this is not knowledge, it is only belief; but it is belief not about actions simply, but about motives as well as actions, and it may be of the greatest use.

How do we gain knowledge about motives, the moving powers of the human machine? Since we cannot take this machinery to pieces, or experiment with it freely, we must derive our knowledge largely from the consciousness of our own motives. Tickling produces laughter in us, and pricking, a cry; affection, and the command of those whom we love, produce in us obedience; desire of a result or reward produces effort; fear of pain or penalty produces avoidance of certain actions, performance of others. Hence we infer that, in others also, similar effects have been produced, or will be produced, by similar causes. In either case, our inference is based partly upon our observation that these causes have preceded these effects in other persons, and partly upon our *faith* that other people's machinery is like our own.

But we have not yet touched one of the most powerful of motives, that power within us which we call Conscience ("joint-knowledge"); as though there were in us an Assessor sitting in judgment by the side of the mysterious "I," the two together pronouncing sentence of "Right" or "Wrong" upon the several propositions and intentions which are, as it were, called up before their tribunal. The development of Conscience and our sensibility to its dictation appears to me largely due to the Imagination. If a philosopher tells me that when Conscience appears to us to say "Right" it really says "Expedient for society and ultimately for yourself," or "Calculated to gain esteem for yourself," or "Conducive to your own peace of mind," I am obliged, with all deference to him, but with greater deference to truth, to assure him that (however correct he may be as to the origin of this feeling in my own infant mind or in the matured mind of my primæval ancestors) he is mistaken, at all events in my own case, as to the action of Conscience now. I may possibly have been long ago guided to my idea of "Right" by my observation of what is expedient: but, to me, now, the sense of "right" is as different from the sense of "expedient," as the eye is different from some sensitive protuberance which may ultimately be developed into an eye, but is at present responsive only to the touch.

How then do we gain this knowledge of right and wrong? For of course it is not enough to reply that we gain it by the voice of Conscience : such an answer only makes us repeat our question in a different shape : " In the very young, Conscience, though it may be existent, is certainly latent ; when and whence does it begin to work ? " I should reply that the first idea of good and evil is communicated to the very young through the habit of obedience to their parents or those who stand to them in the parental position. A child is so created as to be in constant dependence on the favour and good-will of his mother. When he is obedient to her he finds himself at peace and happy, and he welcomes on her face that sunshine which indicates that she is pleased with him. When he is disobedient, harsh sounds follow, a lowering darkness on the countenance close to his, obstacles to his freedom, restrictions of his pleasures, perhaps sharper pains or penalties : and he is now out of harmony with his little Universe. All this strange and subtle evil inside him and outside him he has brought on himself by disobeying the maternal will ; and hence there gradually springs up in his mind an Imagination of some unnameable thing, which is his first idea of right. But as he grows older and widens his sphere of observation he finds—if he is placed in anything like those favourable circumstances which Nature has appointed for most of us—that this parental will is in harmony with the widening world around him. The parents say, " Do not play with fire ; " Nature says the same, and punishes him if he transgresses. The parents say, " Do not touch that knife ; " again Nature confirms their authority by inflicting a penalty on disobedience. Thus, if the parents have anything of parental forethought, the child gradually associates them with the governing powers of his growing Universe, and begins to feel that the parental will is also the will, or order, of Nature. They are as God to him : and the confirmed habit of obedience to them deepens in his heart the conviction—but still a conviction rather springing from Imagination than from Reason—that the power which thus induces him to obey is a great and grand Power, orderly, not to be resisted; wise and justified by results, but to be obeyed without thinking about results; it *ought* to be obeyed; it is *Right*.

Now he steps out into the world of other human beings; and here he learns to widen his idea of Right. Perhaps he also learns to alter it. If he was born and reared among thieves, his conscience may have been altogether perverted so that he actually thought it honourable to steal. But in any case, even though he may come from the best of homes, he often learns that the parental will is not always in harmony with the highest and best will; and gradually he forms a different standard of "Right" from that which he held before. It was once the will of his parents, now it is often the will of Society. Conforming himself to the will of Society he is free from pains and penalties; he is at peace with those around him, and he is generally at peace with himself. I say generally, not always: for by this time he has begun to think for himself and to see that Conscience ought to speak in the interests not merely of his parents, nor of a select circle of his own friends or companions, but of all mankind. His Imagination pictures for him an ideal Order such as he has never actually experienced. He feels that he " ought " to be at peace and in harmony with this imaginary Order, and not with some distorted and narrowed conception of it conveyed to him by his "set," his class, his city, his nation, or his church. In his conscience, he hears the voice of this Moral Order of humanity. Hence it is that men have been sometimes impelled to thoughts beyond, or even against, the conscience of their contemporaries; to protest, for example, against unjust wars, against war of any kind, against slavery, against duelling, against legalized oppression. In every case the impelling power has been the same, a sense of discord between the man's imaginary ideal and the actual environment in which these evils and disorders have existed. Others, his commonplace companions, have been content to go with the world around them—to be kind slave-holders, honourable duellists, moderate oppressors—and they have felt no pangs of conscience. But by a few, a chosen few, there has been acquired a keener sense of the ideal of moral harmony, a keener eye for detecting moral disorder, and an abhorrence of it which will not permit them to live in peace amid such evils: they must either die or mend them.

They often do die in mending them; but while in the process of dying, or preparing for death—with all deference to the clergyman who lately maintained that "if there is no hereafter, and if the only reward of self-sacrifice and the only punishment of crime are those which happen in the present life, *it would have been far better to have been Fouché than Paul*"—they have at least a peace of mind which they could not have attained by conformity with the world. The grosser conscience that "worked" well enough in their companions would not have "worked" in them. Even, therefore, though they appear to be exceptions to the rule that tests truth by its "working," they are not really exceptional. They have been in discord with the world but in concord with themselves. Often they prove to others the truth of their conceptions by raising up the world to their level, and by pointing to the moral order which has issued from the fulfilment of their ideas. But in any case, though they may fail for a time or (apparently) for all time, they have had in themselves a sufficient test of the truth of their ideas: they have followed their conscience and they have found that this course "worked"—that is to say, suited and developed their nature—as no other course could have worked for them. But in order thus to hear and obey the voice of conscience and to discern its highest truths, how much of faith, how much of imagination has been needed!

But this digression about Conscience has led me a little astray from my subject, which was "the knowledge of persons:" I must return to it in my next letter.

V

My dear ——,

Let us now return to the consideration of the "knowledge of persons." How do we gain knowledge of a human being, that is to say of his motives? "By observing his actions in many different circumstances, especially in extremities of joy, sorrow, fear, temptation, and then by comparing his actions with what we, or others, have done in the same circumstances?" But this is a very difficult and delicate business, especially that part of it which involves comparison. Here we may easily go wrong; and we therefore naturally ask what test have we that our knowledge is correct. One test of any useful knowledge of a machine would be, not our power to discourse fluently about it, but our power to "work" it, *i.e.* to make it perform the work for which it is intended : and similarly one test of useful knowledge of a human being must be our power to "work" him, *i.e.* to make him perform the work for which he is intended. A perfectly selfish man of the world may have considerable knowledge of men and "work" them cleverly in a certain sense : he is not cheated by them ; he is perhaps obeyed by some, not thwarted by others ; he knows the weak points of all, jostles down one, persuades another to lift him up, gets something out of every one, and is, in a word, largely successful in making men help him to do *what he intends*. But this is a very poor kind of "working," as compared with that which has been practised by the lawgivers, poets, philosophers, and founders of religion; who have moulded and fashioned great masses of men so as to be better able than they were before to do the noblest works that men can do, the works for *which they are intended*. Now I think it will not be denied that the men who, in this sense, have "worked" mankind have had great ideas of what men could do and ought to do. Sometimes they have had ideas so high that they have seemed impossible of attainment and almost absurd, even as ideas. Yet these are the men, these idealizers of humanity, who have most helped mankind on the path of progress. And this would lead us to the conclusion that the men who have "worked" mankind best have been those who have refused to accept men as they are. Constrained by the Imagination, they have kept before their eyes an Ideal of humanity, towards which they have aspired and laboured with sanguine enthusiasm.

To the same effect tends our observation of mankind in smaller groups, and especially in that smallest of groups called the family. It is generally the parents who have most influence over their child, most power to "work" him; and we can often see that the reason of their influence does not arise from the power to reward or punish, but from their affection for him, and from their faith in him. Especially do we perceive this in the familiar but mysterious process called forgiving. We see parents, yes even wise parents, constantly placing faith in a child beyond what seems to a dispassionate observer to be warranted by facts, treating him as though he were better than he has shewn himself to be, better than he appears to us likely ever to become. And, strange to say, this imaginative system has on the whole proved more successful than the impartial and dispassionate disposition which would take a human being exactly for what he is, and treat him as being that and no more.

I do not mean to say that there have not been blind and fond parents in abundance who—having no high moral standard and being merely desirous to see comfort and bright faces around them—have done their children harm by ignoring their faults and regarding them as perfect: but on the other hand, I call on you to admit the paradox that just, wise, and righteous parents, who have had a high moral standard, have been most successful in enabling their child to rise to that standard, by treating him as though he were better than he really has been. Further, I say that this system has been pursued by all those who have forgiven others, and by Him above all others who has done most to make forgiveness "current coin" among mankind.

I can understand a man of cold-blooded and dispassionate temperament objecting to any such idealization of humanity. "The whole theory," he might say, "is radically unfair and unreasonable. You argue that you ought to love a man and ignore his faults if you wish to know him and move him. You might just as well argue that you ought to hate a man and ignore his virtues for the same purpose. Hate is as keen-eyed as love. Hate spies out the least defects, anticipates each false step, predicts each hasty word, and caricatures beforehand each hasty gesture. Hate makes a study of its objects: hate, therefore, as well as love, might be said to stimulate us to know others. But the right course is neither to hate, nor to love, but to judge. As hate blinds us to virtues, so love blinds us to vices. We ought to be blind to nothing, to extenuate nothing, to ignore nothing, but to be purely and reasonably critical. Thus we shall know humanity as it is."

The answer to this very plausible theory is extremely simple: "Your theory appears to be just and wise upon a cursory and unscientific view of human nature: but it has not endured the scientific test of experiment; it has not *worked.* I believe the reason why it does not work is, that it ignores some faintly discernible but growing tendencies in human nature which are not to be discerned without more sympathy than you appear to possess : no human being can be understood in the daylight of Reason alone ; affection and Imagination are needed to transport us as it were into the heart of a fellow-creature, to enable us to realize him as we realize ourselves, and to treat him as we would ourselves be treated; faith also in the possibilities of humanity is a very powerful help not only towards discerning the best and noblest that men can do, but also towards developing their power of doing it. But in any case, whatever may be the reasons for its failure, your theory does not "work," and must therefore be given up.

"By 'failure,' I do not mean that your theory will prevent you from getting on and making your way in the world, but that it will prevent you from operating on yourself and on mankind, so that you and they may do the work which you are intended to do. You say the business of a student of men is to be critical. I say that such a student is a mere pedant, a book-philosopher : but the scientific student of men is he who knows how to 'work' them : and those who have in the true sense of the term 'worked' men, have not been of the critical temperament which you eulogize, but often quite uncritical, wondrously uncritical, but full of a fervent faith in a high ideal of humanity, and in a destiny that would ultimately conform humanity to its ideal. If you aim at exerting no social ennobling influence of this kind, if you are content, while leading the life of a man of the world, to abide, spiritually speaking, in the cave of a recluse, then keep on your present course. Criticize men dispassionately to your heart's content. Try to persuade yourself that you know them. But you will never succeed—you will never persuade even yourself that you have succeeded—in making a single human being the better for your influence.

"In morals as in mathematics nothing can be done without faith in the Ideal. If you want to operate scientifically upon imperfect men you must keep constantly before your mind the image of the Perfect Man. We have seen that, before we can attain to 'applied mathematics,' which constitute the basis of those sciences by which we dominate the material world, we have to begin with 'pure mathematics.' In that region of study we have to idealize and speak of things, not as they are in our experience, but as they might be if certain tendencies that we see around us could be infinitely—yes, and we must add, impossibly—extended. Yet in the end, if we go patiently onward, we find that our 'pure mathematics' lead us to conclusions of immense practical importance.

"It is precisely the same in the science of humanity, which we may call anthropology. In order to prepare the way for 'applied anthropology' whereby we may dominate the immaterial world, the minds and tempers of men, we must begin with 'pure anthropology'; that is to say, we must idealize and speak of man not as he is but as he would be if certain tendencies which we see in him, conducive to social order and individual development, could be infinitely—yes, and we must add, if we limit our horizon to this present life, impossibly—extended. In the end, if we go patiently onward, we shall find that 'pure anthropology' will be of immense practical importance in helping us to control and develop ourselves and individuals around us and all communities of men. This 'pure anthropology,' having to do with the Ideal of humanity, is necessarily associated or identified with the conception of God; and some would call it 'theology' or 'Christianity.' But that is a mere matter of names. Call it by whatever name you please, but study it you must.

You will never 'work' mankind—that is to say you will never make men do the work for which they are intended —till you have studied the Ideal Man."

You may reply, and with some justice, that there is a danger in this repeated appeal to the test of "working."

What," you may ask, " about the Buddhist and the Mohammedan, the one with his peaceful missions, the other with his victorious sword? Cannot both make the same appeal? In advocating the invariable appeal to "working," do we not come dangerously near urging the acceptance of any doctrine that will afford good leverage to moral effort, regardless of its truth or falsehood? Ought not, after all, the harmony of the doctrine with Reason (in the highest sense—not only syllogistic, but intuitive, imaginative, or whatever you choose to call it) to be the ultimate criterion?"

I suppose there is a "danger" in every means of attaining truth, a danger in observation, a danger in experiment, a danger in inductive, a danger in deductive, reasoning: but it does not follow that any of these means are to be discarded, only that they are to be carefully used. If the Buddhist can appeal to the successes of centuries, that proves, I should say, that there is some element of genuine truth in his religion; if the Mohammedan points to conversions, in India and elsewhere, far more rapid than those made by Christianity and not dependent on "the victorious sword," that also proves that in some important respects—for example in the practical recognition of the equality of all believers without respect to rank or race—Mohammedans have been far more faithful to their teacher than we have been to ours. And generally, any religion that succeeds in making men better with it than they were without it, must be admitted (I think) to contain (so far as it succeeds) some element of divine revelation. And therefore, while admitting the appeal to Reason, I cannot reject the appeal to Experience as well. Do not think that, in laying so much stress on "working," I ignore the difference between the propositions of Natural Science and those of Religion, or forget how much more ready and convincing verification is in the former than in the latter. The means of verifying may differ in different ages: why not? In the earliest period of Christianity, men had, as a test, the contrast between the heathen and the Christian life; the burning zeal of the freshly imparted Spirit of Christ; and the "mighty works" wrought by the Apostles and perhaps by some of their successors. Now, for us in Christendom, the proof from "contrast" is less obvious, and we have lost also something of the fresh and fiery zeal —must we not add the occasionally misguided zeal?—of the first Christians: but, by way of compensation, we have, besides our individual experiences, the collective evidence of many generations shewing what Christ's Spirit can do to help us when we obey it, to chasten us when we disobey. Are we wrong then in inferring that one test of religions is the same which our Lord appointed for testing men: "By their fruits ye shall know them"?

There is undoubtedly a great difference between proof in Science and proof in matters of Religion: and Religion depends, far more than Science, upon Imagination. But I have not ignored this difference. On the contrary, I have attempted to show that, since Religion depends *far more* than Science upon Imagination; and since Science itself depends *largely* upon Imagination; therefore Religion must depend *very largely* upon Imagination, and especially upon that form of Imagination to which we give the name of Faith.

VI

MY DEAR ——,

You suspect that I am "pushing the claims of the Imagination so far as to deprive the Reason or Understanding[1] of its rights;" and you ask me whether I dispute the universal belief that the former is an "illusive faculty." As for your suspicion, I will endeavour to show that it is groundless. As for your question, I admit that the Imagination is "illusive," but I must add that it also leads us to truth. It constructs the hypotheses, as well as the illusions, which, when tested by experience, guide us towards Knowledge.

Imagination is the "imaging" faculty of the mind. It does not, strictly speaking, create, any more than an artist, strictly speaking, creates. But as an artist combines lines, colours, shades, sounds, and thoughts, each one of which by itself is familiar to everybody, in such new combinations as to produce effects that impress us all as original and unprecedented, so does the Imagination out of old fragments make new existences and unities.

Attention impresses upon us the present; Memory recalls the past; but the Imagination is never content simply to reproduce the past or present. It sums up the

---

[1] "Reason" is used, in these letters, in a sense for which Coleridge (I believe) preferred to use "Understanding." But as long as we have a verb "reason," commonly used of mathematical, logical, and ordinary processes of arguing, so long it will be inexpedient, in a popular treatise, to use the word in any but its popular sense. Perhaps some might give the name of "higher Reason" to what I call Imagination.

past of Memory (sometimes perhaps also the present of Attention) and combines it with a conjectured future in such a way as to produce a whole. It is always seeking for likenesses, orderly connections, regular sequences, beautiful relations, suggestions of unity in some shape or other, so as to reduce many things into one and to obtain a satisfying picture.

For example, suppose a large mill-wheel at rest to be almost hidden from my eyes by intervening trees so that, even if it were moving, I could only see one spoke at a time; and at present I am not aware that it is close before me. Something begins to move. I look up. Attention tells me that I see before me, moving from left to right, something like a plank or pole: it passes and I see nothing; but then comes another similar object moving similarly; then a third, rather quicker; then a fourth, quicker still. The mind at once sets to work to find the cause. The Memory tells me that I have seen simply a number of poles or planks moving from left to right with quickened motion; the Attention tells me that I see one now; but the Imagination, taking in the isolated reports of Memory and Attention, includes them in a larger hypothesis of her own, in which, if I may so express it, the constituent elements, the spokes, are subordinated, and the explanatory unity, the wheel, is brought into prominence: and thus the motion from left to right, which explained nothing, is replaced, in my mind, by the motion of revolution, which explains everything.

It is on the basis of the Imagination, aided by Experience and Reason, that we establish our conviction of the permanence of the simplest Laws of Nature. This I have touched on in one of my previous letters. The Memory, recalling the sight of many stones falling to the ground, comes perhaps to the aid of Attention, as a child notes a particular stone falling to the ground, and suggests to the child's imitative nature an experimental attempt to make a stone fall to the ground. The child does it once and again, as often as he likes. Then, as a result of this unvarying experience, there springs up in the child's mind a picture in which he sees reproduced an apparently endless vista of his sensations as to stone-falling and its antecedents, a picture not confined, like the pictures of Memory, to past time, but including future as well as past and present: and thus the childish thought leaps upwards all at once to the conception of that sublime word "always," and dares to promulgate its first universal proposition, and attains to the definite certainty of a Law of Nature.

But you say that the Imagination is "illusive." It is; it rarely conducts us to truth without first leading us through error. Its business is to find likenesses and connections and to suggest explanations, not to point out differences, and make distinctions, and test explanations: these latter tasks are to be accomplished not by Imagination but by Reason with the aid of enlarged experience. The Imagination suggests to the child that every man is like his father, every woman like his mother; that the motion of the sea is like the motion of water in the washing-basin; that the thunder is caused by the rolling of barrels or discharge of coals up above; that a clock goes on of itself for ever: and a multitude of other illusions all arising from the same healthy imaginative conviction in every young mind that "What has been will be," and "The whole world is according to one pattern." The conviction is based on a profound general truth, but the particular shapes which it assumes are often erroneous. It is only after a course, and sometimes a very long course, of experience and experiment, that the child, or perhaps the man, eliminates with the aid of Reason those ideas which will not work, and confirms those that will work, till the latter become at last strong and inherent and quasi-instinctive convictions. None the less, if the Imagination did not first suggest the ideas on which the Reason is to operate, we should never obtain anything worth calling knowledge.

We might express all this by saying that Imagination is the mother of working-hypotheses: and this is true of all working-hypotheses, those of the observatory and laboratory as well as those of the nursery. No one who grasps this truth will henceforth deny the debt of science to Imagination. Knowledge is not worth calling knowledge till it is reduced to Law; and Law, as I have shown you above, is a mere idea of the Imagination. I do not deny the subsequent value of Reason; but Imagination must come first. It was from the Imagination that there first flashed upon the mind of Newton the vision of the working-hypothesis by which the apple's fall and the planet's path might be simultaneously explained. Then came in Reason, with experiment, testing, comparing, prepared to detect discrepancies, unlikelihoods, and any want of harmony between the new theory and the old order of things. Finally, the once-no-more-than-working-hypothesis, having been found to harmonize with countless past and present phenomena and having enabled us to predict countless future phenomena, is now called a Law, and we are practically certain that it will act. The approval of this Law we owe to Reason, but for the suggestion of it we are indebted to Imagination. On the debt owed to Imagination by Mathematics—the foundation of all science—I will not add anything to what has been said in a recent letter.

Next as to the work of Imagination in art. Poets and artists, as well as astronomers, must be, so to speak, *ex analogia Universi;* that is to say, they must be in harmony with that order of things which they long to reveal to their fellow-men ; they must see Law and Unity where others fail to see it ; they must have inherited or received capacities and intuitions which give them an intense sympathy with the deep-down-hidden rhythms and abysmal motions which regulate atoms and sounds, and hues and shapes, and the thoughts and feelings of men. An artist who wishes to paint a hill-side, or a wave, or a face, must have a vision of it. He must see it not only exactly as it is, but how it is : he sympathizes, as it were, with every cleft and runlet and hollow and projection of the hill, with every turn and fold and shade and hue of the ever-varying wave: he realizes the secret of Nature's working. Shall we make a distinction between the secret in the one case and the other? Shall we say the "spirit" of the face, but the "law" of the hill and the "law" of the wave? Or will not the intuition into this complex combination of multitudinous forces, apparently free and conflicting yet all guided and controlled into one harmonious result, be better expressed by saying that he enters into the " spirit " in all cases, the " spirit " of the hill, the wave, and the face ? In proportion as he has this power, a great artist will be less likely to speak about it, and less able to explain it : but have it he must ; and it is a power really not dissimilar, though apparently most different, from the scientific Imagination. It is, in both cases, a power of recognizing Order and Unity. The test also of the artistic, is (roughly speaking) the same as that of the scientific Imagination. Those ideas are right which "work." Does a scientific idea open, like a key, the secrets of Nature ? Then it "works," and is, so far, right. So in art : to imagine rightly is to imagine powerfully so as to sway the minds of men. Those artistic imaginations are wrong which fail to fit the wards of the complicated human lock and to stir the inmost thoughts. There are obvious objections to this definition of what is artistically right ; what stirs the Athenian may not stir the Esquimaux. But, roughly speaking, we may say that the test has held good. What has stirred the Athenian has stirred the great civilising races of the world. There may be a better and a higher test hereafter ; but, for the present at all events, prolonged experience of its "working" is the test of artistic Imagination.

But the Imagination plays, perhaps, its most important part in our conceptions of human emotions and human character. These things cannot be exactly defined, like triangles or circles ; nor can they or their results be predicted like the results of chemical action or the instinctive motions of irrational animals. Yet the Imagination helps us, after a sympathetic contemplation of what a friend *has* done and said and wished, to complete the picture by taking as it were a bird's-eye view of his past, present and future, so as to be able in some measure to realize and predict what he *will* do and say and wish. This mental "imagination," "image," or "idea" of our friend we might describe as the "law" of his being, so far as it was grasped by us : but so much more subtle and variable than any known "law" are the sequences of human thought and conduct, that we generally prefer the phrase which we just now used to describe the intuition of the artist ; and so we speak of "entering into the spirit" of a man. It is usual to say that we do this by "sympathy : " but sympathy is only one form of Imagination tinged with love, the power of imagining the joys and sorrows of others and of realizing them as one's own. Imagination, without love, might realize the sorrows of an enemy to gloat over them : love, if it could be without Imagination—which it cannot be, since love implies at least some imagination of what the beloved would wish— would be a poor lifeless sentiment doing nothing, or nothing to the purpose. But imaginative love, or sympathy, gives us the key to the knowledge of all human nature, and is the foundation of all domestic and social unity and order.

As to the test of Imagination when brought to bear upon human nature, you will remember, I dare say, that it was determined to be the success with which it "worked" human nature, or, in other words, made men do "what they are intended to do." But I was then speaking of the way in which the great prophets, lawgivers, and founders of religions have influenced great masses of mankind, and in which almost every mother influences her children, by idealizing them. I might have added, and I will now add, a word on the manner in which an imaginary ideal of human nature proves its truth experimentally to the imaginer, by "working" *him*, that is, by making *him* capable of doing "the work he was intended to do." It is the more necessary to do this because the illusions of Imagination are nowhere so strong and so lasting as in the study of human Nature; and there is a danger that we may be deterred by the thought of them from steadily pursuing the truth. The cynic tells us with a sneer that babies, and none but babies, think men and women better than they are, and that, the older one grows, the more one is disillusionised about the virtue of human nature. But that is not true, or only a half truth. If we, as children, imagine the men and women about us to be perfections of power, wisdom, and virtue, one reason is, that we have, as children, a most inadequate standard of physical, mental, and moral excellence. As our standard rises, our sense of inadequacy increases; but the reason why, as we grow older, we cease to think people perfect, is, very often, not that we think worse of human beings, but that we think better of human possibilities.

But in some minds defect of Imagination combines with other causes to induce the repeatedly disillusionised man to give up the search after the truth that lies beneath the illusion and to cast away all trust, all thought, of any ideal of humanity. Those who do this make shipwreck of their own lives. Their low ideal or no-ideal of conduct does not " work ;" that is to say, it does not fit them to do the work they were intended to do. Even for the purposes of their own happiness their life is a failure. So far as the spiritual side of their nature is concerned, a dull and stagnant self-satisfaction is the highest prize they can hope to acquire : they have none of the keen joys of spiritual aspiration, of failures redeemed, of gradual progress, and of deeper insight into the glorious possibilities of human nature. But those who, while not rejecting the sobering admonitions of Experience and Reason, can nevertheless so far obey the promptings of Imagination as to retain in their hearts an ever fresh and expansive and healthful Ideal of life, find themselves led on by it from hope to nobler hope, from effort to more arduous effort, until life and effort end together.

Let this suffice as my protest against the popular fallacy that the Imagination is an abnormal faculty, limited to poets and painters and "artists," mostly illusive, and always to be subordinated in the search after truth. I maintain, on the contrary, that it lies at the basis of all knowledge ; that it is no less necessary for science, for morals, and for religion, than for artistic success ; and that the illusions of Imagination are the stepping-stones to Truths.

Now to speak of Reason, or, as some would call it, Understanding. While dealing with Imagination, we recognized that the work of Reason is mostly negative and corrective : but let us come to detail. Reason is commonly said to proceed by two methods ; (1) by Induction, wherein, by "inducing," or introducing, a number of particular instances (*e.g.* "A, B, C, &c., are men and are mortal"),

you establish a general conclusion ("all men are mortal");
(ii) by Deduction, wherein, from two previous statements called Premises, you deduce a third, called a Conclusion.

(i) As regards Induction, surely you must admit that the initial part of the task falls not upon the Reason but upon the Imagination; which sees likenesses and leaps to general conclusions, mostly premature or false, but all containing a truth from which the falsehood must be eliminated. Thus, a child imagines, by premature Induction, that all men are (1) like his father; (2) black-haired; (3) between five and six feet high; (4) white-skinned, and so on. Then comes Reason afterwards, comparing and contrasting these imaginative premature conclusions with a wider and contradictory experience and widening the conclusion accordingly. Hence it is the part of Reason to suggest those varied experiments which are a necessary part of scientific Induction; and this is generally done by pointing out to us some neglected difference: "You say you had a Turkish bath three times, and each time caught a cold: but were the antecedents of these three colds quite alike? If not, how did they differ? Did you not on the first occasion sit in a draught at a public meeting? on the second, forget to put on your great coat? on the third, let the fire out though it was freezing? Consider therefore, not the single point of likeness, the Turkish bath, but the points of *unlikeness* also, in the antecedents of your three colds; and try the Turkish bath again, omitting these antecedents, before you say 'A Turkish bath always gives me cold.'"

You see then that in Induction the positive and suggestive part of the work is done by the Imagination; the negative and eliminative part by Reason.

(ii) As regards Deduction, the business of Reason is to ascertain that the Premises are not only true but also connected in such a way that a conclusion can be drawn from them. But even here Imagination plays a part: for the conclusion of every syllogism (roughly speaking) depends upon the following axiom: "If a is included in b, and b is included in c, then a is included in c; in other words, if a watch is in a box, and the box is in a room, then the watch is in the room." Now this general proposition, like all general propositions, is arrived at with the aid of the Imagination, so that we may fairly say that the Imagination, helps to lay the foundation of the Syllogism. When therefore you bear in mind that in every Syllogism the Premises are often the result of an Induction in which Imagination has played a part, and that the conclusion always depends upon an axiom of the Imagination, you must admit that even Deductive Reasoning by no means excludes the Imagination.

(iii) Practically, errors seldom arise, and truth is seldom discovered, from mere Deductive Reasoning. Any one can see his way through a logical Syllogism, and almost any one can lay his finger on the weak point in an illogical one. But the difficulty is to start the Reasoning in the right direction and to begin the Logical Chain with an appropriate Syllogism.

For example, suppose we wish to prove that "every triangle which has two angles equal, has two sides opposite to them equal": how can our Reason, our discriminative faculty, help us here? At present, not at all. We must first call to our aid the Imagination, which says to us, "*Imagine* the triangle with two equal angles to have two unequal sides opposite to them, and see what follows." And every one who has done a geometrical Deduction knows that we frequently start by "imagining" the conclusion to be already proved, or the problem to be already performed, and then endeavouring to realise, among the many consequences that would follow, which of those consequences would harmonize with, or be identical with, the data to which we are working back.

The same process is common in the reasoning that deals with what is called Circumstantial Evidence. Thus, it is asserted by A that he saw B commit a murder in the midst of a field, five minutes before midnight, on the first day of last month : how can we test the truth of A's assertion? The negative faculty of Reason cannot answer the question. But once more Imagination steps in and says, "*Imagine* the story to be true ; *imagine* yourself to be in A's place ; *imagine* the circumstances which would have surrounded him, the hidden place from which he saw the murder, the light which enabled him to see it, the precise sight that he saw, the voices or sounds that he heard, and, in a word, all the details of a *likely* and coherent narrative." When the Imagination has done this and "imagined" the place—perhaps a hedge—the light—moonlight, and so on, Reason steps in, and corroborates or rejects, by shewing that there was, or was not, a hedge whence the deed could have been witnessed ; that there was a full moon or no moon on the night in question ; that, if there had been a moon, the place in question was open to the moonlight, or in deep shadow : and thus Imagination and Reason (aided by experience of the place and knowledge of the time) arrive at a conclusion, the former making a positive, the latter a negative contribution. Hence it appears that even in those questions which are called pre-eminently "practical"—for what can be more "practical" than a trial in a law-court for life or death?—the Imagination plays so great a part that without its aid the reason could effect little or nothing.

Here I must break off ; but I hope I have said enough to satisfy you that the imaginative faculty, though it needs the constant test of Reason and Experience, is far more intimately connected with what we call knowledge, than is commonly supposed. But if this be so, we ought not (I think) to be surprised if a careful analysis of our profoundest religious convictions should reveal that for these also we are indebted, and intended by God to be indebted, to the Imagination far more than to the Reason.

VII

MY DEAR ——,

I have been very much pained by your sprightly account of the lively and witty conversation between you and your clever young friends, —— and ——, on the proofs of the existence of a God. Bear with me if I assure you that discussions in that spirit are likely to be fatal to real faith. They may often be far more dangerous than a serious collision between untrained faith and the most highly educated scepticism. I do not deprecate discussion, but I do most earnestly plead for reverence.

Young men at the Universities stand in especial need of this warning because their studies lead them to be critical; and habits of criticism may easily weaken the habit of reverence. I remember once being shewn over a great public school by the Headmaster, justly celebrated as a Headmaster once, and much more celebrated since in another capacity. It was a grand school, though a little too ecclesiastical to suit my taste. While we were in the chapel my friend spoke earnestly of the pleasure it gave him on Sundays to see in the chapel the familiar faces of the old boys who came to revisit the old place. At the same time he deplored the contrast between those who went into the army, and those who went to the Universities: "The army fellows," he said, "almost always come to Communion, the university fellows almost always stop away." These words made an indelible impression on my mind, "Who is to blame, or praise, for this?" asked

I, on my journey homeward. " Is it the army that is to be praised for its inculcation of discipline and self-subordination, helping the young fellows to realise the meaning of self-sacrifice? Or is it the University that is to be blamed for its negative and destructive teaching? Or can it be that the school is in part to blame for teaching the boys to believe too much; and the University in part to blame for teaching the young men to criticize too much?"

Over and over again, since that time, I have asked myself these same questions about many other young men from many other public schools. I honour the army as much as most men, more perhaps than many do : but after all the profession of a soldier is the profession of a throat-cutter; throat-cutting in an extensive, expeditious, and honourable way,—throat-cutting in one direction often undertaken merely to prevent throat-cutting in another direction—but still throat-cutting after all : and it seemed very hard to believe that the profession of throat-cutting is, and ought to be, a better preparation than the pursuit of learning at the Universities, for participation in the Holy Communion. On the whole I was led to the conclusion that the young men in the army had retained and deepened the instinctive obedience to authority, the sense of the need of the subordination of the individual to the community, and perhaps also the feeling of reverence, while they had not been taught so fully to appreciate all that was implied in attendance at Communion or to realize the intellectual difficulties presented by the New Testament. In other words—to put it briefly and roughly—the young cadets and officers came to Communion because they had been taught to feel and not taught to think ; and the University men stayed away because they had been taught to think and not to feel. Now I will ask you to excuse me if I suggest that the principal danger to your character at present arises from the want of such discipline as may be obtained by some in the army, and by others in the practical work of life. You need some emotional and moral exercise to counterbalance your mental and intellectual training. You are not aware how much of the most valuable knowledge, conviction, certainty—call it what you will, but I mean that kind of moral and spiritual knowledge which is the basis of all right conduct—springs in the main from spiritual and emotional sources.

In the present letter I should like to confine myself to this subject, the culture, if I may so say, of Christian faith. Let me then ask you first to clear your mind by asking yourself what is the essence of the faith which you would desire to retain. It is (is it not?) a faith or trust in the fatherhood of God. This surely is the Gospel or Good News for which Christ lived and died, in order that He might breathe it into the hearts of men. "Fatherhood" —some of your young friends will exclaim—"What an antiquated notion! Flat anthropomorphism!" By "anthropomorphism" they mean a tendency to make God in human shape; just as Heine's four legged poetic Bruin makes God to be a great white Polar Bear, and the frogs of Celsus imagine Him to be a gigantic Frog. No doubt, this is very funny; but the decryers of anthropomorphism who venture on any conception of a God— are they any less funny? Do not they shew a similar disposition to make God in the shape of human works or human experiences? Shall I be exploring a nobler path of spiritual speculation if I say God is a Rock or a Buckler, or a Centre, or a Force, than if I say God is a Father in heaven? Ask your sceptical companions what conception of God they can mention which is not open to objection, and they will perhaps reply " An Eternal, or a Tendency, not ourselves, which makes for righteousness." Now to reply "an Eternal," appears to me to be taking a rather mean and pedantical advantage of the uninflected peculiarities of English (and Hebrew), which leave it an open question whether you mean your "Eternal" to be masculine, or neuter. And "Tendency"—what is it? Is it not a "stretching," or "pulling," or partially neutralised force—a common human experience? Now we are dealing with the accusation of limiting our conception of God to our experiences as men. And, so far as this charge is concerned, what is the difference between calling God a "Tendency," or a "Rock," or a "Shield," or a "House of Defence," as the old Psalmist does? Are not all these names mere metaphors derived from human experience? In the same way to call God a Father is (no doubt) a metaphor: but is it more a metaphor than to call Him a Tendency?

Some metaphors, which describe God by reference to the relations of man to man, may be called anthropomorphic; others, which describe Him by reference to implements (such as a Shield) may be called organomorphic; others, which assimilate Him to lifeless and inorganic objects (such as a Hill) may be called by some other grand name, such as apsychomorphic; others, which would subtilize Him down to a thought, or a mind, or a spirit, may be called phronesimorphic, noumorphic, pneumatomorphic; but in the name of common sense— or in the name of that sense which ought to be common, and which ought to revolt against bondage to mere words —what is there in that termination "morphic" which should stagger a seeker after divine truth? Do we not all recognize that all terms applied to the supreme God are "morphisms" of various kinds? And the question is not how we can avoid a "morphism"—for we cannot avoid it—but how or where we can find the noblest and most spiritually helpful "morphism." And as between the ancient and the modern metaphors just set before you can you entertain a moment's doubt? Might we not imagine the question put — after the old Roman authoritative fashion—to an assembly of the consciences of universal mankind: "Christ says that God is a Father in heaven; refined thinkers say that He is a Tendency; *utri creditis, gentes?*" To which I seem to hear the answer of the Universe come back, "We will have no Tendencies seated on the throne of Heaven. Give us a Father, or we will have nothing." And you, my dear friend, how is it with you? *Utri credis?*

But perhaps you complain, or some of your friends might complain, that this is not treating the question fairly. "The doctrine of the Fatherhood of God," they may say, "is to be discussed like any other proposition, upon the evidence." I entirely deny it, if from your "evidence" you intend to exclude the witness of Imagination expressed in Faith and Hope. I assert, on the contrary, that it is to be believed in, against what may be called quasi-evidence. It cannot be demonstrated to be either true or false. Do not misunderstand me. There is abundant evidence of a certain kind—as I will hereafter shew—for the Fatherhood of God; but there is also evidence against it: and what I mean is, that the mind is not to sit impartially and coldly neutral between the two testimonies, but is to grasp the former and hold it fast and keep it constantly in view, while it lays less stress on and (after a time) puts on one side the latter. I have shewn you that many of our deepest and most vital convictions are based less upon Reason than upon Imagination. Why then should we be surprised if the most profound convictions of all, our religious certainties, rest upon that imaginative desire to which we have given the name of Faith?[1] If

---

[1] Faith is "desire (approved by the Conscience) of which we imagine the fulfilment, while putting doubt at a distance": see the *Definitions* at the end of the volume.

an archangel (robed in light) were to step down to me this moment and were to cry aloud, "Verily there is no God," I should reply, or ought to reply, "Verily thou art a devil." If the same archangel were to come in the same way and to say "Verily there is a God," I should reply, "I felt sure there was; and now I am more sure than ever." How unfair, how illogical, if our belief is to be a matter of mere evidence! But it is not to be a matter of mere evidence. It is to be a struggle against an evil thought—shall I not say an evil being?—that is perpetually attempting to slander God to men by representing Him as permitting or originating evil.

Does this startle you—this suggestion of an evil being—as being too old-fashioned for an educated Christian? Well then, put it aside for the time (though it is indeed Christ's doctrine): and merely assume as a temporary hypothesis that the essence of Christ's Gospel is a trust in the Fatherhood of God. Now, if this be so, and if this trust or faith is to be kept pure and strong, must it not be regarded with reverence and reserve as being (what indeed it is) a kind of private, domestic, and family relation? Is it to be made the subject for light, casual, frivolous discussions; epigrammatic displays; cut-and-thrust exhibitions of word-fence; logical or rhetorical symposia? What would you say of a young man who should allow his relations with his father and mother to be discussed with humour and epigram on every light occasion? Would he be likely long to retain the bloom of domestic affection unimpaired? I remember reading about some well-educated and enlightened free-thinker—I fancy it was Bolingbroke—on whose table a Greek Testament was regularly placed by the side of the port when the cloth was drawn, and whose favourite topic for discussion after dinner was the existence and attributes of the Deity. Does not your instinct teach you that from such discussions as these no good could possibly come, nothing but a hardening of the conscience, a fatal familiarity with sacred things regarded with a view to witticism—that kind of familiarity which too surely breeds contempt? What a terrible contrast it is—complacent Bolingbroke at his wine, analysing the attributes of God, and the all-pitying Father looking down from heaven and pleading, through Christ, not to be analysed but to be loved and trusted!

May we not go a step further and say that Christian Faith or trust—if it be once recognized as faith or trust, altogether distinct from the kind of assent which we give to a proposition of Euclid—needs not only to be protected from certain evil influences but also to be subjected to certain good influences? It is a kind of plant, and requires its spiritual soil, air, rain and sunshine; in other words it needs good thoughts, noble aspirations, and unselfish acts, to keep it alive. You may retort perhaps that Faith itself ought to produce these results, and not to be produced by them. But I reply that, though Faith does tend to produce these results, it is strengthened by producing them; and it is weakened and finally extinguished by not producing them. "Our faith" has been described as "the victory that hath overcome the world." What is there in the world that it should need to be "overcome"? I suppose the writer meant that this present, visible, tangible, enjoyable system of things— which was meant by the Supreme to be a kind of glass through which we might discern something of the greatness and order of the Maker—has been converted, partly by our selfishness, partly by some Evil in the world outside us, into a mirror shutting out all glimpse of God and giving us back nothing but the reflection of ourselves. On the other hand, there is a different way of regarding the world when, our eyes being opened like the eyes of Aeneas amid burning Troy, we discern in the midst of this present condition of things a great conflict between Good and Evil, and on the side of goodness, we see the forms of Righteousness, Justice and Truth, supported by Faith, Hope, and Charity; amid the smoke and roar of battles and revolutions, the destructions of nations, and the downfall of empires and of churches, we realise that these are abiding influences; that either in this world, or in some other, these things shall ultimately prevail, because these are the Angels that stand about the throne of the Ruler of the Universe. This state of mind is Faith, and it is to be nurtured by effort, partly in action, partly in thought. Bacon bids us nurture it by "cherishing the good hours of the mind." St. Paul says nearly the same thing in different words: "Whatsoever things are honourable, whatsoever things are just, whatsoever things are pure, whatsoever things are lovely, whatsoever things are of good report, if there be any virtue, and if there be any praise, *think on these things.*"

Are you surprised at this? Does faith seem to you, on these terms, a possession of little worth—this quicksilver quality which varies with every variation of our spiritual atmosphere? Why surely everything that lives and grows is liable to flux. You do not disparage bodily health because it is dependent on supports and influences, and liable to changes; why then disparage spiritual health because it is similarly dependent? No doubt one would not be willingly a religious valetudinarian; a man's spiritual constitution ought not to be at the mercy of every slight and passing breeze of circumstance; but at present there is little danger of spiritual valetudinarianism. Physical "sanitation" is on every one's tongue; but no one thinks of the necessity of good spiritual air and of the evils of bad spiritual drainage. We do not recognize that there are laws of our spiritual as well as of our material nature. We wilfully narrow our lives to the sabbathless pursuit of gain or pleasure—self everywhere, God nowhere —and then go about hypocritically whining that the age of faith has passed and that we have lost the power of believing. With our own hands we put the stopper on the telescope and then complain that we cannot see!

Do not however, suppose that I call upon you, because hope is the basis of Christian belief, on that account to hope against the truth and to believe against reason. I bid you believe in the Fatherhood of God, first because your conscience tells you that this is the best and noblest belief, but secondly also because this belief—although it may be against the superficial evidence of the phenomena of the Universe—is in accordance with these phenomena when you regard them more deeply and when you include in your scope the history of Christianity.

I admit that we have to fight against temptations in order to retain this belief; and sometimes I ask myself, "If I and my children had been slaves in one of the Southern States of America; or if I and my family had suffered such indelible outrages as were recently inflicted by the Turks upon the Bulgarians; or if I were at this moment a matchbox-seller or a father of ten children (girls as well as boys) in the East of London—should I find it so easy to believe that God is our Father in heaven?" And I am obliged to reply, " No, I should not find it easy ; " I fear that I might be tempted to say, as a workman did not long ago to a lecturer on co-operation who mentioned the name of God: " Oh, no ; no God for us ; the workman's God deserted him long ago." And perhaps you yourself may remember the answer of one of those wretched Bulgarians to some newspaper correspondent who endeavoured to console him in his anguish by the reflection that " After all there is a God that governs the world : " " I believe you," was the reply ; " there is indeed a God ; and he governs the world indeed ; and he is the

Devil." Or take a spectacle of the Middle Ages as a problem. In the lists are two armed knights; on the one side a man of might and muscle, exulting in conflict; on the other, a slight, weak creature, who never fights save on compulsion, and is to fight now on sternest compulsion, being accused (though innocent) of some gross crime by yonder man of flesh, who combines scoundrel, liar, traitor, oppressor, thief, and adulterer, all in one; and the fight is to begin under the sanction of the Church of Christ. As the trumpets sound, while the heralds are still calling on God to "shew the right," the two men meet, and "the right" is cast to the ground, trampled on by his enemy, and dragged from the lists to the neighbouring gallows, while the muscular scoundrel wipes his forehead and receives congratulations. Do you suppose that the innocent man's wife, if she were looking on, would be able easily to say at that moment, "Verily there is a God that judgeth the earth"?

Can I possibly put the case for scepticism more strongly? I would fain put it with all the force in my power in order to convince you that I have thought often over these matters, and that, although my own life may have been happy and free from stumbling-blocks, I have at least tried to understand and sympathize with those who find it very hard to believe that there is a God. But, in the presence of such monstrous evils as these, I take refuge in a belief and in a fact; first, in the belief (which runs through almost every page of the Gospels and has received the sanction of Christ Himself) that there is an Evil Being in the world who is continually opposing the Good but will be ultimately subdued by the Good; secondly, in the fact that in one great typical conflict between Good and Evil,—where apparently God did not "shew the right," and where, in appearance, there was consummated the most brutal triumph of Evil over Good that the world ever witnessed—there the Good in reality effected its most signal triumph. The issue of the conflict on the Cross of Christ is my great comfort and mainstay of faith, when my heart is distracted with the thought of all the spurns, buffets, and outrages, endured by much-suffering humanity. " At last, far off," I cry, " the right will be shewn, even as it was in the contest on the Cross."

You see then the nature of the conflict of faith. It is a struggle of hope against fear, trustfulness against trustlessness, where strict logical proof is impossible. But I do not call you to set Faith against Reason, or to make hope trample on the understanding, or to shut your eyes to the presence or absence of historical evidence. If religion `comes down from the region of hope and aspiration into the region of fact and evidence, and asserts that this or that fact happened at this or that time and place, then, so far, it appeals to evidence, and by evidence it must be judged.

Half the earnest scepticism of the present day is not really spiritual scepticism but simply doubt about historical facts. Distinguish carefully and constantly between two terms entirely different but continually confused—the *super-natural* and the *miraculous*.

In the super-natural every rational man must believe, if he knows what is meant by the term ; for every rational man must acknowledge that the world had either a beginning or no beginning, a First Cause or no First Cause ; and either hypothesis is altogether above the level of natural phenomena, and therefore supernatural. The theist and the atheist are alike believers in the supernatural. The agnostic, poised between the two, admits that some supernatural origin of the world is necessary, but is unable to decide which of the two is the more probable. All alike therefore believe in the supernatural; but the important difference is that some take a hopeful or faithful, others a hopeless or faithless, view of the supernatural. Proof in this region is not possible, unless the testimony of the conscience may be accepted as proof. If Jesus were to appear to-morrow sitting on the clouds of heaven and testifying that there is a Father in heaven, I can imagine some men of science replying, " This is a mere phantom of the brain," or, " This is the result of indigestion," or "Assertion is not proof." Mere force of logical proof or personal observation can convince no one that there is a God or that Jesus is the Eternal Son of God ; such a conviction can only come from a leaping out of the human spirit to meet the Spirit of God ; and hence St. Paul tells us that "no man can say " —that is, " say sincerely "—"that Jesus is the Lord *save by the Spirit*." Here therefore, in this region of the indemonstrable, I can honestly use an effort of the will to ally myself with the spirit of faith. " I will pray to God ; I will cling to God ; will refuse to doubt of God ; refuse to listen to doubts about God (except so far as may be needful to do it, in order to lighten the doubts of others, and then only as a painful duty, to be got through with all speed) ; I am determined (so help me God) to believe in God to the end of my days : "—in resolving thus I am not acting insincerely nor shutting my eyes to the truth, but taking nature's appointed means for reaching and holding fast the highest spiritual truth.

But I do not feel justified in thus using my will to constrain myself to believe in the miraculous; for here God has given me other means—such as history, experience, and evidence—for arriving at the truth. Nor does a belief in the super-natural in the least imply a belief in the miraculous also. I may believe that God is continually supporting and impelling on its path every created thing ; but I may also believe that there is no evidence to prove that His support and impulsion have ever been manifested save in accordance with that orderly sequence which we call Law. I may even believe that the Universe is double, having a spiritual and invisible counterpart corresponding to this visible and material existence, so that nothing is done in the world of flesh below which has not been first done in the world of spirit above; yet even this latitude of spiritual speculation would not in the least establish the conclusion that the observed sequence of what we call cause and effect in the material world has ever been violated. To take a particular instance, I may be convinced, that Jesus of Nazareth was the Eternal Word of God, made flesh for men; and yet I may remain unconvinced that, in thus taking flesh upon Him, He raised Himself above the physical laws of humanity. In other words I may, with the author of the Fourth Gospel, heartily believe in the supernatural Incarnation while omitting from my Gospel all mention of the Miraculous Conception. Nay, I may go still further. While cordially accepting the divine nature of Christ, I may see such clear indications and evidences of the manner in which accounts of miracles sprang up in the Church without foundation of fact, that I may be compelled not merely to omit miracles from my Gospel and to confess myself unconvinced of their truth, but even to avow my conviction of their untruth. But into this negative aspect of things I do not wish now to enter. I would rather urge on you this positive consideration, that, since our recognition of the Laws of Nature themselves, depends in a very large degree upon faith, we ought not to be surprised if our acknowledgment of the Founder of these Laws rests also on the same basis. And, if this be so, we cannot speak accurately about the "evidence" for the existence of a God, unless we include in that term the aspirations of the human conscience toward a Maker and Ruler and Father of all.

VIII

My dear ——,

I am afraid your notions about "proof" are still rather hazy; for you quote against me a stern and self-denying dictum which passes current among some of your young friends, that "it is immoral to believe what cannot be proved."

Have you seriously asked yourself what you mean by "proved" in enunciating this proposition? Do you mean "made sufficiently probable to induce a man to act upon the probability"? Or do you mean "absolutely demonstrated"?

If you mean the former, not so many as you suppose are guilty of this "immorality." Give me an instance, if if you can, of a man who "believes what cannot be made sufficiently probable to induce him to act upon the probability." Of course some men *say* they believe what they, in reality, do not believe; but you speak, not about "saying" but about "believing;" and I do not see how any man can "believe" what he does not regard as probable. I am inclined to think therefore that, in this sense of the word "prove," your proposition is meaningless.

But perhaps by "prove," you mean "absolutely demonstrate;" and your thesis is that "it is immoral to believe what cannot be absolutely demonstrated;" in that case I am obliged to ask you how you can repeat such cant, such a mere parrot cry, with a grave face.

Do you not see that, as soon as you conceded (as I

understand you to have done) that our belief in the Laws of Nature is based upon the Imagination, you virtually conceded the validity of a kind of proof in which faith and hope play a large part, and in which demonstration is impossible. "Demonstration" applies to mathematics and to syllogisms where the premises are granted, though it is also sometimes loosely used of proof conveyed by personal observation; "proof" applies to the other affairs of life. Demonstration appeals very largely (not entirely, as I have shown above, but very largely) to Reason; proof is largely based on Faith. Having defined "angles," "triangles," "base," and "isosceles," and having been granted certain axioms and postulates, I can demonstrate that the angles at the basis of an isosceles triangle are equal to one another; but I cannot "demonstrate" that, if I throw a stone in the air, it will come down again, though I am perfectly convinced that it will come down, and though I commonly assert that I can "prove" that it will come down.

Why, your whole life is full of beliefs—as certain as any beliefs can be—which it is impossible to demonstrate! When you got up this morning did you not believe that your razor would shave and your looking-glass reflect; that your boiling water would scald if you spilt it, and your egg break if you dropped it; and a score or two of other similar perfectly certain beliefs—all entertained and acted on in less than an hour, but all incapable of demonstration? But you maintain perhaps that "these beliefs are not beliefs, but knowledge based on the uniformity of the laws of nature; you know that the laws of nature are uniform, and therefore you knew that your razor would shave." But how, I ask, do you know that the laws of nature are uniform? "By the experience of mankind during many thousands of years." But how do you know that what has been in the past will be in the future—will be in the next instant? "Well, if a law of nature were broken—say, for example, the law of gravitation—the whole Universe would fall to pieces." In other words, you and I would feel extremely uncomfortable, if we existed long enough to feel anything; but what does that demonstrate? Absolutely nothing. It would no doubt be extremely inconvenient for both of us if any law of nature observed in the past did not continue to be observed in the future; but inconvenience proves nothing logically. It is no doubt extremely inconvenient not to be able to believe that your razor will shave; but what of that? Where is the demonstration? And remember your own *dictum*, "It is immoral to believe what cannot be demonstrated."

Perhaps you may try to writhe out of this application of your own principle by the use of grand terms; "The Laws of Nature have been proved to be true by experiment as well as by observation; they have been made the basis for abstruse calculations and inferences as to what will happen; then the philosopher has predicted 'this will happen,' and it has happened. Surely no one will deny that this is a proof!" A proof of what? Of the future invariableness of the sequences of Nature? I shall not only deny, but enjoy denying, that it is a proof; if you mean by proof such a demonstrative proof as you obtain in a syllogism, where the premises are assumed, or in mathematics, where you are reasoning about things that have no real existence but are merely convenient ideas of the imagination. Believe me, this distinction of terms is by no means superfluous. You and your young scientific friends are continually confusing " proof " with " demonstration;" and you have one use of the word " proof" for religion and another for science. When you speak of religion, you say " it is immoral to believe in it for it cannot be *proved*" (meaning " demonstrated "); when you speak of science, you say, " This can be *proved*" (not meaning "demonstrated," but simply "made probable," or "proved for practical purposes").

You may discourse for hours upon the Laws of Nature, but you will never succeed in convincing any one, not even yourself, that they will remain valid in the moment that is to come, by the mere force of logic. You are certain—so am I practically quite certain—that the stone which I throw at this moment up in the air, will, in the next moment, fall to the ground. But this certainty does not arise from logic. We have absolutely no reason for this leap into the darkness of the future except faith,—faith of course resting upon a basis of facts, but still faith. The very names and notions of "cause" and "effect" are due not to observation, nor to demonstration, but to faith. The name, and the notion, of a Law of Nature are nothing but convenient ideas of the scientific imagination, based upon faith. Take an instance. We say, and genuinely believe, that fire and gunpowder "cause" explosion; that explosion is the "effect" of gunpowder and fire; and that the effect follows the causes in accordance with the "laws of nature;" but you have not observed all this and you cannot demonstrate it. You have merely observed in the past an invariable sequence of explosion following (in all cases that you have seen or heard about) the combination of gunpowder and fire; you have also perhaps predicted in the past that explosion would follow, and demonstrated that it did follow this combination, as often as you pleased; you have found, or have heard that others have found, that this sequence agrees with other chemical sequences, which you are in the habit of calling causes and effects; but all this is evidence as to the past, not as to the future. Your certainty as to the future arises not from any demonstration about the future, but from your faith or trust in the fixed order of Nature, and from nothing else. Now the greater part of the action of life deals with the future.

It follows therefore that, in the greater part of life, we act, not from demonstration, but from a proof in which faith is a constituent element.

Whence arises this trust in the uniformity of the phenomena of the Universe? We can hardly give any other answer except that we could not get on without it. Having been found to "work" by ourselves, and by many generations of our forefathers, this faith is possibly by this time an inherited instinct as well as the inbred result of our own earliest experiences. But when we analyse it we are forced to confess that we can give no logical account of it. Logically regarded, it savours of the most audacious optimism, arguing, or rather sentimentalizing, after this fashion: "It would be so immensely inconvenient if Nature were every moment changing her rules without notice! All forethought, all civilization would be at an end; nay, we could not so much as take a single step or move a limb with confidence, if we could not depend upon Nature!" Does not this personification of Nature, and trust or faith in Nature, somewhat resemble our trust or faith in God? I think it does; and it is very interesting to note that the very foundations of science are laid in a quasi-religious sentiment of which no logical justification can be given.

I might easily go further and shew that, even as regards the past, we act in our daily lives very often on the grounds of faith and very seldom on the grounds of demonstration. On this I have touched in a previous letter; but your dictum about the "immorality of believing what cannot be proved" makes it clear that you are hardly as yet aware of the nature of the ordinary "proofs" on which we act. How few there are who have any grounds but faith for believing in the existence of a Julius Cæsar or an Alexander! Yet they believe implicitly. Many have heard these two great men loosely spoken of, or alluded to; but they have never weighed, nor have they the least power to weigh, the evidence that proves that Cæsar and Alexander actually existed. Now as the unlearned are quite certain of the existence of a Julius Cæsar, so are you too quite certain of many facts upon very slight grounds. You ask one man his name; another, how many children he has; a third, the name of the street in which he lives, and so on; how certain you often feel, on the slight evidence of their answers (unless there be special grounds for suspecting them) that your information is correct! The reason is that all social intercourse depends on faith; if you began to suspect and disbelieve every man who gave you answers to such simple questions as these, social life would be at an end for you, and you might as well at once retire to a hermitage; scepticism in matters of this kind has not worked, and faith has worked; and this has gone on with you from childhood and with your forefathers from their childhood for many generations. Thus faith has become a second instinct with you, and you act upon it so often and so naturally that you are not aware of the degree to which it influences and permeates your actions. The cases in which you act thus instinctively upon very slight evidence, and upon a large and general faith in the people who give the evidence, are far more numerous than those cases in which you formally weigh evidence and attempt to arrive at something like demonstrative proof. In other words, not only as regards the future but also as regards the past, faith is for the most part the underlying basis of action. You believe, to a large extent and in a great many cases, simply because "it would be so immensely inconvenient not to believe."

I claim that I have fulfilled my promise of shewing that people act much more upon faith than upon demonstration in every department of life; and I now repeat and emphasize what I said before, that if all our existence is thus dominated by faith, it is absurd to attempt to exclude faith from any religion. But if our special religion consists in a recognition of God the Maker as God the Father, then it is more natural than ever to suppose that our religion will require a large element of faith or trust. Just as family life would break down if the sons were always analysing the father's character, and declining to believe anything to his credit beyond what could be demonstrated to be true, so religious life will break down, if we treat the Father in heaven as a mere topic for logical discussion and declare that it is "immoral to believe" in His fatherhood if it cannot be proved.

Of course I do not deny that you must have evidence of the existence of the Father before you can trust in Him. You could not trust your parents if you had not seen, touched, heard them—known something of them in fact through the senses : so neither can you trust God if you have not known something of Him through the senses. Well, I maintain that is what you are continually doing. God is continually revealing Himself to us in the power, the beauty, the glory, the harmony, the beneficence, the mystery, of the Universe, and pre-eminently in human goodness and greatness. Contemplate, touch, hear ; concentrate your mind on these things, and especially on the perfection of human goodness, power, and wisdom : thus you will be enabled to realize the presence of the Father and then to trust in Him. Contemplate also the Evolution of the present from the past : the ascent from a protoplasm to the first man, from the first man to a Homer, a Dante, a Shakespeare and a Newton ; do not entirely ignore Socrates, St. Paul, St. Francis. You cannot indeed shut your eyes to the growth of evil simultaneously with the growth of good : but do not fix your eyes too long upon the evil : prefer to contemplate the defeat of evil by goodness, especially in the struggle on the Cross ; and

Letter 8] FAITH AND DEMONSTRATION 79

with your contemplation let there be some admixture of action against the evil and for the good. Do this, and I think you will have no reason to complain of the want of "evidence" of the existence of One who has made us to trust in Him.

I have told you what to do: let me add one word also of warning as to what you are not to do. You are not to regard the world from the point of view of a neutral and amused spectator. You are not to detach yourself from the great struggle of good against evil, and to look on, and call it "interesting." That attitude is fatal to all religion. Reject, as from the devil, the precept *nil admirari;* better be a fool than a dispassionate critic of Christ. Again, you are not to regard the world from the mere student point of view, looking at the Universe as a great Examination Paper in which you may hope to solve more problems and score more marks than anybody else. High intellectual pursuits and habits of enthusiastic research are sometimes terribly demoralizing when they tempt a man to think that he can live above, and without, social ties and affections, and that mere sentiment is to be despised in comparison with knowledge. This danger impends over literary as well as other students, over critical theologians as well as over scientific experimenters; we all sometimes forget—we students— that, if we do not exercise the habit of trusting and loving men, we cannot trust and love God. To harden oneself against the mute but trustful appeal of even a beast is not without some spiritual peril of incapacitating oneself for worship.

IX

MY DEAR ——,

Your grounds of objection appear to be now changed. You say you do not understand my position with regard to Evolution, as I described it before, and referred to it in my last letter. If I admit Evolution, you ask how I can consistently deny that every nation and every individual, Israel and Christ included, " proceeded from material causes by necessary sequence according to fixed laws ; " and in that case what becomes of such metaphors as "the regulating hand of God," "God the Ruler of the Universe" and the like? It is a common saying, you tell me, among those of your companions who have a turn for science, that " Evolution has disposed of the old proofs of the existence of a God : " and you ask me how I meet this objection.

I meet it by asking you another question exactly like your own. I take a lump of clay and a potter's wheel and "from these material causes by necessary sequence according to fixed laws" I mould a vessel ; is there no room in this process for "the regulating hand of man" and for "man the creator of the vessel"? In other words, may not these "fixed laws," and that "necessity" of which you admit the existence, represent the perpetual pressure of the Creator's hand, or will, upon the Universe?

By Evolution is meant that all results are evolved from immediate causes, which are evolved from distant causes, which are themselves evolved from more distant causes ;

and so on. In old times, men believed that God made the world by a number of isolated acts. Now, it is believed that He made a primordial something, say atoms, out of which there have been shaped series upon series of results by continuous motion in accordance with fixed laws of nature. But neither the isolated theory nor the continuous theory can dispense with a Creator in the centre. We speak of the "chain of creation;" and we know that in old days men recognized few links between us and the Creator. Now, we recognize many. But, because a chain has more links than we once supposed, are we excused for rejecting our old belief in the existence of a chain-maker? Whether things came to be as they are, by many creations, or by one creation and many evolutions, what difference does it make? In the one case, we believe in a Creator and Sustainer: in the other case, in a Creator and Evolver. In either case, do we not believe in a God?

What then do your young friends mean—for though they express themselves loosely, I think they do mean something and are not merely repeating a cant phrase—when they say that Evolution has "disposed of the old proofs of the existence of a God"? I think they mean that Evolution is inconsistent with the existence of *such a God as the Christian religion proclaims, that is to say, a Father in heaven.* The old theory of discontinuous creation (in its most exaggerated form) maintained that everything was created for a certain benevolent purpose—our hair to shelter our heads from the weather, our eyebrows and eyelashes to keep off the dust and the sun, our thumbs to give us that prehensile power which largely differentiates us from apes; in a word, paternal despotism was supposed to do everything for us with the best of intentions. The new theory says there is no sufficient evidence of such paternal benevolence. Our hair and our eyebrows and eyelashes and thumbs came to us in quite a different fashion. Life, ever since life existed, has been one vast scramble and conflict for the good things of this world: those beings that were best fitted for scrambling and fighting destroyed those that were unfit, and thus propagated the peculiarities of the conquerors and destroyed the peculiarities of the conquered. Thus the characteristics of body or brain best fitted for the purpose of life were developed, and the unfit were destroyed. Although therefore a purpose was achieved, it was not achieved as a purpose, but as a consequence. There is no room, say the supporters of Evolution, in such a theory as this for the hypothesis of an Almighty Father of mankind, or even of a very intelligent Maker. What should we think of a British workman who, in order to make one good brick, made a hundred bad ones, or of a cattle-breeder whose plan was to breed a thousand inferior beasts on inadequate pasture, in order ultimately to produce, out of their struggles for food, and as a result of the elimination of the unfittest, one pre-eminent pair?

When he expresses himself in this way, my sympathies go very far with the man of science, if only he could remember that he is protesting, not against Christ's teaching about God, but against some other quite different theory. Though God is called "Almighty" in the New Testament, we must remember that it is always assumed that there is an opposing Evil, an Adversary or Satan, who will ultimately be subdued but is meantime working against the will of God. The origin of this Evil the followers of Christ do not profess to understand; but we believe that it was not originated by God and that it is not obedient to Him. We cannot therefore, strictly speaking, say that God is the Almighty ruler of "the Universe *as it is.*" God is King *de jure,* but not at present *de facto* (metaphors again! but metaphors expressive of distinct realities).

His kingdom is " to come: " He will be hereafter recognized as Almighty ; He cannot be so recognized at present.

I know very well that I can give no logical or consistent account of this mysterious resistance to the Supreme God. But I am led to recognize it, first, by the facts of the visible world ; secondly, by the plain teaching of Christ Himself. Surely the authority of Christ must count for something with Christians in their theorizing about the origin of evil. Would not even an agnostic admit that as, in poetry, I should be right in following the lead of a poet, so in matters of spiritual belief (if I am to have any spiritual belief at all) I am right in deferring to Christ? It is a marvel to me how some Christians who find the recognition of miracles inextricably involved in the life and even in the teaching of Christ, nevertheless fail to see, or at all events are most unwilling to confess, that the recognition of an evil one, or Satan, is an axiom that underlies all His doctrine. In the view of Jesus, it is Satan that causes some forms of disease and insanity ; Satan is the author of temptation, the destroyer of the good seed, the sower of tares, the " evil one "—so at least the text of the Revisers tells us—from whom we must daily pray to be delivered. The same belief pervades the writings of St. Paul. Yet if you preach nowadays this plain teaching of our Lord, the heterodox shrug their shoulders and cry "Antediluvian ! " while the orthodox think to dispose of the whole matter in a phrase, " Flat Manichæism ! " But to the heterodox I might reply that Stuart Mill (no very antiquated or credulous philosopher) deliberately stated that it was more easy to believe in the existence of an Evil as well as a Good, than in the existence of one good and all-powerful God ; and the orthodox must, upon reflection, admit that in this doctrine about Satan Christ's own teaching is faithfully followed.

Of course if any one replies, " Christ was under an

illusion in believing in the existence of Satan," I have no means of logically confuting him. But I think there must be many who would say, with me: "If I am to have any theory in matters of this kind which are entirely beyond the sphere of demonstration, I would sooner accept the testimony of Christ than the speculations of all the philosophers that ever were or are. Christ was possibly, or even probably, ignorant (in His humanity) of a great mass of literary, historical, physiological, and other scientific facts unknown to the rest of the Jews. But we cannot suppose Him to be spiritually ignorant; least of all, so spiritually ignorant as to attribute to the Adversary what ought to have been attributed to God the Father in Heaven.

It would be easy for you to shew that any theory of Satan is absurdly illogical; nobody can be convinced of that more firmly than I am already. Whether Satan was good at first and became evil without a cause; or was good at first and became evil from a certain cause (which presupposes another pre-existing Satan); or was evil from the beginning and created by God; or evil from the beginning and not created by God—in all or any of these hypotheses I see, as clearly as you see, insuperable difficulties. If you cross-examine me, I shall avow at once a logical collapse, after this fashion: "Were there then two First Causes?" I believe not. "Did the Evil spring up after the Good?" I believe so. "Did the first Good create the Evil?"[1] I believe not. "Did the Evil then spring

[1] Some passages in the Old Testament (notably Isaiah xlv. 7) state that God "created evil;" and results attributed by one author to Satan (1 Chron. xxi. 1) are attributed by another to "the anger of the Lord" (2 Sam. xxiv. 1). Much of course depends upon the meaning of the word "evil;" and I am knowingly guilty of talking absurdly when I first define evil as "that which is not in accordance with God's intention," and then proceed to say that "God did not create evil." But all people who discourse philosophically on this subject talk far more absurdly than I do: for I am consciously, but they are unconsciously, illogical. The belief that God "created evil," whether held or not by the authors of any of the books of the Old Testament, is against the whole tenour of the teaching of Christ.

up without a cause?" I cannot tell. "Did the Good, when He created the Goodness that issued in Evil, know that he, or it, contained the germ of evil, and would soon become wholly evil?" I do not believe this. "Whence then came the Evil, or the germ of the Evil?" I do not know. "Are you not then confessing that you believe, where you know nothing?" Yes, for if I knew, there would be no need to believe.

Here you have a sufficiently amusing exhibition of inconsistency and ignorance: but this seems to me of infinitely little concern where I am dealing not with matters that fall within the range of experience, but with spiritual and supernatural things that belong to the realm of faith, hope, and aspiration. I could just as easily turn inside out my cross-examiner if he undertook to give me a scientific theory on the origin of the world. No doubt he might prefer having no theory about the origin of the world, and might recommend me to imitate him by having no theory about the origin of Evil, or about the nature of the Supreme Good. But my answer would be as follows: "I have a certain work to do in the world, and I cannot go on with my work without having some theories on these subjects. Most men feel with me that they must have some answer to these stupendous problems of existence. As the senses are intended to be our guide in matters of experience, so our faculty of faith seems to me intended to guide us in matters quite beyond experience." There is another answer which I hardly like to give because it seems brutal; but I believe it to be true, and it is certainly capable of being expressed in the evolutionary dialect so as to commend itself to the scientific mind: "An agnostic nation will find itself sooner or later unsuited for its environment, and will either come to believe in some solution of these spiritual problems or stagnate and perish. And something of the same result will follow from agnosticism in the family and in the individual."

From this doctrine of Christ then I am not to be dislodged by any philosophic analysis demonstrating that good and evil so run into one another that it is impossible to tell where one ends and the other begins. "Is all pain evil? Is it an evil that a sword's point pains you? Would it not be a greater evil that a sword should run you through unawares because it did not pain you? Is not the pain of hunger a useful monitor? Has not pain in a thousand cases its use as a preservative? Is not what you call "sin" very often misplaced energy? If a child is restless and talkative and consequently disobedient, must you consequently bring in Satan to account for the little one's peccadilloes? If a young man is over-sanguine, reckless, rash, occasionally intemperate, must all these faults be laid upon the back of an enemy of mankind? Is animal death from Satan, but vegetable death from God? And is the death of a sponge a half and half contribution from the joint Powers? And when I swallow an oyster, may I give thanks to God? but when a tiger devours a deer, or an eagle tears a hare, or a thrush swallows a worm, are they doing the work of the Adversary? Where are you to begin to trace this permeating Satanic agency? Go back to the primordial atom. Are we to say that the Devil impelled it in the selfish tangential straight line, and that God attracts it with an unselfish centripetal force, and that the result is the harmonious curve of actuality? If you give yourself up to such a degrading dualism as this, will you not be more often fearing Satan than loving God? Will you not be attributing to Satan one moment, what the next moment will compel you to attribute to God? Where will you draw the line?" To all this my answer is very simple: "I shall draw the line where the spiritual instinct within me draws it. Whatever I am forced to pronounce contrary to God's intention I shall call evil and attribute to Satan." Herein I may go wrong in details, and I may have to correct my judgments as I grow in knowledge; but I am confident that, on the whole, I shall be following the teaching of Christ. My spiritual convictions accord with the teaching of that ancient allegory in the book of Genesis, which tells us that Satan, not God, brought sin and death into the world. There was a Fall somewhere, in heaven perhaps as well as on earth—"war in heaven" of the Evil against the Good—a declension from the divine ideal, a lapse by which the whole Universe became imperfect. It has been the work of God, not to create death, but upon the basis of death to erect a hope and faith in a higher life; not to create sin, but out of sin, repentance, and forgiveness, to elicit a higher righteousness than would have been possible (so we speak) if sin had never existed. Similarly of disease, and pain, and the conflict in the animal world for life and death: good has resulted from them; yet I cannot think of them, I cannot even think of change and decay, as being, so to speak, " parts of God's *first intention*." Stoics, and Christians who imitate Stoics, may call these things "indifferent:" I cannot. And even if I could, what of the ferocity, and cruelty, and exultation in destruction, which are apparent in the animal world? "Death," say the Stoics, "is the mere exit from life." Is it? I was once present at a theatre in Rouen where the hero took a full quarter of an hour to die of poison, and the young Normans who sat round me expressed their strenuous disapprobation: "C'est trop long," they murmured. I have made the same remonstrance in my heart of hearts, ever since I was a boy and saw a cat play with a mouse, and a patient stoat hunt down and catch at last a tired-out rabbit: " It is too long," " It is too cruel." " Did God ordain this?"—I asked: and I answered unhesitatingly "No." These are but small phenomena in Nature's chamber of horrors: but for me they have always been, and will always remain, horrible. I believe that God intends us to regard them with horror and perhaps to see in them some faint reflection of the wantonly destructive and torturing instinct in man.

Those are fine-sounding lines, those of Cleanthes :—

οὐδέ τι γίγνεται ἔργον ἐπὶ χθονὶ σου δίχα, δαῖμον,
πλὴν ὅποσα ῥέζουσι κακοὶ σφετέρῃσιν ἀνοίαις.[1]

I should like to agree with them; but I cannot. The picture of the cat and the mouse appears—fertile in suggestions. "This at least," I say, "was not wrought by 'evil men in their folly;' and yet it did not come direct from God." Isaiah pleases me better with his prediction, physiologically absurd, but spiritually most true: "The lion shall eat straw like a bullock." That is just the confession that I need: it comes to me with all the force of a divine acknowledgment, as if God thereby said: "Death and conflict must be for a time, but they shall not be for ever: it was not my intention, it is not my will, that my creatures should thrive by destroying each other."

Applying this theory to Evolution, I believe that Satan, not God, was the author of the wasteful and continuous conflict that has characterized it; but that God has utilized this conflict for the purposes of development and progress. This is what I had in my mind when I said that Evolution diminished the difficulties in the way of acknowledging the existence of a God. The problems of death, destruction, waste, conflict and sin, are not new; they are as old as Job, perhaps as old as the first-created man; but it is new to learn that good has resulted from

---

[1] "Naught is on earth, O God, without thy hand,
Save deeds of folly wrought by evil men."

those evils. In so far as Evolution has taught this, it has helped to strengthen, not to weaken, our faith. But then, if we are to use this language, we must learn to think, not of "Evolution by itself," but of "Evolution with Satan." "Evolution without Satan" would appal us by the seeming wastefulness and ubiquity of conflict and the indirectness of its benefits; but "Evolution with Satan" enables us to realize God as our refuge and strength amid the utmost storms and tempests of destruction.

If any one says that the belief in Satan is inexpedient, I am ready to give him a patient hearing; but I find it difficult to listen patiently to what people are pleased to call arguments against it. For example, "Duty can exist only in a world of conflict;" to which the reply is obvious, "But God might have made men for love and harmonious obedience, and not for duty and conflict." This, of course, is a very presumptuous statement, such as Bishop Butler would have condemned; but it is a fitting reply to a still more presumptuous implied statement. God has revealed Himself as Righteousness and Goodness without internal conflict; He has also revealed His purpose to conform us to Himself; and the Bible speaks of Him as being opposed by an Adversary who caused men for a time to differ from the divine image; is it not then a very presumptuous thing to imply that "God *could* not have created men but for conflict and duty," or, in other words, "God *could* not have made us better than we are, even had there been no Adversary opposing His will?" Again, we hear it said that, "An evil Spirit contending against a good Spirit must needs have produced two distinct worlds, and not the one progressive world of which we have experience:" to which the answer is equally obvious, "The orbit of every planet, or the path of any projectile, shews that two different forces may result in one continuous curve."

The only consistent and systematic way of rejecting a belief in the existence of Satan is to reject the belief in the existence of sin. Then you can argue thus, "The notion of a Satan arises from the false and sharp antagonism which our human imaginations set up between 'good' and 'evil,' whereas what we call 'evil' is really nothing but an excess of tendencies good in themselves and only evil when carried to excess. The difference therefore between good and evil is only a question of degree." That theory sounds plausible; but it ignores the essence of sin, which consists in a rebellion against Conscience. It is not excess, or defect, the more, or the less; it is the moral disorder, the subversion of human nature, which is so frightful to contemplate that we cannot believe it to have proceeded from God. But perhaps you reply, "That very disorder is merely the result of energy out of place or in excess." Well, in the same way, when gas is escaping in a room in which there is a lighted candle, there is first a quiet and inoffensive escape of the gas, and secondly a violent and perhaps calamitous explosion; and you might argue similarly, "The difference was only one of degree; the explosion was merely the result of a useful element out of place and in excess." But I should answer that no sober and sensible householder would justify himself in this way for allowing a lighted candle and escaping gas to come together; and so I cannot believe that God is willing that men should justify Him for tolerating theft, murder, and adultery, on the ground that these things are "only questions of degree." I think we please Him better, and draw closer to Him, when we say, "An Enemy hath done this." And besides, for our own sakes, if we are to resist sin with our utmost force, it seems to me we are far more likely to do so when we regard it as Christ and St. Paul regarded it than when we give it the name of "misplaced energy," or "an excessive use of faculties, in themselves, good and necessary."

To me it seems that if we are to have a genuine trust in God, it is almost necessary that we should believe in the existence of a Satan. I say "almost," because there may be rare exceptions. A few pure saintly souls, of inextinguishable trust, may perhaps be able to face the awful phenomena of Evil and to say, " Though He hath done all this yet will we trust in Him ; what may have moved Him to cause His creatures to struggle together, and to thrive, each on the destruction of its neighbour, we know not, and we are not careful to know ; our hearts teach us that He is above us in goodness, and in wisdom, as in power ; we know that we must trust Him ; more than this we do not wish to know." Such men are to be admired—but to be admired by most of us at a great distance. For the masses of men, and especially for those who know something of the depth of sin, it must be a great and almost a necessary help to say, "The Good that is done upon Earth, God doeth it Himself ; the evil that is upon earth God doeth it not : an Enemy hath done this."

One evil resulting from the rejection of Christ's doctrine is that we consequently fail to understand much of His life and sufferings. If Christ was really manifested that He might destroy the works of the Devil, then much is clear that is otherwise incomprehensible. There was then no delusion nor insincerity in the parables of the Sower and the Tares. God did not first cast the good seed and then blow it away with His own breath. God did not sow wheat with the right hand and tares with the left. "An Enemy" had done the mischief. There was no fiction when Jesus spent those long hours by night on the mountain top in prayer. He needed help, and needed it sorely. He was fighting a real battle. It was not the mere anticipation of pains in the flesh, the piercing nails, the parching thirst, the long-protracted death, that made the bitterness of Christ's passion. Even when He had regained composure, and in perfect calm was going forth to meet His death, we find Him declaring that Satan had asked for one of his Apostles "to sift him as wheat," and implying that all His prayers were needed that the faith of the tempted disciple should not "fail." But in Gethsemane the battle for the souls of men was still pending. There was an Enemy who was pulling down His heart, striving hard to make Him despair of sinful mankind, perhaps to despair of we know not what more beyond; forcing Him in the extremity of that sore conflict to cry that He was "exceeding sorrowful even unto death," and afterwards, on the Cross, to utter those terrible words, "My God, my God, why hast thou forsaken me?" All this is full of profound meaning, if there was indeed an Enemy. But if there was no Enemy, what becomes of the conflict? What meaning is left to the Crucifixion, except as the record of mere physical sufferings, the like of which have been endured, before and after, by thousands of ordinary men and women?

This belief in the existence of Satan appears to me to be confirmed by daily present experience as well as by the life of Christ. It "works." It enables us, as no other belief does, to go to the poor, the sick, the suffering, and the sinful, and to preach Christ's Gospel of the fatherhood of God. All simple, straightforward people who are acquainted with the troubles of life must naturally crave this doctrine. If you ascribe to Providence the work of Satan, they will consciously or unconsciously identify Providence with the author of evil, and look to One above to rescue them from Providence. Instead of attempting to console people for all their evils by laying them on the Author of Goodness, we ought to lay them in part upon themselves, in part on the author of evil.

"God, the Father in heaven, did not intend you to be thus miserable"—thus we can begin our message—"your sufferings come from an Enemy against whom He is contending. Do not for a moment suppose that you are to put up in this life with penury, disease, misery, and sin as if these things came from God. Very often they are the just punishments of your own faults, as when drunkenness brings disease; but as the sin, so also the punishment, was of Satan's making, though God may use both for your good. You are to be patient under tribulation; you are to be made perfect through suffering; you are to regard the trials and troubles of life as being in some sense a useful chastisement proceeding from the fatherly hand of God. But never let your sense of the need of resignation lead you to attribute to the origination of God that which Christ teaches us to have been brought into the world by God's adversary. Satan made these evils to lead men wrong; God uses them to lead men right. Death, for example, came from Satan, who would fain make us believe that our souls perish with our bodies, that friends are parted for ever by the grave, and that there is no righteousness hereafter to compensate for what is wrong here: but God uses death to make men sober, thoughtful, steadfast, courageous, and trustful. It remains with you to decide whether you will bear your evils so as to succumb to the temptations of Satan, or so as to prevail over them and utilize them to your own welfare and to the glory of God. On which side will you fight? We ask you to enlist on the side of righteousness."

I feel sure that this theory of life would commend itself to the poor, that it would be morally advantageous to the rich, and that it would be politically useful to the State. There has been too prevalent a habit—among those believers especially who ignore Satan and attribute all things to God—of taking for granted that the social inequalities and miseries of the lower classes which have come down to us from feudal and non-Christian times, can never pass away. I remember once in my boyhood how, when I represented to a farmer that the condition of his labourers was not a happy one, he met me with a text of Scripture, " The poor shall never depart out of the land ; " and that seemed to him to leave no more to be said. It is this provoking acquiescence of the comfortable classes in the miseries of the suffering classes, which irritates the latter into a disbelief of the religion that dictates so great a readiness to see in the miseries of others a divinely ordained institution.

The time will soon come (1885) when the very poor will demand a greater share in the happiness of life : and the question will arise whether they can be helped to obtain this by their own individual efforts or by the co-operation of those of their own class, or by the State, or by the Church. Caution must be shewn in trying experiments with nations ; but as some experiments will assuredly have to be tried, it is most desirable in this crisis of our history that the Church at all events should faithfully follow Christ by regarding physical evil, not as a law of fate, but as a device of Satan. If, by descending a step or two lower in the scale of comfort, the comfortable classes could lift the very poor a step or two higher, the Church ought not to help the rich to shut their eyes to their obvious duty by giving them the excuses of such texts as " The poor shall never depart out of the land," or, " Man is born to trouble as the sparks fly upward." Poverty is often a good school : but penury is distinctly an evil ; and the Church should regard it as an evil not coming from God, and should make war against it, and teach the poor not to acquiesce in it. The Gospel of Christ would be made more intelligible to the poorer classes than it has been made for many centuries past, if it could be preached as a war against physical as well as moral harm. Such a crusade would call out and enlist on the right side all the combative faculty in us; it would inspire in us a passionate allegiance towards Christ, as our Leader, desiring, asking, yes, and we may almost say, needing our help in a real conflict in which His honour as well as our happiness and highest interests are at stake; it would attract the co-operation of all faculties in the individual, of all classes in the country. In other words the theory would work; and so far as a religious theory works, so far have we evidence, present and intelligible to all, that it contains truth.

I have recently heard views similar to mine controverted by an able theologian, who contended that, although they professed to be illogical, they went beyond the bounds even of the illogicality permissible in this subject. But the controverter's solution of the problem was this: "*Evil is a part of God's intention. We have to fight, with God, against something which we recognise to be His work.*" Is not this a "hard saying"? Is it not harder than the saying of Christ, "An enemy hath done this"? I say nothing about its being illogical and absurd: but does it not raise up a new stumbling-block in the path of those who are striving to follow Christ?

It may be urged that the belief in Satan has been tested by the experience of centuries and has been found to be productive of superstition, insanity, and immorality; but these evils appear to me to have sprung, not from the belief in Satan, but from a superstitious, disorderly and materialistic form of Christianity, which has perverted Christ's doctrine about the Adversary into a recognition of a licensed Trafficker in Souls. The same materialistic and immoral tendency has perverted Christ's sacrifice into a bribe. But, just as we should not reject the spiritual doctrine of Christ's Atonement, so neither should we reject the spiritual doctrine of an Evil in the world resisting the Good, although both doctrines alike have been grossly and harmfully misinterpreted.

Of course it is possible that in our notions of spiritual personality, and therefore in our personification of Satan, we may be under some partial illusion. The subject teems with difficulties; and I have not concealed from you my opinion that some passages in the Old Testament appear to support a view at variance with the tenour of the New. The real truth, while justifying our Lord's language, may not accord with all our inferences as to its meaning; and I should myself admit that it would be most disastrous to attempt to personify the Adversary with the same vividness with which we personify the Father in heaven. Still,—in answer to the taunt of the agnostic or sceptic, "Is this, or that, the work of the God whom you describe as Love?"—I think we avail ourselves of our truest and most effective answer, when we resolve to separate certain aspects of Nature from the intention of God, and to say, with Christ, "An enemy hath done these things."

X

MY DEAR ———,

I see you are still violently prejudiced against illusions, that is to say against recognising the very important part which they have played in the spiritual development of mankind. You clearly believe that, though the world may be full of illusions, Revelation ought to be free from them. "The Word of God," you say, "ought to dispel illusions, not to add to them." I maintain on the contrary, that the Word of God, if it comes to earth, must needs come in earthen vessels; and that the most divine truth must needs be contained in illusion. Let illusions then be the subject of my present letter. At the same time I shall attempt to answer your prejudice against the natural worship of Christ as being a "new religion." Not of course that I admit that it is a "new religion;" on the contrary I regard it as the old religion, the predestined God-determined religion to which we are to return after extricating ourselves from the corruptions of Protestantism, as our forefathers extricated themselves from the corruptions of Romanism. I shall not deal here with the special illusions of Christianity, but with your evident *a priori* prejudice against any admixture of illusion with Revelation.

But first, what do I mean by "illusion," and how does my meaning differ from "error" or "mistake" generally, and from "fallacy," "delusion," and "hallucination" in particular? I say "my meaning," because the word is

H

often used loosely (I do not say wrongly) for any of these synonyms: but I restrict it to a special sense.

"Illusion," then, is wholesome error tending to the ultimate attainment of truth; "delusion" is harmful error arising from a perverted Imagination; "hallucination" is a wandering of the Imagination, without any guidance or support of fact, involving "delusion" of the most obstinate character; "fallacy" is an error of inference or reasoning; "mistake" is the result of mal-observation or weak memory; and "error" a general name for any deviation from the truth.

Illusion, in many cases, is an exaggerative and ornative tendency of the mind. It leads the very young to think their parents perfection, and the young to think them far better and wiser than they really are; it constrains the lover to exaggerate the beauty, accomplishments, and qualities of the woman whom he loves; it tends to the distortion of history by inclining all of us to accommodate facts to the wishes and preconceptions of our idealizing nature, which is always longing for "a more ample greatness, a more exact goodness, and a more absolute variety than can be found in the nature of things;"[1] and it lures us onward, young and old alike, over the rough places of life, even to the very brink of the grave, by the ever-fleeting, ever-reappearing suggestions of a bright to-morrow that shall make amends for the dull and commonplace to-day.

These illusive hopes, beliefs, and aspirations are never fulfilled in this life; but even the cynic and the pessimist must acknowledge, with Francis Bacon, that they constitute the very basis of all poetry that "tends to magnanimity and morality." Those who believe in God will further recognize in illusion a divinely utilized integument for the preservation and development of aspirations that shall

[1] *Advancement of Learning*, ii, 4, 5.

ultimately find a perfect fulfilment in a harmonious cooperation with the divine Love and in the unending contemplation of the divine Glory. Nor are illusions without a present practical purpose. Men are more hopeful, more active, more loving on account of them. On the other hand, even optimists must acknowledge that no man should shut his eyes to the truth in order to remain in what he knows to be no more than a comfortable error. The venial illusions of childhood, youth, and ignorance, become unpardonable or hypocritical in experienced age. Do you ask how we are to distinguish "illusions" from "delusions"? The answer is easy—on paper; but, in practice, often difficult to apply. However, the test is the same as that by which we distinguish knowledge from ignorance. Illusions "work;" that is to say, men are on the whole the better for them, and they prepare the way for truth. Delusions fail; men are in no way the better for them, and they often prepare the way for insanity and for physical or spiritual death.

We have spoken of moral illusions; let us touch on another kind of illusions to which some (I do not say rightly) have given the name of "illusions of sense."

I doubt whether the name is correctly given; for to me it seems that the illusion proceeds not from the senses (which, as far as I can judge, never deceive us) but from the imaginations and inferences which we base upon the report of the senses. Take an extreme case, fit rather to be called "delusion" than "illusion." If I see the phantom of a cat before the fire, which cat nobody else in the room can see, do my senses deceive me? No; but I am deceived by the imaginative inference which leads me to assume from past experience that the object which I see is visible to, and can be touched by, everybody else. My visual sense (which has to do with images only) reports—and can do no otherwise—that it discerns the image of a

H 2

cat. That report is true. But then my imagination forces on me the belief that this is an ordinary tangible and visible cat. That belief is false. Or take again the not infrequent case of colour-blindness. I am a signalman, and cannot tell a green light from a red: do my senses deceive me when I call a red light green? No; my sense reports inadequately for my necessities, and coarsely as compared with those who possess a finer sense of colour, but not deceitfully. My error arises from having loosely and servilely used the distinctive words "red" and "green" from childhood to manhood, although my senses continually protested that they could not distinguish two colours corresponding to the two words: but I imagined that there must be some such distinction for the two, and that I must be capable of recognizing it, because everybody around me recognized it. If we are to say that the signalman's senses deceive him we must be prepared to admit that every man's senses deceive him more or less. Do you suppose, when you see anything, that you see that which the thing *is?* "This is a yellowish-green," say you. "Of course," a Superior Being might reply; "but which of the one hundred and fifty shades of yellowish-green is it? You might as well tell me, when I shew you a sheep, 'This is a *being*,' as tell me simply this is 'yellowish-green.'" We do not see things as Superior Beings see them; but we are not on that account to say that our sight deceives us. Our visual sense reports the truth more or less adequately: but our Imagination, prompted by insufficient experience and inference, leads us sometimes to illusive conclusions.

Still, although "illusions of sense" ought perhaps to be rather called "illusions *from* sense,"—*i.e.* illusions arising "from" the report of the senses, but not illusions in which the senses are themselves deceived—no one will deny that such illusions exist. Sometimes they are exceptional, but sometimes so common as to be almost universal. Let us enumerate a few and ask whence they spring, and what purpose they serve?

They spring from a very strong conviction—erected upon the basis of Experience by Faith, but absolutely necessary for healthy life and spontaneous action—that the ordinary inferences which we almost instinctively derive from the report of the senses, are true, that is to say, will correspond to experience; and that we can act upon them without formally reasoning upon them.

Take the following instance. Shut your eyes, and get a friend to prick the back of your hand with the two points of a pair of compasses simultaneously, so that the two points may be about the eighth of an inch apart when they touch you; you will feel—and if you could not correct the inference by the sense of sight, you would infer—that only one point is pricking you. The reason is that the skin of the back of the hand only reports one sensation; and the mind leaps to the conclusion—owing to the multitude of past instances where one sensation has resulted from one object—that, in this instance also, one object alone is producing the sensation. A more curious instance is the following: Place the middle finger over the first finger, and between the two fingers thus interlaced place a single marble or your nose: you will appear to be touching two marbles or two noses. The reason is this: when the two fingers are in their usual position (not thus interlaced) and touching marbles or similar objects, two simultaneous sensations on the right side of the right finger and on the left side of the left finger would always imply *two* marbles; now you have constrained the two fingers to assume an unusual position where these two simultaneous sensations can be produced by *one* marble; but you, following custom, would infer the presence of two marbles, if sight, or other evidence, did not shew there was only one.

But illusions from the sense of touch are far less

common than illusions from the sense of sight. We all know how a cloud or sheet or coal may be converted by the Imagination into an image of something entirely different and visible only to the imaginer, although he supposes that others "must see it" too. But these are, so to speak, private illusions: the great public and, at one time, universal illusion, was the conviction that the sun and the stars move and that the earth does not move. There is scarcely any illusion more natural than this. Our senses give no indication whatever of the earth's motion; but they do indicate that the sun and the stars are moving. So complicated a process of reasoning, and so much experience, are needed before a man can realize (as distinct from repeating on authority) the causes for believing in the earth's motion that it is by no means surprising that, even now, only a minority of the human race believe that they are dashing through space at the rate of some thousands of miles an hour; and, except during the last three hundred years, the illusion that the earth is at rest was universal. Another common illusion from sight is that which leads us to suppose that, when we see anything in the air, a straight line from our eye towards the image which we see would touch the object itself: whereas, in reality, the image is raised by refraction so that in misty weather we see an object considerably higher than it is, and I suppose (to speak with strict exactness) we never "see" an object precisely where it is.

I have mentioned a few of the "illusions from the senses;" and now you will probably ask me what purpose they serve, how they can be called "wholesome," and how they "tend to the ultimate attainment of truth."

They appear to me to be "wholesome" because they represent and spring from a wholesome belief that "Nature will not deceive us; Nature does not change her mind; Nature keeps her promises." Sent into the world with but little of the instinctive equipment of non-human animals, we are forced to supply the place of instincts by inferences from sensation. Now if we were always obliged consciously to argue and deliberately to infer, whenever the sensations hand over a report to the Imagination, we should be at a great disadvantage as compared with our instinct-possessing compeers, whom we call irrational. " This inkstand which I see before me was hard yesterday, and the day before—but will it be hard if I touch it to-day or to-morrow?"—if a child were to argue after this fashion every time he reached out his hand to touch anything, the life of Methuselah would be too short for the ratiocinations necessary as a basis for the action of a week. For healthy progress of the human being, trustful activity is needed, and for trustful activity we must trust Nature, or, in other words, we must trust these quasi-instinctive inferences about Nature which we derive from our sensations. This trust or faith in the order of material things within our immediate observation, I have already described as being the germ of a trust or faith in a higher order altogether, that universal order, at present imperfectly realized, which we call the Divine Will.

Now when we say to Nature, "We trust you ; you will not deceive us," Nature replies for the most part, " You do right ; I will not deceive you ; you will be justified in your faith." But occasionally she replies in a different tone.

" Yes, I have deceived you; you did not use the means you had of obtaining the truth ; therefore you deceived yourselves, or, if you please to say so, I deceived you, in order that, after deceiving yourselves by a prolonged experience, you might learn, while trusting my order and permanence in general, not to trust every conception of your own about that order and permanence in particular.

"Yet in reality, what you call my 'deceptions' were, in part, the results of your own defects (some blameworthy, some perhaps inherent and not blameworthy), in part the results of my method of teaching mankind, by line upon line and inference upon inference. How does a child gain knowledge? By generalizing from too few instances: by inferring too soon; then by enlarging the circle of instances from which he generalizes; by correcting his inferences with the aid of experience: thus the progress of every child towards truth is through a continuous series of illusions. But when I break each one of your false and rudimentary conceptions of my Order, I always reveal to you, concealed in the husk of it, the kernel of a better conception. Thus while I teach you daily to distrust your own hastily adopted and unverified assumptions or inferences about my Order, I give you no cause to distrust my Order itself; and by the self-same act I strengthen both your faculty of scientific reason and also your faith in me. You may find fault with me that I did not bestow on each one of you, even in the cradle, the perfection of all knowledge and wisdom. Deeper laws, deeper than I can now speak of, forbade that rapid consummation: but, since that could not be, since it needs must be that imperfection should be in the intellectual, as well as in the moral, world, rejoice at least that illusion is made subject to truth."

Well, after this long but needful account of "illusions," in the sense in which I use the term, let me now recur to your objection that "the Word of God ought to dispel illusions, not to add to them." I suppose those who believe in a God at all, will in these days regard Him as the Maker of the world, as a whole, in spite of the evil that is in it. Some of the Gnostics, as you know, believed that the good God who had *not* made the visible world was opposed to the bad God who had made it; but with them we need not at this time concern ourselves, as there are probably none who now entertain that belief. Those then who believe in a God, Maker of heaven and earth, will not deny that God partially reveals Himself to men by the things He has made. Now by which of all His creatures does God reveal Himself most clearly? You will say perhaps—indeed I have heard you say it—" By the stars and their movements." I do not believe it. I say, " By the life of the human family first and by the stars of heaven, second." But I will assume that your answer is correct, and that God reveals Himself mainly by the movements of the stars of heaven ; and I will try to shew you that in this revelation God leads men to truth through illusion. Then I think it must seem reasonable to you that, if God does not dispense with illusion in that intellectual revelation of Himself which most closely approaches to a direct spiritual revelation, illusion may also have been intended or permitted by Him to play an ordained part in spiritual revelation itself.

Where, then, I ask, in all the teaching of Nature's school, has there been more of illusion than in her lessons of astronomy? When I was a boy, I remember, in the midst of a hateful sum of long division that would not come out right, devoting my attention to the sun moving through the branches of certain trees, and announcing to my tutor that " The sun moves." " No, you are mistaken." " But I cannot be mistaken, for I saw it." I rivalled—I exceeded—the obstinacy of Galileo ; I was ready to be punished rather than consent to say what seemed to me a manifest falsehood, that the sun did not move. Surely this boyish experience represents the experience of mankind, except that the tutor who has corrected their astronomical illusions, has been their own long, very long experience. Does it not seem sometimes as if God Himself had said, when He made the heavens to declare

His glory, "Being what they are, my children must be led to knowledge through error, to truth through illusion"? It may be said that in some cases men have fallen into astronomical mistakes through their own fault; through haste, for example, through the love of neat and complete theories, through carelessness, through excessive regard for authority; and so indeed they have. But is it always so? When you and I last walked out together on Hampstead Heath, you took out your watch, as the sun went down over Harrow, and said, "Now he's gone, and it's just eight." I remember replying to you, "So it seems; but of course you know he 'went' more than eight minutes ago." You stared, and I said no more; for something else diverted your attention at the time, and I felt I had been guilty of a little bit of pedantry. But I said quietly to myself as we went down the hill, "I don't suppose he knows it, but the sun certainly 'went' eight minutes ago; and what my young friend saw was an image of the sun raised by the refraction of the mist, like the image of a penny seen in a basin of water." Well now, was this your fault, this error of yours? No, it was, in the second place, the fault of the University of Oxford, which has bribed the schools to desist from teaching mathematics to any boy with a taste for classics and literature, so that you had to give up your mathematical studies before you came to optics; and it was, in the first place, the fault of—what shall I say? Shall I say the fault of Nature? That means the fault of God. Say, if you like, that it was the fault of Matter, or of an Evil principle. Say, it was no one's fault. Say that more good than harm results from it, in the way of stimulating thought and research. Deny it was a fault at all. Yet do not deny that it represents a Law, the Law of the attainment of truth through illusion—a Law which it is folly to ignore.

So far I have been going on the assumption that your answer was correct as to the means by which God mainly reveals Himself. But now let us assume that my answer, and not yours, is correct, and that God reveals Himself mainly by the relations of the family. In that case we must agree that each rising generation is led up to the conception of the divine fatherhood mainly by the preliminary teaching of human fatherhood. Now surely in the domestic atmosphere refraction is as powerful and as illusive as in the material strata of the air. Nay, the better and purer the family, the stronger is the illusion. Unloving children may be logical and critical; but what loving child does not idealise a good mother as perfectly good, and a strong wise father as the perfection of wisdom and strength? To the good child the parents stand in the place of God; and it is his illusive belief in these earthly creatures, which, when it has been corrected and purified, is found to have contained and preserved the higher belief in the eternal Father. You see then that in the family no less than in science, in the spiritual as in the intellectual side of Nature's school, the pupils pass upwards through illusion to the truth.

I have promised to say nothing of the special illusions of Christianity which I must reserve for a later letter.

But let me say thus much from the *a priori* ground on which we are now standing, that *if* illusions in Nature are most powerful in her noblest and most spiritual teaching, then, so far from there being a prejudice *against* finding illusion in religion, *we ought on the contrary to be prepared to find illusion most potent* in the early stages of the purest religion of all. Was ever people so illusively trained as the faithless children of faithful Abraham, the rejected Chosen People? Is not the Promised Land to this day a proverbial type of illusion? Do we not recognize illusion in every age of Christian revelation? And if the very

Apostles of the Lord Jesus—so much I will here assume—
had their illusions both during, and after, the life of their
Master; if the early Christians had their illusions also
concerning the speedy coming of Christ; if in the Mediæval Church and in the later Roman Catholicism there
have predominated vast illusions about transubstantiation, the powers of the priesthood, and the infallibility of the Pope; if the Protestant Churches themselves
have not been exempt from illusions about the literal inspiration and absolute infallibility of the Bible; is it not
the mark of astounding presumption to suppose that for
the Anglican branch of the Reformed Church there should
have been reserved a unique immunity from an otherwise
universal law?

But possibly you think that the Gospels have been so
long in our hands, and the Christian religion so long in
practice and under discussion, that nothing new can now
be said or thought about them? Just so Francis Bacon, in
1603, expressed his conviction (the innocent philosopher!)
that there had at last come about a complete "consumption of all things that could be said on controversies
of theology." Reflect a moment. How long have the
stars been with us "under discussion"? And how recent
have been our discoveries of the real truth about them!
How recently have these discoveries been even possible?
In the same way the exact criticism of the New Testament
has only become recently practicable. The subject matter
and thought could of course be appreciated centuries ago,
and often perhaps by the simple-minded and unlearned as
well as by the subtle and profound theologian; though,
even as to the thought of the New Testament, I often
think that we are greatly to blame if our increased
knowledge of history and psychology does not illuminate
much that was dark in its pages for those who had not
our advantages. But we are speaking of that kind of

intellectual criticism which dispels illusions; and for the purposes of the critical analysis of the First Three Gospels, Bruder's Concordance was as necessary as Galileo's telescope was for the discovery of Jupiter's moons, or the thermometer for the investigation of the laws of heat. Other influences have been at work, as well as mere mechanical aids, to throw light on the central event of the world's history. And surely if Abraham could wait nineteen hundred years for the coming of Christ, the spiritual descendants of Abraham —for such we claim to be—may well wait another nineteen hundred years to realize His nature and enter into the full meaning of His worship.

You see I am not now trying to prove the existence of any illusion in our present form of Christianity; I am simply *arguing against your prejudice* that, if the present form of Christianity be not true, then any new form must necessarily be false. You say, or perhaps till lately you were inclined to say, "If I could only breathe the atmosphere of Augustine! If only I could have been a companion of the Ante-Nicene or (better still) of the Apostolic Fathers! Or (best of all) of the Apostles! Or of Christ Himself! Then I should have been free from illusions." I reply, "No, you would not; and your aspiration is a mark of ingratitude to God. You deliberately reject the commentary He has given you in the History of the Church during these eighteen centuries. You think the story of Christ is completely told and completely explained. It is not so. All the created world is intended to bear witness and illustration to His life and work. Shakespeare and Newton and Darwin, as well as Origen, Augustine, and Chrysostom, have added to the divine commentary. All the good and all the evil of eighteen hundred years have borne witness to the divine nature of His mission; to the impotence and ruin which await the nations that cast Him off; to the blessing that attends those who follow His Spirit; to the mischief that dogs those who substitute for His Spirit a lifeless code of rules or a fabric of superstitions."

And now one last word as to the special illusion from which (in my belief) we must in the short remnant of this century strive to deliver ourselves. I think we have worshipped Christ too much as God, and too little as Man. We have erroneously supposed that He exempted Himself during His manhood from the laws of humanity. Like the Roman soldiers, we have stripped from Him the carpenter's clothes, and put upon Him the purple rags of wonder-working imperialism, and placed in His hand the sceptre of worldly ostentation, and in that guise we have bowed the knee to the purple and the sceptre, and, doing homage to these things, we have cried, "Behold our God." But now the time has come when we must take from off Him these tawdry trappings, and give Him back His workman's garments. Then we may find ourselves constrained to bow the knee again in a purer homage offered no longer to the clothes but to the Man.

Call this homage by what name we will, it is already of the nature of worship. And as we grow older and more able to distinguish the realities from the mirage of life, more capable of trust, love, and reverence, and better able to discriminate what must be, and what must not be, loved, trusted, and revered—looking from earth to heaven, and from heaven to earth, we shall ask in vain where we can find anything, above or below, nobler, and better, and more powerful for good, than this Man to whom our hearts go forth in spontaneous love and trust and reverence. Then we shall turn once more to the Cross finding that we have been betrayed into worship while we knew it not, and while we cry, "Behold the Man," we shall feel "Behold our God."

XI

MY DEAR ——,
Admitting the doctrine of illusion, and dismissing all prejudice against what is new, you declare that still my position remains absolutely unintelligible to you. I will set down your objection in your own words: "Apparently you maintain that Christ is a mere man who came into the world, lived, worked, and died according to the laws of human nature; even His resurrection you apparently intend to explain away till it becomes a mere vision, and therefore not a sign of any other than a human existence. Now worship is a tribute conceded to God alone. To a mere man, who lived eighteen centuries ago, how can you force yourself, by any effort of the will, to pay worship simply because you have reason to believe that this individual was pre-eminently good"?

In reply, I ask you, "What else is more worthy of worship?" There is no question of "forcing myself" at all. I worship Christ naturally. That is to say I love, trust, and reverence Him more than I love, trust, and reverence any other person or thing or universe of things. This I do because I cannot help it; and if I have brought myself to do this naturally by fixing my thoughts on the power of Goodness, and on Christ as the incarnate representation of Goodness, this causes me no shame and involves me in no conflict with my Reason.

But you—have you not omitted some important features in the description of this "mere man"? Jesus was not only pre-eminently good, He was also pre-eminently powerful and wise for spiritual purposes. His influence regenerated the civilized world; it is manifest around us. He Himself spoke of Himself in language which shews that He believed Himself to be endowed with a divine authority over men, and to stand in a unique relation to God. In a fanatic or a fool that would mean nothing: in one so wise, so soberly wise, so utterly unselfish, so marvellously successful, it must needs count for much. Although I reject the miraculous, I do not reject—nor understand how any one can reject—the supernatural. I regard Jesus as being a "mere man" indeed, if by "mere man" you mean a "real man;" non-miraculous, subjected to all the material limitations of humanity; but still a man such as is described in the first chapter of the Fourth Gospel; the Word of God incarnate; the Man in whom was concentrated God's expression of Himself; the Divine Perfection made humanly perceptible. This I believed once upon the authority of the Fourth Gospel; but I believe it now on the testimony of history and my own conscience.

Put yourself in my place. Suppose, as I suppose, that Christ was what He was, and did what He did, naturally and without miracles. Does not that make His personality in a certain sense more wonderful and certainly more lovable? It is comparatively easy, with miracles at command, to persuade men to anything; but, without miracles, to introduce a new religion, to bring in a new power of forgiving sins, to offer up one's life, not for friends, nor for country, but for mankind, to manifest oneself so to one's disciples during life that after your death they shall see you and shall be convinced that you have triumphed over death; to disarm an armed world by non-resistance, and to breathe a spirit of enthusiasm for righteousness and a passionate love of mankind into myriads of a remote posterity—these surely are feats which, if natural, should make us exclaim, "Verily we have here a divine nature."

I trust I am not being goaded into any exaggeration of what I really feel, by the hope of inducing you to share my feelings. Perhaps it is not possible to worship any man, not even such a one as Jesus, as long as he remains in the flesh. Not till death takes a friend from us do we seem to know the real spirit that lay behind the flesh and blood; not till Jesus was taken from us could that Spirit come which was to reveal the real Being that underlay the humanity of the Nazarene. I will admit that I should not have worshipped Jesus of Nazareth on earth—in Peter's house for example at Capernaum; for though love might have been present, the trust and awe that were to be developed by His resurrection would have been wanting. Jesus does not claim our worship nor even our recognition, as an isolated being, but as inseparably linked to One without whom He Himself said He could "do nothing". It was not till He was removed from the visible world and enthroned in the hearts of men by the side of the Father, that men could perceive His real nature; and He is to be worshipped not by Himself, but as the Son of God, and one with God. Christ did not merely *tell* us about the Father; He revealed the Father *in Himself;* and, if we worship the Father as Christ revealed Him, we are, consciously or unconsciously, worshipping the Son.

Almost all language about all spiritual existences is necessarily metaphorical. What is "righteousness" except a *straightness*, and what is "excellence" except *pre-eminence?* The proposition "Christ is the Son of God" is a metaphor; it is a metaphor to say that "God is our Father in heaven," and that "God is Love." Perhaps even to say that "God *is*" is a metaphor, expressing a truth, but expressing it inadequately. But it would be the ignorance of a mere child to suppose that a metaphor means nothing. There is no deeper truth in heaven or earth than the metaphor that God is the Father of man, and that the Lord Jesus Christ is His Eternal Son. When I try to think of God and to pray to God as my Father, I can think of Him as being without the seas, without the stars, without the whole visible world; but I can never think of Him aright, nor ever conceive of Him as being Love, without conceiving also of One whom He loves, who is with Him from the beginning; whom when I try to realize, I can realize only in one shape; and hence it comes to pass that I find myself without any "effort of the will," spontaneously worshipping God through, and in, and with, that one shape, I mean the Lord Jesus Christ. Worshipping the Father I find that I have been unconsciously worshipping, and must consciously continue to worship, the Eternal Son.

But there is another difference between us, besides your failure to recognise the spiritual power and spiritual wisdom of Christ. You do not know what you mean by worship; you do not know what you ought to worship; and you do not know how little you know of God.

You tell me that "worship is a tribute conceded to God alone." But what is God? The absolute God no one knows. Our most perfect conception of Him is only a conception of a Mediator of some kind by which we approach Him. To each man, that which he worships, and that alone, is God. I worship Christ, therefore to me Christ is God. What will you say to that? I suppose you will say " A non-miraculous Christ *ought not to be* God to you"? Why not? How does He differ from your conception of God? Is He less loving, less merciful, less just? "No," you reply, "but He is less powerful." How is He less powerful? Has He less power of pitying, loving, forgiving, raising men from sin to righteousness? Is He less powerful in the spiritual world? "Perhaps not; but He is less powerful in the material world. He never, according to your account, rose above, never even for a moment suspended the laws of nature." Indeed? And God, the Maker of the world—did He ever rise above, or suspend the laws of nature? When? "Well, He is said to have done so frequently in the records of the Bible". But many men deny that, and you yourself are disposed to agree with them. "At all events He did so when He made the world."

Here at last we can come to an understanding. You look up to God as to the Maker of the world, and are more ready to worship Him, as such, than to worship a non-miraculous Christ. If by "the Maker of the world" you mean—as I am quite sure many mean—"the Maker of the mere material forces of Nature," or even "the Maker of *all things apart from Christ*," then words fail me to express how entirely I differ from you. But let me try to put your view into my own language, in order to shew you that I do not condemn it without understanding it. "We cannot," you say, "worship a mere non-miraculous man, who did nothing but talk and lead a good life, and perhaps perform a few acts of faith-healing, however beneficial may have been his influence on posterity. The fact that, after his death, visions of him were seen by excited and enthusiastic followers, and in one case by an enemy of highly emotional tendencies, cannot alter this decision. It is impossible to worship a being so helpless, so limited, so aweless as this. What is such a creature in comparison with the mysterious Maker of the stars or Ruler of the ocean? Surely the sight of a storm at sea ought to suffice to turn any one from the imaginary and self-deceiving worship of the merely human Jesus of Nazareth to the worship of One whose greatness and glory and terror surround us on every side with material witnesses, One in comparison with whom no mere man may be mentioned."

Natural as such an argument may seem to you and to many others who call themselves Christians, it is in reality based upon a diabolical prejudice in favour of power. I can understand our forefathers, worshippers of Thor and Odin, arguing thus; and so great is our own inherited and inbred admiration of mere force, that even to us Christians the temptation is still very strong to bow down before the whirlwind and the fire, rather than before the still small voice. But it is a temptation to be resisted and overcome. You call upon me to worship the Ruler of the waves. Now the sea is full of the gifts of God to men; yet if I knew nothing more of the Creator than that He had made and rules the sea, then—with all the knowledge of the death and destruction that reign beneath the depths of ocean among its non-human tenants, and of the destruction that reigns on its surface when it wages war against man and conquers—I should say, " So far as the sea alone reveals the nature of Him who made it, I would a thousand times sooner worship Jesus of Nazareth, the non-miraculous man, than the Maker of the ocean." It is the most vulgar and contemptible cowardice to cringe before the Maker of the destroying ocean—who might be the Devil and not a good God, so far as the ocean's destructive power reveals its Maker—rather than to do homage to the best of men. I grant that in a storm at sea, with the lightning blinding my eyes, and the pitiless waters tearing my companions from my side and threatening every instant to devour me—I grant that I might, and should, feel tempted to exclaim, "A mightier than Christ is here." But, if I did, I should be ashamed of it. It would be a traitorous tendering of allegiance to Satan. When force and terror and death come shrieking on the wave-crests, and proclaiming that " Power after all is Lord of the world," then is our faith tested ; it is "the victory of our faith" to overcome that lie and to make answer thus : " No, Goodness is Lord over the world ; Love is Lord over the world ; and therefore He who is one with Love and Goodness, the Lord Jesus Christ, He is Lord over the world. Do with me as thou wilt, thou Mighty Maker of all things ! If Christ was not deceived, thou art His Father and I can trust thee. But if Christ was deceived, then art thou Satan and I defy thee, be thou the Maker of a world of worlds. Better to perish and be deceived with Christ, than to be saved and caressed by a Maker who made Christ to perish and to be deceived ! If there be in truth any opposition of will between the Maker and the Lord Jesus Christ, then is the Lord Jesus the superior of the two ; and in the Lord Jesus alone will I put my trust, and to Him alone will I cleave as my Lord and my Saviour and my God."

Have I made my meaning clear to you? I do not say, Have I persuaded you that I am right? But have I made you understand that it really is possible for one who has apprehended even imperfectly the illimitable extent of the goodness of Christ and the divine nature of that goodness, to feel heartily and sincerely that, of all things in heaven and earth and in the waters under the earth, the goodness and power and wisdom of God in Christ are the fittest objects for our love, our trust and our reverence, in other words, for our worship? Can you name any fitter object? If you will not worship God in the man Jesus, you will hardly worship Him in Socrates, or Paul, or any other specimen of humanity. Will you then turn to inanimate nature, and worship him in that ? Then you will be turning from the higher to the lower conception of God. Before I knew Christ, I might perhaps have worshipped God the Maker, being led to him, so to speak, by the world as Mediator. Inspired by awe for the Creator of so vast and orderly a machine, I might have adored Him as the artificer of the stars and this terrestrial globe. But now, Christ has made this kind of "natural religion" impossible. He, the ideal Man, has revealed to me depths of love, pity, mercy, self-sacrifice, in comparison with which the ocean is but the "water in a bucket," and the stars of heaven are as "a very little thing." If therefore I try to conceive of God as alien and apart from Christ, God becomes at once degraded and inferior to man.

How shall I try to express myself more clearly? Let me use words not my own, in which a man of recognized ability once summed up for me my own conceptions ; " I see," he said, " you do not, as most do, worship Christ out of compliment to God ; you worship God out of compliment to Christ." The words then sounded to me a little profane, though they were not meant to be so ; but I had to confess that they exactly expressed my meaning. Since then, it has seemed to me that these words were but an incisive way of saying, what every one says and few realize, that Christ is the Mediator between us and God: we worship God the Father because we attribute to Him the character that we adore in God the Son.

By this time you will have seen that while answering the question, "Whom, or what, ought we to worship?" I have indirectly answered a preliminary question, "What do we mean by worship?" You have also probably noticed what answer I have given to this question: worship appears to me a combination of love, trust, and awe. Do you accept this? I have never seen any serious objection taken to this definition except by those who refuse practically to define it at all and who would simply say " Worship is the homage paid by man to the Creator: and it has nothing to do with, and cannot be explained by, the feelings with which we regard man." If I had not seen this in the columns of a theological journal, I should not have believed it possible that modern superficiality and conventionalism could achieve quite so transparent a shallowness. The sum total of our feelings towards God—more especially our awe for Him—cannot indeed be adequately expressed in the same language which expresses our feelings for men : but that is a very different thing from saying that the former " have nothing to do with " the latter. I believe that a large part of most men's worship consists of a shrinking from an Unknown, the sort of dread that children feel for " the dark." But righteous worship must imply other feelings ; and these feelings—some of them at all events—must have names ; and whence are the names to be derived but from our feelings towards men and things—towards men, surely, as well as towards things ? We must either love God, or hate Him, or be indifferent to Him ; we must either trust, or distrust Him. I do not see how the people who would sever worship from all reference to human relations can look upon it as other than a mere homage of the lips or knees, a going to church, and attendance at religious services. Need I say that, when I define worship, I am defining the worship of the heart, not the attitude of those who honour God with their lips but whose heart is far from Him ?

Now the attitude of man to God has varied greatly in accordance with their conception of God, according as they have conceived Him to be Moloch, or Apollo, or Jehovah, or the Father of the Lord Jesus Christ. In some men worship has been mere terror ; in some, it has been a desire to bribe ; in some it has been faint gratitude and strong admiration ; in some it has been intense awe and reverence. All such forms of worship have been imperfect, and some have been very bad. At the best, none of them have combined all the best and noblest feelings of aspiration which Nature tends to develop in us by means of human and non-human agencies. Human nature—acting through the relations of the family—should elicit love and loving trust; non-human nature—acting through the seas and skies, with their suggestions of vastness and power—should elicit awe and awful trust; and the combination of these two natural influences should elicit love, trust and awe, which three-fold result constitutes worship.

Has the worship of God through the mediation of Christ entirely superseded—was it intended to supersede—the worship of God through the mediation of the visible World? I think not yet. It will in the end but not now. There may come a time, in some future existence, when we shall see righteousness like the sun, when we shall have visions of the beauty and order of holiness like the stars, and behold the glory of sacrifice spread out before our eyes like the firmament of heaven; and then the revelation of God through visible Nature will be swallowed up in the revelation of God through invisible Nature. But now, not many of us can pretend to such a power of spiritual insight. We feel that, if we learned the story of Christ without the help of the commentary of the awful powers of material nature, we might be in danger of repeating it with a glib familiarity which would hinder us from penetrating its meaning. Those who live in the stir of cities where they are doomed never to be alone, never to realize perfect silence, never to see more than a few square feet of sky, are living as the Word of God did not intend them to live; they may have—they often have—great spiritual compensations; they certainly have some spiritual disadvantage in these unnatural negations. As long as we have eyes and ears and the faculties of wonder and admiration, so long must we suppose that the revelation of the Word of God through Jesus of Nazareth has not dispensed with the revelation of the Word of God through the forces of material nature. If we wish to approach

God we should not despise the Mediation of the Word of God in its entirety, that is to say, the mediation of "the World with Christ."

Now what practical inferences follow from our definition of worship, if we are satisfied that it is roughly true? Here let me put in a caution. Our definition cannot be exactly true; for, in its exactness, worship means the sum total of all the feelings that should be felt by the mind of man, when he contemplates God through the mediation of "the World with Christ." Who can enumerate these without confessing that he may have passed over some so subtle and so deep that language itself has left them unnamed? We must therefore be content with a rough definition. But if it be roughly true that worship means love, trust and awe, what practical inferences may we thence deduce as regards our own conduct?

First, then, worship is not the formal thing it is generally supposed to be. It is not a mere smoothness of the hinges of the knees, or a readiness to take the name of God within one's lips. It is a natural going forth of the heart to that which one loves, trusts, and reverences most. Some men have little power of reverencing; others, of trusting; others, of loving; such men's worship must necessarily be maimed and imperfect. If a man who is destitute of reverence loves and trusts money more than anything else, money really is that man's God; it is no hyperbole, it is the fact; the man does actually worship money; he does not say prayers to it, does not go down on his knees to it, but he loves it and trusts it more than anything else; therefore, so far as he can worship anything, he worships money. Similarly another man worships pleasure; another, his children; another, power. We are accustomed to apologize for such expressions as if they were metaphors or exaggerations; but they are not; they are plain statements of spiritual realities.

Thousands of men who say they worship Christ, and who honestly suppose they worship Christ, do nothing of the kind. This is the dark side of the self-delusion of worship, but there is a brighter. There are many men at the present day who call themselves agnostics, but who would hardly deny that they love and reverence Jesus of Nazareth more than any other being. They worship Him then. Their worship is tinged with hopelessness, and therefore imperfect; but so far as it goes, it is a genuine worship of Christ. Perhaps, too, some who profess mere Theism feel, in their hearts, that though they dislike to say they worship Christ, they love Christ more than they love their conception of " God without Christ ;" if so, may we not say that, so far as that element of love goes, they worship Christ? Thousands of thousands of people, before Christ was born, worshipped Goodness and a good God in their lives and hearts, though they were, in name, worshippers of Apollo or Moloch. Thousands of people in the same unconscious way have been, and still are, worshipping the Incarnate Christ. They may not acknowledge this, they may not even know it: but their hearts have gone out to Him in love and trust and awe, more than to any other person or thing in heaven or earth.[1]

Search your own soul and acknowledge how little you know of God; I do not mean how little you profess to know, but how little you really know; how very much of

---

[1] It is a strange but common mistake to expect a purer morality from a conventional Christian than from a heathen or an atheist. One ought to expect less, much less. The man who can be familiar with the character, and acknowledge the claims, of Christ, without really loving Him or serving Him, and who can believe all that the Church teaches *about* Him, without at all believing *in* Him, must surely be far below the atheist who now and then does a good turn for humanity, out of mere pity and without the least hope of any ultimate triumph of goodness. For my part, I am quite surprised at the apparent goodness of conventional Christians: but I think they are not so good as their actions would imply. They are forced, by tradition and the example of a few, to keep up an artificial standard of morality in some departments of life.

what you think you know, is but second-hand knowledge, scraps of sayings repeated on authority, but not representing any heartfelt faith. Then—after deducting all the verbiage that you once esteemed a part of your own belief—take the poor residuum of your conception of the Godhead, and put it by the side of your conception of the Word of God incarnate in Christ, making some faint attempt at the same time to realize the stupendous life and character of Jesus. Then ask yourself in what respects the former conception differs from the latter for the better. Lastly ask yourself what you mean by worship—not lip-worship, or knee-worship, but the worship of the heart; and whether your heart does not go out in heart-worship as much towards the latter as to the former of these two conceptions. If you will do this fairly and honestly, my only fear would be that you might find that your conception of God Himself was too weak to retain its grasp on you; but if God still held His place in your heart, then I should feel confident that Christ would sit enthroned by His side, as being the Son without whom the Father could not be known, worshipped in virtue of a claim which no mere performance of miracles could establish, and which no mere non-performance of miracles could invalidate.

The sum is this. In Nature there is evil as well as good. I cannot therefore worship the Author of *all* Nature, but must worship the Author of *Nature-minus-the evil.* Where is He to be found? He is revealed in what we recognize to be good, true, and beautiful. Now no one man can include in his life all that we mean by scientific truth, and artistic beauty, as well as moral goodness. But, truth being a harmony, there is no deeper and nobler truth than the harmony of a human will with the will of the Supreme; and, beneath perishable artistic beauty, there is an eternal beauty to be discerned in righteousness. It ought not therefore to surprise us that the Eternal Word, after endeavouring for thousands of years to lead creation up from the worship of Power to the worship of Goodness, should at last take upon Himself the form of a creature, conspicuously powerless from the world's point of view, ignorant of science, and destitute of outward beauty, but of a goodness so divinely beautiful and so true to the underlying Laws of spiritual Nature, that when He held out His arms and called upon wandering mankind to come to Him, the enlightened conscience of humanity sought refuge in His embrace.

THE WORSHIP OF CHRIST 125

XII

MY DEAR ——,

Your letter of yesterday raises two objections, which I will do my best to meet. First, if I regard Christ as God, I ought not, you think, to stumble at the miracles, but to welcome, and even to require, them; and secondly, you are not satisfied with my definition of worship. Let me deal first with your first objection, restating it in your own words.

"I admit," you say, "that Jesus, even without miracles, would be worthy of worship in your sense of the word; but that is not the same thing as regarding Him as the Eternal Son of God, the Creative Word. I agree with Plato that there is nothing more like God than the man who is as just as man may be; but you demand more of me than this; you wish me to regard Him not as being merely '*like* God' but as '*being* God,' 'very God of very God.' Surely you must therefore admit that Jesus was exceptional, and not 'in the course of nature;' and the introduction into the visible world of such an exceptional and supernatural Being surely makes it antecedently probable, if not necessary, that He would bring with Him some quite exceptional phenomena in the way of evidence. The Miraculous Conception and Resurrection of Christ's Body (if only they were true) would supply just the requisite evidence that Jesus was the Creative Word, Lord over the issues of life and death. If the creative

Power of God, no less than the Righteousness and the Love of God, was incarnate in the person of Jesus, it would have been no less manifest in His life and works. But you desire to reduce Him to a being in no way distinguishable from other men except by superior moral excellence. There is, it seems to me, no logical connection between moral excellence and creative power. The two attributes, being generically different, demand different kinds of evidence to substantiate them.

"Again," you continue, "even if I put aside your contention that Jesus is the Word of God, there remains your assertion that He is sinless. Now a sinless Jesus is, in Himself, a miracle; and if you call on me to believe that Jesus was without sin, you ought to see no antecedent improbability, nay, you ought to see an antecedent probability, that He would work miracles."

Well, I feel that we are walking in a slippery region—this land of antecedent metaphysical probabilities; but I will try to follow you. Let me take your second objection first. Does it then really seem to you no less antecedently probable that the Word of God, made man, should have the power (say) of walking on water, than that He should be sinless? Surely we see in the best men approximations to sinlessness, but no approximations at all to what spiritualists (I believe) call "levitation"! In proportion as men approximate to our conception of God, in that proportion they are free from sin, but they do not "levitate;" hence, while we are led to believe that the Man who completely represents God (the Word of God Incarnate) will be absolutely sinless, we are led to no such conclusion as to "levitation." Or will you maintain that the best men shew any germ of any the least power to suspend any the least law of nature? There is no vestige of any such tendency around us; and your only support for such a belief would be found in the miracles of the Old

Testament, which you yourself deny, and as to which I shall have something to say in a future letter.

I admit however that there is one seeming argument derived from the "mighty works" of healing undoubtedly worked by the disciples of Jesus as well as by Jesus Himself. Without anticipating a subject that must be deferred to a future letter, I will merely ask you at this stage to distinguish between those "mighty works" on the one hand which were marvellous but not miraculous, and the "miracles" on the other hand which, if true, involved suspensions of the laws of nature. That Jesus may have healed certain diseases through faith, would be acknowledged by the most sceptical physiologists as quite possible in accordance with the laws of nature ; and this power would be consistent with such a faith-inspiring personality as we attribute to our Lord. Even from ordinary men and women there "goes out virtue," we scarcely know how, to the sick and suffering who are imbued with their hopefulness, their cheerfulness, their faith ; much more might we suppose that from the Ideal of Humanity "virtue" would probably go forth in unique measure and produce unique results, though always in accordance with those laws of material nature to which He had submitted Himself. But this is no argument for real "miracles ;" and—even while arguing—I protest against this method of arguing about facts, from metaphysical "antecedent probability." I do not object to the argument from "antecedent probability" where you can appeal to experience and argue from what happened in the past to what is likely to happen in the future. But where you can have no such evidence (because the Son of God was not twice incarnate) ; where the question is, "Did Jesus do this or did He not ?" and where we have history and evidence to guide us, as to what He did and said ; it seems to me we ought to be guided by evidence and not by "antecedent probabilities," especially when these "probabilities" are derived from nothing but metaphysical considerations.

But you tell me that you see "no logical connection between moral excellence and creative power;" and another passage in your letter says that "we have no reason for thinking that the best men shew any tendency to approximate, in creative power, to the co-eternal Word." What do you thence infer? Apparently this, that, as Christ revealed God's righteousness and love by His own righteousness and love, so He must have revealed God's creative power by His own creative acts. I, too, believe that. But by what creative acts? By changing water into wine, or seven loaves into seven thousand loaves, or three fishes into three thousand fishes? Think of it seriously. Do these two or three abrupt and dislocated achievements appear to you adequately to represent the quiet, gradual, orderly, creative power of the true Word of God, by whom the heavens were made? For my part I see a noble meaning in your words, but the meaning I see in them is not what you mean. It was necessary—so far I agree with you—that the Incarnate Word should manifest God's creative Power as well as His Love and Righteousness. But how? Can you not answer for yourself without my prompting? Does not your own conscience suggest to you what is the highest effort of creative power? Are we not taught—and do not our hearts respond to the teaching—that God is a Spirit? And, if God is a Spirit, must not the highest kind of creation be, not material, but spiritual?

Now I maintain that it is a greater, more sublime, and more God-like act to create righteousness in accordance with God's spiritual laws than to create loaves and fishes and wine against God's material laws. And I maintain also—in opposition to your opinion—that "the best men" *do* manifest "a tendency to approximate in creative power to the co-eternal Word," so far as concerns this, the highest kind of creation. It is hard, very hard, for us to realize—in spite of the teaching of the prophets in old times and of the great English poets in our own days—that the creation of the heaven and the earth is "a very little thing, a drop of a bucket," as compared with the creation of righteousness. It is a desperate struggle, this battle of the spirit against matter, of the invisible against the visible, before we can believe, with all our being—with our minds as well as our hearts—that the creation described in the first chapter of the Fourth Gospel was more divine than that described in the first chapter of the Book of Genesis. But it was so. The first creation of orderly matter was but a shadowy, unsubstantial metaphor, predicting the second creation of orderly spirit. "All things were made by him, and without him was not anything made that was made:" so writes the Evangelist, describing the first, and proceeding to describe the second, creation : and he continues thus, "In him was life, and the life was the light of men." To the same effect writes St. Paul : "The first Adam became a living soul. The last Adam became a life-giving spirit." Is it not possible, on the testimony of one's own conscience, and on the testimony of history present and past, and on the testimony of the Apostles and Evangelists— even when critically reviewed and disencumbered of the miraculous element—to acknowledge that Jesus has been indeed "a life-giving Spirit" to mankind, and to worship Him as representing the Creative Word who has moved on the face of the material and of the spiritual waters, creating order alike in the matter of the Universe and in the minds and consciences of men?

And now to deal with your second objection (directed against my definition of worship) which I will repeat in your own words :—" You define worship as consisting of the sentiments of love, trust, and awe. I confess this does not express *all* my notion of worship. Such sentiments I have felt towards my teachers, whether dead or living, but I do not consider that I worship them. When we apply the word to God, we mean by it a direct act of communion—or at least a real effort after communion—between two minds. When I pray to God, I believe myself to be directing my thoughts towards a Being with whom I am spiritually in direct and immediate relation—the Maker of all, *my* Maker and Father. But I cannot persuade myself that I stand in a like relation to Jesus of Nazareth. We do not pray to Paul or Plato, and I do not see any such difference in the historical manifestations of Jesus as should lead me to believe that I, and millions of other believers, can make my thoughts known to him, and can receive back impressions from him, when we cannot do so to other minds which have helped to change the world's history and have been revealers of the Father."

Are you not here confusing a state of mind with an action resulting from that state of mind? We have been speaking, not of lip-worship, but of heart-worship, defining it as a state of mind. Now is not prayer the result of worship, rather than identical with worship, as we have defined it above? A child feels love, and trust, as well as reverence, for its parents; and, in consequence he asks them to grant his desires, or he thanks them for kindnesses; but yet the asking and thanking are not identical with the feelings of the children towards their parents, but spring from those feelings. Similarly we, feeling a trust and an awe for the Maker and Father, far beyond what we can feel for Paul or Plato, impart to Him our petitions for our highest needs, or offer Him our thanks: but this asking and this thanking are not identical with, but the results of, the feelings we entertain towards God. What you really mean is that your love, trust, and awe towards God so far transcend those corresponding feelings when entertained by you for your fellow-creatures, that you ask from Him things which you would never dream of asking from them. Moreover you consider (rightly or wrongly) that a dead or absent man cannot enter into communion with you, but that God is superior to death and to the limitations of space, and that He alone can always hear and always answer; and this you appear to think a non-miraculous Christ cannot do.

Well, here I confess there is a vast difference between us; for I feel sure that Christ can do this. You say, I do not "pray to Paul and Plato:" I do not, though I sometimes think that it would be better to pray to Paul or Plato than to the sun or moon. But I do not find Paul, I do not find Plato, claiming power to forgive sins; or declaring that he came to die for mankind and that his blood was to be shed for the remission of sins; or predicting that he should be slain and that he should rise from the dead; or promising that whatsoever his disciples asked from the Father in his name should be performed; or promising to give his disciples, after his death, a spirit, the Holy Spirit of the Father, which should enable them to resist all adversaries after he had left them; or, in other words, making a manifest preparation to prepare his disciples for his death on the ground that after death he would still be present with them and still their guide and helper. Now even when I set aside the Fourth Gospel, and eliminate all miraculous narrative from the first three Gospels, I find myself in the presence of One who, I am convinced, both said these things, and made them good in deeds. I am penetrated with the conviction that He said them and had a right to say them; and that this is proved by literary and historical evidence, and by the history of the Church, and by my own experience. The miracles I can easily disentangle from the life of Christ; but His divine claims to be our Helper and Saviour after death and to all eternity, I cannot. Accepting them, I can neither deny Him worship nor myself the right of access to Him in prayer.

Christ's whole life and doctrine, His plan (so to speak) for the establishment of spiritual empire over the hearts of men, appear to me imbued with divinity; but if I were forced to choose some one particular discourse or incident in His life as a reason for my adoration of Him, I should not choose any of His mighty works of healing, nor any of His parables or discourses, nor even His death upon the cross : I should point to the institution of the Lord's Supper. As the years pass over my head, the picture of that mysterious evening becomes more and more powerful and vivid with me and more and more inexplicable unless Jesus was verily the Life of the world. It is ten times more vivid and more powerful now than it was when I believed in a miraculous Jesus. When I kneel down at the altar-rails there rises up through the distance of eighteen centuries that strange scene in the guest-chamber at Jerusalem, where Jesus portioned out His flesh and blood, bequeathing Himself to His disciples for ever. Then follows the thought of the countless myriads of souls who have derived spiritual strength from this rite and have lived again in Christ, and I say to myself, " Truly God was in the self-doomed man who thus gave us His flesh and blood for mankind. A mere man devise so strange a rite ! So (at first) repellently strange ! so profoundly simple ! so perfectly and spiritually successful !" I solemnly protest to you that the inexpressible depth of the divine intuition which found utterance in the Lord's Supper, impresses me more and more—far more than all the miracles put together—as a proof that we have in Christ a Being in initial and fundamental harmony with the very source of our spiritual life ; and, rationalist though I am, I find myself, nevertheless, praying naturally and spontaneously after this fashion : "Master, my only true Lord and Master, grant that I may feed on thy body and be quickened by thy blood, and live in thee a new and spiritual life ! Thou One Forgiver of sins, thou Bearer of all the burdens of mankind, bear Thou the burden that I cannot bear, and blot out all my offences; Thou who sittest at the right hand of the Majesty on high, lift me in thyself even to the throne of heaven, and present me to the Father as His child ! Thou who didst die in the flesh and rise again in the spirit never to die, rise thou in my heart and soul ; take my whole being into thyself and cause me there to die unto sin and to live with thee unto righteousness ! Grant me eternal life, thou Lord of Life ! Say within my soul, ' Let there be righteousness,' and there shall be righteousness ! Create me anew, O Lord, thou ever-living, co-eternal Word of the Creator."

You may object that many of these prayers, with slightly different wording, might equally well be addressed to the Father through the Son. They might, and, as a rule, they probably would be so addressed. But in moments of unusually deep emotion prayers of this kind go forth I think, more naturally to the Father in the Son than to the Father through the Son ; and surely your very objection, and my answer to it, shewing that prayers may be indifferently addressed to the Father or to the Son, constitute a strong argument for the unity (in the heart of the person praying) of Son and Father. And if I can pray like this, do I not worship, must I not worship, Christ as the Creative Word, the Eternal Son of God ? And is there anything to prevent me from praying like this in the fact that He to whom I pray, when He received our humanity, received it in truth and honesty, with all its material limitations?

XIII

MY DEAR ——,
Desiring to approach the subject of miracles, you ask me whether I do not accept the following sentence as a statement of my views concerning nature: "The Universe is perennially renewed and created afresh by an active energy of the Spirit of God, and what we call 'laws of nature' are the mode in which our limited minds are enabled to apprehend the working of Creative Power." If I accept it, you declare you cannot understand why I should stumble at miracles. "It is a matter of every-day experience," you say, "and natural, that the human will should suspend the laws of nature, as for example by arresting the motion of gravitation; and consequently it seems unreasonable for you, or for other believers in a personal God, to be scandalized if He also now and then permits Himself the same liberty."

I accept your statement, so far as concerns the perennial energy of the Spirit of God upon the material and immaterial Universe; but I do not quite agree with the thought, or perhaps I should say with the expression, of the last part of your sentence—"the mode in which our limited minds are enabled to apprehend the working of Creative Power." I should prefer to call the Laws of Nature "a revelation of Himself by God to men, on the recognition of which our very existence depends." The Laws of Nature are indeed nothing but ideas of our own Imagination; but they appear to me, more or less, true ideas, through which God has revealed Himself to us as a God of Law and Order. I believe in the fixity of natural Law as much (I think) as the man of science does; I reverence a Law of Nature, not as a result of necessity, but as an expression of God's will. But your own remarks about the ordinary "suspension of the law of nature by the human will" appear to me to imply a little confusion of thought arising from a confused use of the word "nature" in two or more senses. On this point therefore I should like to say a few words.

1. Nature

i. *Nature sometimes means the ordinary course of things apart from us and from our intervention;* as when we say that "*Nature* looks gay"—an expression which we might use of fields and even of a not too artificial garden, but not of a city or a street.

In this sense it may be occasionally applied to the ordinary course of things in our own bodily frame, so far as it goes on without our deliberate intervention; as when a physician tells a fussy patient to cease from medicining himself and to "let *Nature* take its course."

ii. *Nature sometimes means the ordinary course of things in ourselves, not in our bodies but in some other part of us, but still apart from our deliberate intervention;* as when we say that "*Nature* impels us to avoid pain, to preserve our lives, to cherish our children, to love and revere our parents, and to seek the esteem and friendship of our neighbours."

But sometimes in human beings one "natural" impulse is opposed by another: as when the desire to preserve one's life is opposed by the desire to gain the esteem of one's neighbours. When these two conflict, which is to be called the more "natural"?

The answer will be different, according as we use the word "natural" in the sense of "ordinary" or "orderly." One class of natural impulses, which may be called selfish or self-regarding, is perhaps more *ordinarily* predominant; another class, those which regard the good of others, contributes more to the progress and *order* of society. In the individual, as well as in society, the former or "ordinary" impulses, if unchecked, often tend to excess of passion, and what we call mental "disorder"; the latter (which are seldom in excess) tend to self-control and a well-ordered mind. In the former sense, it is more "natural," because more "ordinary," to laugh when we are tickled, or to seize food when we are hungry, than to die for our country or to provide food for our children; but, in the latter sense, the nobler actions are more "natural" because more in accordance with order.

What do we mean by a well-ordered mind? We mean one in which the Will does not at once yield to the impulses from the things which seem nearest to ourselves; in which the Imagination vividly presents to us the wants of our neighbours as well as our own; in which the Reason states what can be said for and against each proposal, and the Conscience finally decides the course to be taken. Here then we see an entirely new notion of Nature, at least so far as man is concerned; a course or order of things no longer apart from human intervention, but entirely dependent upon the supremacy of the Will and Conscience aided by Reason and Imagination: and hence we are led to a double definition of human Nature as follows:—

iii. *Human Nature means, sometimes the ordinary, sometimes the orderly, course of human things.*

Even as to non-human Nature we sometimes find a popular tendency to call, or think, "unnatural," some phenomena which strike us as being contrary to the general order and beneficence of things : and hence we are less fond of saying that Nature prompts the cat to torture the mouse or the moth to fly into the flame, than that she implants in the animal race the parental instinct to protect the young. I confess I sympathize with this tendency, and with all those who in their hearts look upon death and pain as being contrary to the ideal order of things and ultimately destined to be destroyed. But for the present, apart from sentiment, let us simply note the fact that in our popular language we sometimes say that it is the nature of a clock to indicate the right time, but sometimes that it is its nature to deviate from the right time : whence we deduce the conclusion that :—

iv. *The Nature of a thing means sometimes its object, sometimes its custom.*

Laws of Nature

Many of those unbroken sequences of phenomena around us, which have been most frequently observed, have been made the subject of the Imagination and have received an imaginative name. When we find Nature, upon an invariable system, dealing out rewards for one course of action and penalties for another, there is suggested to us the thought of a great Lawgiver laying down laws and affixing rewards for obeying, and penalties for disobeying. Hence the sequences of natural phenomena have been called " Laws of Nature."

Every action of every moment of our lives is performed for the most part in the instinctive and unconscious confidence that Nature will not deceive us by breaking her Laws : and hence they might, from another point of view, be called " Promises of Nature," or " Expressions of the Will of Nature ; but " Law of Nature " has been selected—not perhaps altogether happily—as suggesting something more fixed and definite than even the Promises or Will of the Maker of the world.

Law of Nature is a metaphorical name for a frequently observed sequence of phenomena (apart from human Will), implying, to some minds, regularity; to others, absolute invariability.

Suspension of Laws of Nature

Does human Will ever suspend a Law of Nature?

I am standing, we will suppose, under a tree in autumn. If a leaf flutters down and rests upon my head, the Law of gravitation is no more suspended by my Will, than if it rests upon some intercepting bough. The result of the Law is modified; downward motion is replaced by downward pressure: but the Law itself is not suspended.

But if, upon the command of a man, the leaf were arrested in mid air and remained immovable for an hour together, and if I were led to the conclusion that this was effected by no force which I could conceive as being consistent with the ordinary course of Nature and with the limitations of human power, then I should be obliged to say that the Law of gravitation, in this particular instance, did not work. Using a metaphor, I might say that the Law was "suspended," and the phenomenon itself I should call a miracle.

In reality the true explanation might be quite different. It is conceivable that an extraordinary man, once in a thousand or once in ten thousand years, might be endowed with the power of arresting the motion of a stone in the air, without the intervention of the body and by the mere exercise of Will; and this might be done by him as easily, as regularly, and (for him) as naturally, as we ordinary men stop a stone in the air by the exercise of Will acting upon our bodily machinery. In that case gravitation would still act, pressing the stone, so to speak, upon an invisible hand: and the explanation would be, not that the Law was suspended, but that the results of the Law were uniquely modified by the peculiar action of a unique human nature, in the same way in which they are commonly modified by the regular action of an ordinary human nature. This, I say, is conceivable. Yet if we find (1) in past history, a general tendency to believe in miracles on very slight evidence; (2) in the present time, a general and, as many think, a universal refutation of the evidence on which miracles have been accepted; (3) an increasing power of explaining many so-called miracles in accordance with natural Laws—it becomes our obvious duty to regard miraculous narratives with a very strong suspicion until cogent evidence has been produced for their truth.

The Action of the Will

Hitherto we have been considering the action of the Will upon external Nature; but now what as to the action of our Will upon our own Nature, upon the machinery of our own body? Is that to be called a Law of Nature or a suspension of a Law of Nature?

It is to be called neither. Our definition of "Law of Nature" was "a metaphorical name given to the ordinary course of things *apart from the intervention of human will:*" consequently the action of human will (about which we are now speaking) is expressly excluded from the province of Nature, in this sense, and can neither be called "a Law of Nature," nor a "suspension of a Law of Nature." The action of the Will falls under the head of "human Nature;" and, discussing it under that head, we may call it by any metaphor we please, a custom, habit, law of human Nature.

This distinction between the name given to the course of non-human Nature and the name given to the action of the human Will on the bodily framework, is based on our distinction between the regular and (if I may use the word) the anticipable sequences of the former, as contrasted with the irregular and unanticipable sequences of the latter. When the Will is undeveloped or enfeebled; when the human being is a baby, or one of an excited and undisciplined crowd, or mad, or drunk, or narcoticized, or mesmerized, or reduced to the bestial level by some overpowering instinct; we can occasionally prophesy his actions or movements with something of the certainty and accuracy with which we predict the motions of a machine: but we cannot thus calculate the actions of a mature, healthy, and reasonable man. Hence it has been usual to contrast with the "Laws of Nature" the "freedom of the human Will." We cannot demonstrate the freedom of the Will any more than the fixity of the Laws of Nature: the belief in both is suggested by Imagination, tested and approved by Experience and Reason, and finally retained by Faith. Of course, when I speak thus, you will not suppose that I assume that my mind, or being, is divided into distinct parts (as the body consists of distinct limbs) called Will, Reason, &c.: you will understand that I merely use the ordinary brief and convenient phraseology which says "The Will does so-and-so," meaning "I do so-and-so with a certain consciousness which appears to me to result from a faculty inherent in me of choosing between two or more courses of action, which faculty I call Will." With this precaution, I assert that the action of the Will is natural as regards human Nature, but outside Nature or "extra-natural" as regards non-human Nature, and that it does not involve the suspension of what are technically called "the Laws of Nature."

It is thus shewn that the human Will acts directly on the human body in accordance with the Laws of human Nature, and that it does not interfere with the external world except indirectly, through the body, in accordance with the Laws of Nature (as technically defined). There is nothing therefore in the action of the human Will that would justify the *a priori* inference that the divine Will would, *by any direct intervention,* disturb or suspend that fixed Order in the external world which constitutes a large part of the revelation of God to mankind.

If indeed we are to draw any kind of parallel between divine and human action, we shall have to ask ourselves what is there appertaining to the divine Spirit which can in any sense be said to correspond to its "Body"? And I suppose we shall reply, in Pauline language, that Mankind, which is said to have Christ for its Head, might be mystically and spiritually called the Body of the divine Will or Holy Spirit. If this be so, proceeding with our parallel, might we not repeat, word for word, with the needful proportionate changes, the language of the last paragraph: "The divine Will or Spirit acts directly on the divine body (that is on mankind) in accordance with the Laws of Spiritual Nature, and it does not interfere with the external world, except indirectly, through mankind, in accordance with the Laws of Nature (as technically defined)"? I do not say that this analogy is logic-proof: for what can be called a "body," or what "external," in relation to the all-pervading God? Nevertheless, as it falls in with our actual experiences, this mystical parallel seems as well worth recording as most *a priori* notions on this subject, though we take it as no more than an illustration of possibilities. But, if we are to confine ourselves to certainties, the one thing certain is, that Nature, in the fullest sense, human as well as non-human, emphatically discourages us from expecting "miracles."

XIV

My dear ——,

Your last letter now comes to the point which I have been long anticipating, or rather it recurs to the point from which our correspondence started—the credibility of the miracles attributed to Christ. You tell me that during the long vacation you have been rapidly reviewing my letters and attempting to enter into my views. There is much, you say, that is new, and there is something that improves on acquaintance, in this form of "Christian Positivism" as you call it; its intellectual security has attractions for you, and it seems to you to satisfy at once the aspirations of those who are drawn to worship humanity, and of those who are drawn to worship something above humanity. All this looks very well on paper, you say; but when you take up the Gospels, it seems to fade away into a mere student's dream: and you state the objection thus: "For our knowledge of Christ, we depend almost entirely upon the New Testament; now the New Testament contains accounts of miracles; these miracles we are unable to accept as historical; consequently the New Testament must be regarded as non-historical, and the whole story of Christ becomes a myth."

In return for this argument about the New Testament let me supply you with a similarly sceptical one about the Old Testament, and ask you whether you are prepared consistently to adopt it. "For our knowledge of the children of Israel, we depend almost entirely upon the Old Testament; now the Old Testament contains accounts of miracles; these miracles we are unable to accept as historical; consequently the Old Testament must be regarded as non-historical, and the story of the descendants of Israel becomes a myth."

Now are you really satisfied with this argument? The so-called Law of Moses, the wandering in the Wilderness, the conquest of Canaan, the lives of the wonder-working Gideon and of Barak, the wars and songs of David, the denunciations, warnings, consolations, sorrows, visions, of Isaiah, Jeremiah, Ezekiel and the other prophets, are they indeed, in your judgment, converted into mere myths by the admixture of the miraculous element? Are they even made so far mythical as not to reveal the story of the training of one of the most remarkable of nations, a nation theologically quite singular upon earth? I contend on the contrary, that the removal of the miraculous element results in a two-fold advantage, on the one hand placing the story of Israel in the province of history, and on the other hand, not bringing it down to the level of the common-place, but elevating it to a pinnacle among the histories of nations, and making it in a certain sense more wonderful than before. If Moses was a plenipotentiary miracle-worker from God, then there was nothing unexpected or wonderful in the spiritual results that he achieved; and the wonder rather is that he achieved so little. Give me the thunders of Sinai, with power to burn, blast, and plague my opponents; add to these the power of producing without labour and without delay miraculous supplies of manna, quails, and water, and I myself would undertake to terrify or allure any nation into obeying a far less noble and attractive code of laws than was set forth in the name of Moses. But when I see a lawgiver with no such powers, doing what Moses did, and shaping, or preparing the way for shaping, one of the most carnal and unspiritual of races into a nation of Priests and Prophets for the civilised world, then I am ready to fall upon my face and to take my shoes from off my feet, saying from the depth of my heart, " Truly God is in this place." " But," say you, " the so-called Law of Moses is no more due to Moses than trial by jury is due to Alfred." That matters not. It is not any one Israelite ; it is Israel as a whole, Israel and its lawgivers and poets and prophets collectively ; it is the evolution of the spiritual from the carnal Israel that I revere ; and all the more, if that evolution be natural. Regarded as miraculous, the history of Israel is somewhat of a failure and a bathos ; but, regarded as non-miraculous, it becomes a most miraculous triumph of divine intention and persistence, even though the walls of Jericho succumbed to the trumpets of Israel only in hyperbole, and although the sun stood still at the bidding of Joshua only in the impassioned language of an Oriental poet.

I am quite sure you must feel this as strongly as I do ; you cannot honestly and sincerely put aside all the history of Israel as a myth because it contains a non-historic element of miracles, any more than you put aside the battles of Salamis and Regillus because they too have received their miraculous adornment. But some are probably perplexed and scandalized at the task that is apparently set before them of disentangling the true from the false, the myth from the non-myth : " How strange," they say, " that the story of the training of the Priests of the world, that story which should have been a light to guide our feet, has been suffered to shed darkness instead of light and falsehood instead of truth ! Is it probable, is it even decent and reverent, to suppose that God should have allowed the Book of Revelation to be so falsified that the simple and unlearned cannot depend upon it without the aid of scholars and specialists?"

My reply is that, as long as men reason in this way, assuming that Revelation ought to have been conveyed by some perfect medium, and therefore that it must have been conveyed by some perfect medium, so long it will be as impossible to refute them as it was to refute the Aristotelian astronomers who argued that " The planets ought to move in perfect curves; and the circle is a perfect curve; and therefore the planets must move in circles." We are like children crying for the moon if we demand that this world, or that anything in this world, shall be arranged as if the world were the best of all possible worlds. It is not the best possible world, and we know it is not. Some things attest the glory of God more perfectly than others; but nothing attests it quite perfectly. You might as well hope to remove refraction from the atmosphere, as to remove from the human mind the prejudices which compel and always have compelled mankind to exaggerate and misrepresent divine truth by forcing us to think that God must have acted as we should have acted had we been in His place.

If you and I were omnipotent and had to re-make the Universe, I suppose there is no question but we should make man perfectly good (according to our notions of goodness) and that we should force him to remain good. And if you or I were omnipotent and had to reveal anything to men, we should write it large and clear in the sky, or in the heart, legible to all without effort, so that men should be forced to understand it. But God has neither done this nor anything like it. Therefore, since in other respects He has departed so very far from our notions of the best method, we cannot be surprised if He has not composed the Old Testament quite in the manner which would commend itself to us as the best. From our point

L

of view the Bible teems with obvious imperfections. In the first place there are none of the modern arrangements for securing accuracy. No special newspaper reporters, not even contemporary writers of memoirs or histories, have handed down to posterity the exact words and deeds of Moses, David, Isaiah, and the great heroes and prophets of Israel. Might we not almost say that there have been as it were arrangements for securing inaccuracy? The authors wrote, in many cases, long after the events they recorded, under conditions which rendered accuracy of detail quite impossible. They have often been lengthy where we could have desired brevity (as for example in the enumerations of pedigrees and in the details of the furniture and ritual of the Temple or the Tabernacle) and very brief where we should have prized amplitude. Writing as Orientals for the most part write history, without statistical exactness, they have sometimes made mistakes (sometimes self-contradictory mistakes) in numbers and names, which it is now impossible to rectify. Nay, we can hardly acquit them sometimes of moral error; they have at all events sometimes appeared to praise, or at least not to blame, sometimes even to impute to God, acts that would seem to us—even when all due allowance is made for difference between ancient and modern standards of morality—deserving of express and severe censure.

But their special error which we are now considering remains yet unmentioned. You know that nations, like individuals, in their infancy have very vague notions of the uniformity of Nature, and very strong notions of the personality of Nature or of some Beings behind Nature. Even in modern times Orientals would say that God or Allah did this or that, where we say that this or that "happened;" and I remember hearing not many years ago that some Jews of Palestine, suffering from the consequences of extensive conflagration, wrote to England for relief in a letter which declared—in perfect good faith, and without any intention to imply a miracle—that God had "sent down fire from heaven upon their town." An Eastern traveller of modern times tells an amusing story to the same effect how a camel-driver, when questioned as to the cause of his rheumatism, could not be induced for a long time to make any other answer except that " Allah had caused it ; " and even when the traveller had elicited the immediate cause, the man would still persist that " Allah had sent the rheumatism, though it had followed upon drinking a great quantity of camels' milk when he was in a violent heat." You should therefore accustom yourself, if you want to understand the Bible, to look at Western narrative from an Oriental point of view. Take for example the interesting account given by the African traveller Mungo Park of the manner in which a trifling incident saved his life in the desert. Alone and desperate, faint and famished, he had thrown himself down to die, when he suddenly caught sight of a small but exquisitely shaped plant of great rarity and interest : " And can God have taken so much thought and care for the creation of this little plant," he cried, "and have no thought or care for me?" In the strength of this suggestion he started up, pressed on his way, and reached safety. Now compare this striking little story with the similar incident of the gourd, recorded in the Book of Jonah, and imagine how a prophet of Israel could have described the message of salvation. He would have told us (as the prophet Jonah tells us) how the Lord God in the same day caused a plant to grow up before the face of the man, and how the Lord God said unto the man " Hath the Lord thy God taken thought for this plant, and shall He take no thought for thee ? Arise, go on thy way " – giving, as from God, the actual words of the thought which the Western traveller describes as suggesting itself or occurring to his mind. You must surely see how naturally this conversion of the natural into the seemingly miraculous would have been effected by a penman of Israel, without the least intention to imply a real suspension of the laws of nature.

Keeping yourself still in the position of an Oriental historian, consider what you would be called on to describe, in setting down the story of Israel. You would find, as your materials, various traditions, mostly oral, mostly perhaps poetic, describing a great deliverance wrought in every particular by the hand of Jehovah Himself: you would find the nation around you, and yourself among the rest, believing that Jehovah Himself had drowned the Egyptians in the Red Sea, that His terrible voice had given the Law from Sinai, that He had been to wandering Israel a cloud in the noontide to protect them from the sun, and a light in the darkness to give them guidance, that He had supplied them with food from Heaven and spread a table for them in the wilderness, that He had Himself given them water from Himself (the Rock of Israel!) to quench their thirst. If the Jordan's fords, unusually shallow, had allowed the whole nation to pass across, as upon dry land, you would be taught as a child to hear and sing, in hymns that reiterated the national deliverance, that the Lord Himself had done this: "The waters saw thee, O Lord, the waters saw thee, and were afraid." If, in the general terror of the Canaanites, a strong city suffered itself to be taken on the mere onset and war cry of the invaders as easily as though it had been an unwalled hamlet, the traditions would tell how the walls fell flat at the sound of the trumpets of Joshua; if some sudden storm, accompanied with hail and immediately followed by an inundation of swollen streams, threw the chariots and horses of the enemy into confusion and ensured their speedy rout; or if, on another occasion, the sudden gloom of a storm had been succeeded by a long evening of peculiar brightness and clearness facilitating the pursuit and destruction of the foe, then you would hear that the "stars in their courses" fought against Sisera, or that in the day of Beth-horon the Lord Himself sent down hailstones upon the enemy and stopped the sun at the prayer of Joshua:—

> "The sun and moon stood still in their habitation ;
> At the light of thine arrows as they went,
> At the shining of thy glittering spear."[1]

All these materials, expressed in terse poetic phrase, you, as a historian, would have to amplify into prose. Is it not easy to see how, in the process, without any fraud or conscious exaggeration on your part, you would transmute the natural into the miraculous?

To go through the whole of the miracles in the Old Testament and to attempt to shew how in almost every case the miraculous part of the story may have crept in without intention to deceive, would be a task far above my powers ; and it would require a book not a letter. If you were to study with care the articles in the *Encyclopædia Britannica* on the books of the Old Testament they would give you a good deal of light on this subject. But the problem is complicated by the fact that the causes that originated the miraculous element are not always the same. For example the seven miracles of Elijah and the fourteen miracles of Elisha (the latter number being exactly the double of the former in order to fulfil the prayer of Elisha for a "twofold" portion of the spirit of his master) cannot be explained in the same way as the miracles of the Wanderings or as those in the life of Samson. The eminent Hebraist to whom we are indebted for the Articles above-mentioned would confer on all students of the Bible a very great benefit, if he would give us a separate treatise on the Old Testament miracles. Meantime I must content myself with shewing how some

[1] Habakkuk iii. 11

miracles, of what I may call a "grotesque" kind, may be explained as the mere result of misunderstood names. You must be familiar with this kind of explanation, I think, in ancient history, and even in modern English history, although you have never thought of applying it to the Bible. Perhaps you have read in Mr. Isaac Taylor's *Words and Places* how the sexton in Leighton Buzzard used to show the eagle of the lectern as the identical *buzzard* from which the place derived its name—little guessing that "Buzzard" is a mere corruption of "Beaudésert;" and the porter at Warwick Castle, when he shows you the bones of the "dun cow" slain by Guy of Warwick, hands down a similar erroneous tradition probably derived from a misunderstanding of "dun."[1] A far more famous instance connects itself with the Phœnician name of "Bosra," belonging to the citadel of Carthage. This name meant, in the Phœnician language, "citadel;" but the Greeks confused it with the Greek word "Bursa," a "hide;" and then they proceeded to invent a story to explain the name. Queen Dido, they said, had bought for a small price as much ground as she could encompass with a hide; she had cut the hide into thin thongs and thereby purchased the site of a city for a trifle: hence the city received the name of "Hide." Thus subtilized the Greeks; but it may interest you to know that our own ancestors consciously or unconsciously followed in their footsteps. There is near Sittingbourne a castle called Tong or Thong Castle, situated on a "tongue" of land (Norse, *tunga*) which has given it its name. But tradition has invented or imitated the old Greek story, and has declared that the castle was so-called because the site was bought like Dido's, a trifling price being given for so

[1] "The legend of the victory gained by Guy of Warwick over the dun cow most probably originated in a misunderstood tradition of his conquest of the *Dena gau* or Danish settlement in the neighbourhood of Warwick."—Taylor's *Words and Places*, p. 269.

much land as could be included in the "thong" made from a bull's hide.

But now to come to the particular instance which is the only one I shall give from the Old Testament. You must recollect, and I think you ought to have been perplexed by, the astounding incident in the life of Samson, connected with the "ass's jawbone." The hero is said first to have slain some hundreds of men with the jawbone of an ass, and then to have thrown away the jawbone in the anguish of a parching thirst. Upon this, the Lord is said, (in the Old Version of the Bible) to have opened a fountain of water in the hollow of the jawbone in answer to his cry: and the fountain was henceforth named En-hakkore, *i.e.* the "fountain of him that calleth," because Samson "called upon the Lord." Moreover, when he cast away the jawbone, he is said to have called the place Ramath-lehi ; which the margin (not of the New Version but of the Old) interprets, " the lifting up of the jawbone" or "the casting away of the jawbone." Without pausing to dwell on the extreme improbability of the details of the story, I will merely state the probable explanation. It is probable that the valley containing the "hollow" in which the fountain lay, was called, from the configuration of the place, "the Ass's Jawbone," before the occurrence of any exploit of Samson in it. Indeed we find it actually called "Lehi," or "Jawbone," in the narrative now under discussion, just before the supposed incident of the jawbone took place: "The Philistines went up, and pitched in Judah, and spread themselves in *Lehi* (*Jawbone*)," Judges xv. 9. This latter fact indeed is not conclusive (as the narrator, living long after the event, might possibly use the name of the place handed down to him, even in writing of a time when he believed the name to have been not yet given) : but the probability of a natural explanation of the origin of the name receives strong confirmation from a passage in Strabo (303) who actually mentions some other place (I think in Peloponnesus) called the "Ass's Jawbone." I need not say that Strabo narrates no such Samsonian incident to explain the name, and that it was probably derived (like Dog's Head, Hog's Back and many other such names) from some similarity between the shape of an ass's jawbone and the shape of the valley. Moreover, the word translated "hollow," though it might represent the cavity in an ass's jawbone, might also represent the hollow in a valley, as in Zephaniah (i. 11) "Howl, ye inhabitants of the *hollow*." Again, the name Ramath-lehi cannot mean "casting away of the jawbone;" it means "lifting up," or "*hill*," of Lehi: and accordingly the Revised Version translates, "that place was called Ramath-lehi;" and the margin interprets the name thus, "*The hill* of the jawbone." I should add also that the Revisers—instead of the Old Version, "clave an hollow place *that was in the jaw*"—give us now, "clave the hollow place that *is* in *Lehi*." You must see now surely how on every side the old miraculous interpretation breaks down and makes way for a natural and non-miraculous explanation of the legend. But we have still to explain the name of the fountain, said to have been given from the "calling" of Samson. This is easily done. It appears that the phrase "him that calleth," or "the Caller," is a Hebrew name for the Partridge, so named from its "call," or cry. The "Fountain of the Caller," therefore, in the "hollow place" of the "Ass's Jawbone," was simply, as we might say, Partridge Well in Jawbone Valley, which lay below Jawbone Hill.

But now, many years after the champion of Israel had passed away, comes the legendary poet or historian, who has to tell of some great exploit of deliverance wrought by the hero Samson in this Valley of the Jawbone of the

Ass by the side of the Fountain of the Caller. Straightway, every local name must be connected with the incident that fills his mind and the minds of all his countrymen who live in the neighbourhood. And so "Jawbone Valley" became so called because it was there that Samson smote the Philistines with "the jawbone of an ass;" and "Jawbone heights" are so-called because on this spot Samson "lifted up" the jawbone against his foes, or "threw it away" after he had destroyed them; and "the Well of the Caller" derives not only its name but even its miraculous existence from "*the calling* of Samson upon Jehovah."

I think you will now perceive the kind of reasoning which has compelled me to give up the miracles of the Old Testament. It is not in any way because I have an *a priori* prejudice against miracles: on the contrary, I started with an *a priori* prejudice for miracles in the Bible, though against miracles in general. It is not simply because there is not sufficient evidence for them; it is in great measure because there is evidence against them. For, when you can shew how a supposed miracle may naturally have occurred, and how the miraculous account may naturally and easily have sprung up, I think that amounts to evidence against the miracle. And of course when you find yourself compelled to explain in this way a large number of miracles in the Old Testament, it becomes far more probable than before that the rest are susceptible of some natural explanation. I do not pretend to have investigated in detail every miraculous narrative in the Old Testament. I am ready to admit that at the bottom of the miraculous, there may have been in many cases something very wonderful. Being for example personally very much inclined to the mysterious, I would not deny that in the Hebrew race, as in some others, there may have been some strange power, natural but at present inexplicable, of "second sight;" but, on the whole, looking at the evidence for and against the miracles of the Old Testament, I have now no hesitation in rejecting them as miracles, however much I may admire the spirit that suggested the narratives, as exhibiting a profound and spiritual sense of the sympathy of God with men.

But we may perhaps be called upon to believe in the miracles of the Old Testament on the authority, so to speak, of the miracles of the New Testament. Such at least I take to be the meaning of the following extract from an author who has done so much good educational as well as episcopal work, and has manifested such an openness to new truth, that I differ from him with diffidence where I may possibly have misunderstood his meaning, and with regret where I am confident that I have understood him correctly. The passage is from Bishop Temple's Bampton Lectures,[1] and I will give it at full length, partly because I may have to refer to it again, partly because I am afraid of misinterpreting it if I separate one or two sentences from the context:

"We have to ask what evidence can be given that any such miracles as are recorded in the Bible have ever been worked? It is plain at once that the answer must be given by the New Testament. No *such* [2] evidence can now be produced on behalf of the miracles of the Old Testament. The times are remote: the date and authorship of the Books not established with certainty; *the mixture of poetry with history, no longer capable of any sure separation into its parts;* and, if the New Testament did not exist, it would be impossible to show such a distinct preponderance of probability as could justify us in calling many [? any] to accept the miraculous parts of the narrative as historically true."

If I understand this argument, I fear I must dissent from it. But let us try at least to understand it. Dr. Temple admits (what I should not be disposed to have admitted without a good deal of qualification) that "the mixture of *poetry with history*" (and the context makes it clear that he is referring to the miraculous accounts of

[1] Page 206.
[2] The italics are in the text. In the next sentence, the italics are mine.

Letter 14]   MIRACLES OF THE OLD TESTAMENT   155

the Old Testament) is "no longer capable of any sure separation into its parts." This is a very important admission indeed. A plain Englishman may miss, at first sight, the full importance of it. He may be disposed to say, "What does this matter to me? What do I care whether a miracle is told in poetry or in prose, provided only it is true?" But by "poetry" Dr. Temple does not mean "verse;" he means hyperbole, poetic figures of speech and metaphors; in plain English, he means language that is literally and historically untrue. Consequently the admission amounts to this, that it is now no longer possible in the miraculous narratives of the Old Testament to separate what is historically true from what is historically untrue. If this be so, I cannot understand how the question is substantially affected by the New Testament. Let us suppose for a moment that, many centuries after the times of Moses and Samson, real miracles were wrought by Christ and the apostles; suppose even, in addition, that the reality of the miracles wrought by Christ and his followers could constitute any evidence for the Mosaic Miracles or could refute the evidence against such stories as that of the Ass's jawbone; yet even then, what is the use of knowing that there may be a miracle somewhere concealed in an Old Testament narrative in which it is impossible to "make any sure separation" of the historically true from the historically untrue?

But for my part I am quite unable to adopt either of these suppositions. I cannot see how "a distinct preponderance of probability" for the Samsonian myth or the story of the stopping of the sun could be secured by the fact that miracles were really, long afterwards, performed by Christ. All that could fairly be said, as it seems to me, would be this, that since miracles were actually wrought by the Redeemer of the race, who was

Himself a child of Israel, it is not so improbable as before that miracles might have been also wrought by other previous deliverers of Israel. But this could not go far, and certainly cannot constitute "a distinct preponderance of probability," if we find positive evidence for a miracle almost wanting, and negative evidence against it very strong.[1]

So far as Dr. Temple's argument has weight, so far it appears to me to be capable of being used in the opposite direction to that which he intended. For if there is any connection between the miracles of the Old and of the New Testament, so that the probability of the latter may be fairly said—I will not say to constitute "a distinct preponderance of probability," but to contribute slightly to the probability of the former, then surely we must also admit that the demonstrated improbability of the former must contribute slightly to the *a priori* improbability which we ought to attach to the latter. If the Bible is to be regarded as a whole, and Bible miracles as a whole, then the fact that the Divine Author of the Bible allowed revelation in the earlier part of the Book to be conveyed through an imperfect and non-historical medium will constitute a reasonable probability that He may also have conveyed His later revelations through the same means. In other words, the acknowledged presence of the law of "Truth through Illusion" in the Old Testament should prepare us not to be disappointed if we find

---

[1] A more plausible argument might be derived from any expressions of Jesus which might appear to imply a belief in the historical nature of the Old Testament miracles. This argument appeals strongly to our sense of reverence. We do not like to think that Jesus was mistaken even in a purely intellectual matter. Yet do we really suppose that Jesus, in His humanity, was exempt from the popular intellectual and scientific errors of contemporary humanity? For example, do we really suppose that Jesus was exempt from the popular belief that the sun moves? For those who realize His humanity it is hard to think that He was intended to be so far separated from the men and women around Him; and, if He was not so separated, I find little more difficulty in supposing that He would have had the same belief as was held by all His countrymen concerning the historical character of the Old Testament.

the same law traceable in the New Testament: and the collapse of miracles in the former should prepare us for a collapse of miracles in the latter.

Do not however suppose for a moment that a collapse of miracles implies a collapse of the Bible, and do not be disheartened by such expressions as that "the mixture of poetry with history is no longer capable of any sure separation into its parts." If that expression refers merely to some of the legends of the times of the Patriarchs, or to a few isolated passages elsewhere, it may be accepted without fear; but it cannot apply to the great bulk of the history of the Chosen People. Here you will find very little difficulty in rejecting the obviously non-historical and miraculous element; and you will lose nothing by the rejection. Read through Stanley's *Lectures on the Jewish Church* and ask yourself whether you have missed anything from the campaigns of Joshua and the exploits of Gideon and Samson because the miracles have vanished from his pages. Where miraculous narratives are manifestly not deliberate fabrications, but (as here) late prosaic interpretations of early poetic traditions, they very often afford trustworthy evidence of ancient historical events which imprinted themselves upon the hearts of a simple people. Certainly I can say for myself that I never realized Israel as a nation and had not half my present appreciation of the wisdom and wonder of the deliverance and training of Israel by Jehovah till I had learned to interpret the miracles as being nothing more than man's inadequate attempt to set forth in visible shape the unique redemption of the Chosen People. Spiritually as well as intellectually, my enjoyment of the Old Testament has been doubled ever since I have been able, however imperfectly, to separate the historical element in it from the non-historical, and to interpret the prose as prose and the poetry as poetry.

XV

MY DEAR ——,

You demur to the parallel that I draw between the Old Testament and the New Testament: "The Battle of Beth-horon can be disentangled from the miracle of the stopping of the sun, just as the battles of Salamis and Regillus can be disentangled from the visions which are said to have accompanied them: and so of other Old Testament narratives. But is it possible," you ask, "that the life of Christ can be disentangled from miracles? Do not His own words and doctrine imply a continual assumption that He had power to do 'mighty works' superior to those of ordinary men?"

You could not have put your question more happily: for you unconsciously illustrate the almost universal confusion—common to a great number of theologians and agnostics as well as to the ordinary Bible reader—between "miracles" and "mighty works." You are really asking not one but two questions. Your first question asks about "miracles;" by which you mean some kind of suspension of a law of nature, or, if you prefer it, some act not conceived as explicable in accordance with any natural law by the person who is attempting explanation. Your second question asks about "mighty works," a phrase of constant occurrence in the New Testament, by which phrase we may understand works superior to the works of ordinary persons, but not necessarily suspensions of the laws of nature. Works may be "mighty" and yet quite explicable in accordance with natural law.

You seem to expect a No to your first question and a Yes to your second. I answer Yes to both. (1) The life of Christ can be disentangled from " miracles." (2) Christ always assumed that He could do "mighty works," and from them His life cannot be separated.

It is a law of human nature that the mind influences the body. By acting on the imagination and the emotions men have in all ages consciously or unconsciously effected instantaneous cures in accordance with natural laws. There has been much quackery and deception mixed up with cures of this kind ; but no physician, and no man of any general information, would doubt that such cures have been and still are performed. The Jansenists, subjected to the test of hostile observation, had some undeniable successes of this nature. Every one has heard of the so-called " miracles " of Lourdes ; and no unprejudiced person would deny that amid possible exaggerations and (I greatly fear) some frauds, they have contained an element of reality. "Faith-healing" is going on in England during this very year ; and in the very place where I am now writing I heard a captain of the Salvation Army just now give out a notice that, besides a "free and easy meeting," and a " holiness meeting," and sundry other meetings, there is to be a meeting on one evening this week for the purpose of "casting out devils." If I go there, I shall probably see attempts, with partial success, to excite a paralytic to motion, or to arouse some one from a dull stupor approximating to insanity. These attempts, even though immensely assisted by the intense interest and sympathetic demonstrations of the spectators, will probably produce only a temporary effect ; and when it passes away the patient will very likely be worse than before. But the law of nature is the same with all; in modern times with the Jansenists, the miracle-workers of Lourdes, the "faith-healers," and the Salvation Army, and in ancient times with the priests of Æsculapius. Cures can be effected by a strong emotional shock, sometimes of a gross kind such as mere terror or violent excitement, sometimes of a much purer kind, an ecstatic hope and trust. A marked distinction must of course be made between those cures which can, and those which cannot, be effected by appeal to the emotions. Paralysis (called in the New Testament "palsy"), mental disease (often called in the New Testament "possession"), and various kinds of nervous disorder, are all susceptible of emotional cure: but the loss of a limb cannot be so cured. The cure of a man sick of the palsy by the emotional method would be a miracle for spectators of the first century, but it would not be a miracle for us now; that is to say, it would be explicable by us, but not by them, in accordance with known natural laws: but the restoration of a lost limb by faith would be a miracle for them and for us alike: we know nothing of any natural law in accordance with which such an act could be performed by any degree of faith.

Now it will be admitted by all that the great majority of Christ's "mighty works" were acts of healing, and that many of these were expressly attributed by Him to faith. "Seeing their faith" is the preface, in each of the three Synoptic Gospels, to the account of the cure of the paralytic man, and it is a very curious preface; for it seems to shew that Jesus recognized a kind of sponsorial and contagious efficacy of faith in that instance (as also in the case of the father of the epileptic boy); and we know by modern experience of "faith-healing" how great is the influence of a sympathetic and trustful audience. Elsewhere, "Thy faith hath made thee whole," "According to your faith be it unto you," "Great is thy faith, be it unto thee even as thou wilt," "Thy faith hath saved thee," "If thou canst believe, all things are possible," "Believe ye that I am able to do this?" "Be not afraid, only believe"—these and similar expressions lead us to conclude that many of the "mighty works" of Jesus were conditional on faith. Perhaps it might startle you if I were to say that Jesus was not able to perform a "mighty work" unless faith was present; yet if I said this, I should only be repeating what St. Mark (vi. 5), the earliest of the Evangelists, says on a certain occasion, that on account of the general unbelief at Nazareth Jesus *was not able* (οὐκ ἐδύνατο) to do there any mighty work, "save that he laid his hands upon a few sick folk and healed them." This confession is so frank and almost scandalizing in its plainness that we cannot be surprised that the later Evangelist, in his parallel narrative, softens it down by omitting the words "was not able," and by inserting "many."[1] We need by no means infer from this narrative that Jesus attempted "mighty works" and failed. It may be that He did not attempt them because He discerned the faithlessness of those around Him, and felt His own consequent inability. But, interpret it as we may, this passage remains a most important confirmation of the other passages in which Jesus Himself implies the necessity of faith. Where there was no faith, there Jesus "*was not able* to do any mighty work;" and this limit to His power Jesus Himself recognized.

Here then we find at once a remarkable difference between most of the "mighty works" of Jesus and the "miracles" of the Old Testament. The former were conditional on faith, and, this condition suggests that many of them may be explicable on natural laws; the latter

[1] St. Matthew ix. 58. "And he *did not many* mighty works there because of their unbelief." For a demonstrative proof that the Gospel of St. Mark contains the earliest tradition, see the beginning of the article "Gospels" in the *Encyclopædia Britannica*.

M

have no condition attached to them and there is nothing to suggest that they are explicable on any natural law. Indeed the miracles of the Old Testament are very often wrought, not as a natural response to belief, but as a rebuke to unbelief: thus the hand of Moses is made leprous one moment and pure the next, in order to inspire him with faith; Gideon lays out a fleece on the grass, and the laws of nature are suspended for the purpose of making it wet to-day and dry to-morrow, simply in order that his unbelieving heart may be encouraged by a sign from God; the faithless Ahaz is encouraged by God in the Old Testament to ask for that very favour which Christ in the New Testament systematically refused to the Pharisees—a sign from heaven : and for the sake of Hezekiah (who asks "What shall be the sign that the Lord will heal me?") the dial goes miraculously backward! Could contrast be more complete?

It follows that we shall be acting hastily if we place the "mighty works" of Jesus on the same level as the "miracles" of the Old Testament, inasmuch as the former are (in the strict sense of the term) "mighty works," while the latter (again in the strict sense of the term) are "miracles." But in addition to this reason, derivable from the nature of the works themselves, there is another reason, derivable from the evidence, for drawing a distinction. Besides the direct testimony of the Gospels, we have other testimony, indirect but even more cogent, to prove that Jesus wrought wonderful cures. The earliest of the Gospels was probably not composed in its present shape till more than a generation had passed away after the death of Christ; and, during the lapse of thirty years evidence—especially if handed down by oral, and that too Oriental, tradition—may undergo many corruptions. But the letters of St. Paul are earlier, some of them much earlier; and many of them are of such an unaffected, personal, informal nature that it is absolutely impossible to suppose that they were written to express a conviction that the writer did not feel, or to make the readers believe in truths which were no truths. Now in his letters St. Paul quietly assumes that many of his fellow-Christians, and he himself in particular, had the power of working wonderful cures without the ordinary means.[1] He even sets down this power as one among many "gifts" or "graces" vouchsafed to the Church, and he places it by no means high in the list. A man must be absolutely destitute of all power of literary and historical criticism, if he can persuade himself that these expressions in St. Paul's letters had no basis of fact, and that they were inserted, though unmeaning both to the writer and to the hearers, in order to delude posterity into a false belief. There is nothing in the Epistles to indicate the nature of the diseases which were cured by St. Paul and his followers. We may conjecture with much probability that they were nervous diseases, paralysis, "possession," and the like, such as might be acted on by the "emotional shock" of faith: and the conjecture is confirmed by the fact that, in the time of Josephus, healers of demoniacs were very common in Palestine; and certain Jews of Ephesus are recorded in the Acts of the Apostles to have tried an experiment, after Paul's manner, in attempting to cure a case of one "possessed." But be this as it may, the fact that St. Paul and St. Paul's contemporaries unquestionably cured some kinds of diseases in the name of Jesus, and did this after some sort of

---

[1] To the same effect is *James* V. 14, 15: "Is any among you sick? Let him call for the elders of the church; and let them pray over him, anointing him with oil in the name of the Lord: and the prayer of faith shall save the sick, and the Lord shall raise him up." There can be no doubt that this refers to literal healing; and it is interesting as an indication that probably these early Christian attempts at healing were often tentative. For it will hardly be maintained that *all* who were thus anointed were healed: otherwise death would have been exterminated in the early Christian church.

system, by the utterance of the name of Jesus, without the ordinary means, is a very strong confirmation of the accuracy of the Gospels in attributing to Jesus the power of working instantaneous cures. It would be strange indeed that the Disciples, and not the Master, should have had such powers.

I have laid stress upon the fact that Jesus wrought "mighty" but natural cures, in the first place, because it ought to increase our appreciation of His personal influence and power over the souls of men, to know that He not only possessed this power in an unprecedented degree but also communicated it to His disciples; and secondly, because the fact that He performed these "mighty works" has naturally led people, from the earliest times down to the present day, to infer that He performed "miracles." Even at the present time you will find that the great mass of Christians make no distinction at all between healing a paralytic or a demoniac or a dumb man, and restoring a severed ear or blasting a fig-tree: all alike seem to them "miracles." If this is so even in these days, in spite of physiology, you cannot be surprised that the first Christians and their followers made no such distinction; they assumed that the man who could heal a paralytic by a word could heal any other disease in the same way, and do any other work he pleased contrary to the course of nature. This belief would prepare the way for attributing to Jesus other works of a very different kind, real "miracles," that is, suspensions of the laws of nature. Considering the multitude of such acts recorded in the Old Testament as having been performed by Moses, Elijah, Elisha and others, we may well be surprised to find how very few have been attributed to Jesus: and I believe it can be shewn that each of these few has originated from some misunderstanding, and without any intention to deceive. Of almost all of these real "miracles," said

Letter 15] MIRACLES OF THE NEW TESTAMENT 165

to have been wrought by Christ, I believe we are justified in saying with Bishop Temple that, if we take each by itself, we cannot find for it any "clear, and unmistakeable, and sufficient evidence."[1] So far from being an exaggeration this is rather an understatement of the case: there is not only no "clear and unmistakeable and sufficient evidence" for them, there is also very strong indirect evidence against some of them. In some future letter I may deal in detail with these miracles; for the present I will select only one.

This one shall be the most striking of all the miracles in the New Testament, a miracle exceeding in wonder even the raising of Lazarus. It is found only in St. Matthew's Gospel, and describes an incident that followed immediately on the death of Jesus. Here are the exact words:

"And the earth did quake, and the tombs were opened; and many bodies of the saints that had fallen asleep were raised; and coming forth out of the tombs after his resurrection they entered into the Holy City and appeared unto many."

Have I at all exaggerated this miracle in declaring it to be more startling than even the raising of Lazarus? It records the resurrection, not of one man, but of many. Nor are we allowed by the author to suppose that he referred to visions of the dead, appearing unto friends; for he tells us that "the *tombs were opened*, and many *bodies* of the saints arose." Moreover this would appear to have been a miracle not wrought in private as many of the mighty works of Jesus were, nor a sight vouchsafed to a chosen few (like the manifestations of Jesus after death); for these "bodies" went into Jerusalem,

[1] Bishop Temple excepts only the Resurrection, which is not here under consideration. His words are: "It is true too that, if we take each miracle by itself, there is but one miracle, namely our Lord's Resurrection, *for which clear, and unmistakeable, and sufficient evidence is given.*"— *Bampton Lectures*, p. 154.

during the Passover, at a time when the city was thronged with visitors, and "appeared unto many." What subsequently became of these "bodies"—whether they remained on earth till the Ascension when they ascended with Jesus, or whether they lived their lives over again and were buried a second time, or whether they went back to their tombs again after they had appeared in Jerusalem—is a question of some difficulty, which has exercised the minds of commentators and has been answered rather variously than satisfactorily. Be this as it may, the miracle must be confessed by all to be stupendous.

Now for the evidence of it. I have been quoting from St. Matthew's account of this miracle. What would a dispassionate and intelligent heathen say of it, coming for the first time to the study of our four Gospels? Would it not be something of this sort: "Here you call on me to believe a miracle that appears to me to be motiveless and is certainly singularly startling: but I will suspend my judgment of it till I hear the accounts given by your other three Evangelists. What do they say of the effect produced upon the disciples and bystanders by this earthquake and this most extraordinary resurrection? There were present the women that loved and followed Jesus, there was the Roman centurion, there were 'many' who witnessed the appearances of the dead: even to those who were not present, an earthquake rending the rocks in the neighbourhood could not be imperceptible: what therefore is said on these points by other contemporary authors as well as by your four Gospels? Tell me that first; and then I will tell you what I think of the miracle."

In answer to this request, which I think we must characterize as a very natural one, we should have first to admit that no profane author makes any mention of the resurrection of these numerous "bodies," nor of the earthquake that accompanied it. Then we should have to set down the four records of the four Evangelists as follows :

Mark xv. 37-39.	Matt. xxvii. 50-54.	Luke xxii. 46-7.	John xix. 30, 31.
37. And Jesus uttered a loud voice and gave up the ghost. 38. And the veil of the temple was rent in twain from the top to the bottom.	50. And Jesus cried again with a loud voice, and yielded up his spirit. 51. And behold the veil of the temple was rent in twain from the top to the bottom [*and the earth did quake, and the rocks were rent;* (52) *And the tombs were opened; and many bodies of the saints that had fallen asleep were raised;* (53) *And coming forth out of the tombs after his resurrection they entered into the holy city and appeared unto many.*]	46. And when Jesus had cried with a loud voice, he said, Father, into thy hands I commend my spirit: and having said this, he gave up the ghost.	30. And he bowed his head and gave up his spirit.
[*A blank.*]		[*A blank.*]	[*A blank.*]
39. And when the centurion, which stood by over against him, saw that he so gave up the ghost, he said, Truly this man was the Son of God.	54. Now the centurion, and they that were with him, watching Jesus, when they saw [*the earthquake and*] the things that were done, feared exceedingly, saying, Truly this was the Son of God.	47. And when the centurion saw what was done, he glorified God, saying, Certainly this was a righteous man.	31. The Jews therefore, because it was the preparation, &c.

You see then that this extraordinary incident, startling enough to be the very centre of a galaxy of wonders, is omitted by *three out of the four Evangelists*. You see also that two of the Evangelists agree with St. Matthew in placing a centurion at the foot of the cross, and in assigning to him expressions of faith: but neither of them mentions the "earthquake" as being even a partial cause of the centurion's faith, nor is there so much as a hint of any resurrection of the "bodies of saints" from the tombs.

Now if you and I, with full knowledge of the facts, were writing a biography of a great man, we might undoubtedly exhibit many variations and divergences in our story. Every biographer who knows everything about a man must omit something; many things therefore that you would omit, I should insert, and *vice versâ*. But suppose we were writing in some detail the description of the great man's execution (as the crucifixion is written in great detail by the Evangelists), and, in particular, the emotion and utterances of the soldier who superintended the execution. Is it possible under these circumstances that you should relate (and with truth) that the soldier's emotion was caused in part by an earthquake which happened at the moment of the man's death—adding also that a large number of people rose at the same time bodily from the graves—and that I, with a full knowledge that both these facts are true, should make no mention at all either of the earthquake or of this stupendous resurrection? I say that such an omission of facts is absolutely impossible in any sincere and straightforward biographer, *on the supposition that he knows them*. The argument that "it is unsafe to argue from silence" is quite inapplicable here: nor is it in point to allege the silence of a courtly historian who writes the life of Constantine but omits the Emperor's execution of his son. The answer is that we have not here to do with courtly historians, but with simple unsophisticated compilers of tradition whose main object was to set down in truth and honesty all that could shew Jesus of Nazareth to be the Son of God. Now it is impossible that the Evangelists should not have recognized in this miracle, if true, a cogent proof—cogent for the minds of men in these days—of the divine mission of Jesus: we are therefore driven to the conclusion that they omitted it either because they had never heard of it, or because although they had heard of it, they did not believe it to be true.

You must not however suppose that this evidently legendary narrative was added with any intent to falsify. Like many of the miraculous accounts in the Old Testament, this story is probably the result of misunderstanding —an allegory misinterpreted. The death of Christ abolished the gulf between God and man ; it tore down the veil between the Holy Place and the Holy of Holies, whereby Christ took mankind, in Himself and with Himself, into the direct presence of the Father: and this spiritual truth found a literal interpretation in two of the Gospels which mention the "rending of the veil." But Christ's death did more than this. It struck down the power of death itself : it broke open the tombs, and prepared the way for the Resurrection of the Saints ; and this spiritual truth, being misinterpreted as if it were literally true, gave rise to a tradition (which does not however seem to have been widely received) that at the moment of Christ's death certain tombs were actually broken open, and certain of "the Saints" rose bodily from the dead and walked into Jerusalem.[1]

[1] In the early apocryphal work called *Christ's Descent into Hell*, a striking description is given of the joy of the saints and the terror of Satan, when Christ descends to Hades and rescues the dead, leading them up to Paradise. In one of the versions of this work, the number of those "risen with the Lord" is mentioned as "twelve thousand men."

XVI

MY DEAR——,

You force me to digress. My object just now was to shew that the life of Christ (no less than the history of the redemption of Israel) can be disentangled from "miracles", although not from "mighty works"; and I proposed to take the six or seven principal miracles attributed to Christ by the Synoptists and to shew of each account that it may have naturally and easily crept into the Gospels without any intention to deceive.

But you will not let me go on in my own way; for you ask a question that claims immediate answer, and something more than a mere Yes or No: "Did or did not, the Publican and Apostle St. Matthew write the Gospel attributed to him? And if he did, how can he have suffered a 'legendary' miracle to 'creep into' his narrative? The same question," you add, "applies to the Gospel of St. John. If these two Gospels, as they stand, were written by Apostles, that is, by personal disciples of Jesus and eye-witnesses of the events they profess to describe, then there is no alternative; either Jesus wrought miracles, or the Apostles lied. No eye-witness can err as you suppose some one (I know not whom) to have erred, by interpreting metaphor as though it were literal statement. Imagine Boswell, for example, misinterpreting some metaphorical expression concerning Dr. Johnson to the effect that 'the great lexicographer was exalted by his countrymen to the pinnacle of honour and fame' and consequently inferring that his statue was set up on a column like Lord Nelson or the Duke of York! The notion is too grotesque. If then Jesus did not perform miracles we are forced to conclude either that the Apostles deceived us or that the Gospels bearing their names are forgeries. Which is it?"

In order to meet this objection I must say a few words about the composition of the Gospels. For indeed your question shews a complete misapprehension of the manner in which the Gospels grew up, and of the ancient notions about authorship. In particular, you are far too free in the use of the word "forgeries." The book called the *Wisdom of Solomon* contains some of the noblest sentiments that have ever found eloquent expression, and yet the philosophic author who composed it (probably in Alexandria about eight or nine centuries after Solomon's death) does not hesitate to appeal to the Almighty in words by which he ascribes the authorship to Solomon himself: "Thou hast chosen me to be a king of Thy people and a judge of Thy sons and daughters: Thou hast commanded me to build a temple upon Thy Holy mount," (ix. 7, 8). Now do you call him a forger? The book of Ecclesiastes, one of our own canonical books, declares that it was written by "the son of David, king in Jerusalem" and that the author was a "King over Israel in Jerusalem," (i. 1—12). No one now (worth mentioning) believes these statements to be true. Yet would you call the composer of Ecclesiastes a forger? Probably in both cases the authors felt that they were honouring the memory of the great king in thus introducing new truths to the world under the protection of his name. I believe many other instances might be given of the literary laxity of ancient times. But besides, in the case of the Gospels, you must remember that authorship hardly came into question at all events for a long time. The story of the life of Christ would be, in some shape, current among the Church as the common property of all, as soon as the Apostles began to proclaim the Gospel. Probably it was not, for some time, reduced to writing. Among the Jews the Old Testament was spoken of as Writing or Scripture; but their most revered and sacred comments on it were retained in oral tradition: and hence all through the New Testament you will find that "Scripture" refers to the Old Testament, and that no mention is made of the doctrine about Christ except as "tradition" or "teaching." What therefore would probably at first be current in the Church, perhaps for thirty or forty years after Christ's death, would be simply a number of "traditions" or oral versions of the Gospel, current perhaps in different shapes at the great ecclesiastical centres, such as Jerusalem, Antioch, Ephesus, Alexandria, Rome, yet presenting a general affinity, and all claiming to represent "the Memoirs of the Apostles" or to be "the Gospel of the Lord Jesus Christ."

It ought not to seem strange to you that the Church could exist, and the Good Tidings be preached for some years without the aid of written Gospels. Did not St. Paul preach the Gospel in his letters? Surely he preached it very effectually: yet his letters do not contain a single quotation from any written Gospel.[1] The same may be said of the letters attributed to St. Peter, St. James, and St. John: not one quotes a single saying of Christ, or contains a phrase that can be said, with certainty, to be borrowed from our Gospels. The book of the Acts of the Apostles, the earliest summary of Church history, contains many speeches by Apostles, one by St. James, some by St. Peter and several by St. Paul: in all these speeches only one saying of our Lord is quoted; and

---

[1] If 1 *Tim.* v. 18 were an exception, it would shew that that letter, quoting a Gospel as "Scripture," was later than St. Paul. But it is possibly not an exception.

that is a saying not found in any of our extant Gospels. Conjecture might have led us to conclude that this would be so. We might reasonably have inferred that, as long as the Church had in its midst the Apostles and their companions, and as long also as they daily expected that Christ would " come," the notion of committing the Gospel to writing for posterity would seem superfluous, distasteful, almost implying a want of faith. But when we find this conjecture confirmed by the undeniable fact that the earliest teachers and preachers of the Gospel, in their teaching as it is handed down to us, made no use whatever of our written Gospels, we may regard it as a safe conclusion that, during the first generation after the crucifixion, written Gospels were neither widely used nor much needed.

But soon the need would arise. One after another the Apostles and their companions would pass away, and Christ's immediate "coming" would now be less and less sanguinely anticipated. The great mass of the earliest Christians were either Jews or proselytes to the Jewish religion; but now the Gentiles, who had come to Christ without first passing through the Law of Moses, would become the majority in the Church; and for them the Old Testament would not have the same pre-eminent title as "Writing" or "Scripture." For these Gentiles too the old Rabbinical prejudice against committing the teaching of the Church to writing would have no weight. Now therefore in several churches simultaneous efforts would be made to write down the traditions current amongst the brethren; and hence we find St. Luke prefacing his own Gospel with the remark that he was induced to attempt this task because "many" others had attempted it. St. Luke could hardly have written thus if one authentic and apostolic document already occupied the ground and stood pre-eminent in the Church as the written record of Christ's life by an eye-witness. That there was no such document, known to St. Luke, we may also infer from his acknowledgment of his obligations to those who were " eye-witnesses and ministers of the word." It says that he shapes his narrative " as they handed down the tradition "—for that is the meaning of his word—not " as they *wrote* the tradition." You must have noticed that the extant titles of the Gospels declare them to have been written not " by," but " according to " their several authors. The explanation (which has not been successfully impugned) is that, even in the later times in which their titles were given, the old belief continued, that the men who compiled them did no more than commit to writing their version of a tradition already current. They did not compose, they reported, the tradition; the Gospel was supposed to be the same in all Churches, but here " according to" one version or writer, there "according to" another. The Apostles, being with one or two exceptions mere fishermen and unlearned men, ignorant of letters, could not very well be supposed to be authors of written compositions; but St. Matthew, being a tax-gatherer, would necessarily be an expert writer, and therefore one of the earliest traditions committed to writing would be naturally attributed to his penmanship. But the evidence for St. Matthew's authorship appears, when tested, to be extremely slight. It was the universal belief of the early Church that the Gospel according to St. Matthew was originally written in Hebrew, and Jerome has quoted, as coming from the Hebrew original, a passage not found in our Greek Gospel of St. Matthew. Even when this Gospel is quoted by the earliest writers, it is frequently quoted inexactly, and never connected by them with the name of St. Matthew as the author. We ought not to infer from these unnamed and inexact quotations that the writers did not recognize St. Matthew as the author, for their habit is almost invariably to quote Gospels,

Letter 16] THE GROWTH OF THE GOSPELS 175

simply as Gospel, inexactly, and without mentioning the name of the Evangelist. But this unfortunate habit leaves us without any early and trustworthy evidence for St. Matthew's authorship. On the whole, then, there is very little evidence for supposing that any part of our present Gospel according to St. Matthew was written by an Apostle or by an eye-witness of Christ's life, and there is very much evidence tending to shew that such a supposition is extremely improbable.

Even if we grant that parts of the Gospel were composed by an Apostle, it by no means follows that the whole was. There was a very natural tendency, in the earliest days of the Church—when the traditional Gospel was as it were everybody's property and had not yet acquired the authority of Scripture—to make the tradition as full, as edifying, and as correct, as possible. If we may judge from the style of the book of Revelation (which is said on rather more substantial grounds than are generally alleged for the authorship of most of the books of the New Testament, to have been the work of the Apostle John) the earliest Greek traditions must have been composed in an ungrammatical, mongrel kind of Greek, which must have been as distasteful to the well-educated Christian as cockney English or pigeon English would be to us. This could not long be tolerated in traditions that were repeated in the presence of the whole congregation; and alterations of style, for edification, would naturally facilitate alterations of matter, also for edification. The love of completeness would introduce many corrections and sometimes corruptions. Often, in those early times, the teacher, catechist, or scribe, who knew some additional fact tending to Christ's glory, and not mentioned in the tradition or document, would think that he was not doing his duty if he did not add it to his oral or written version of the tradition. Even in

MSS. of the fourth or fifth centuries we have abundant instances to shew how this tendency multiplied interpolations; principally by interpolating passages from one Gospel into another, but sometimes by interpolating traditions not found now in any Gospel with which we are acquainted. Occasionally there are also corruptions of omission, arising from the desire to omit difficult or apparently inconsistent passages; but by far the more common custom is to add. If this corrupting tendency was in force in the fourth century when the Christian religion was on the point of becoming the religion of the empire, and when the sacred books of Christianity had attained to a position of authority in the Church not a whit below the books of the Old Testament, you may easily imagine what a multitude of interpolations and amplifications must have crept into the original tradition at a time when it was still young, unauthoritative, and plastic, during the first two or three generations that followed the death of Christ. The result of all these considerations is that we are not obliged—and this, to my mind, is a great relief—to suppose that any passage which we may be forced to reject from our Gospels as false, was written by an Apostle.

I say this is to me a great relief, but perhaps it is not so to you. Your notion of what the Gospels ought to be, is perhaps borrowed from a passage in Paley's Evidences where he likens the evidences for the miracles of Christ to that of twelve eye-witnesses, all ready to be martyrs in attestation of the truth of their testimony; and you are shocked perhaps when you find that the Gospels fall very far indeed below the level of such a standard of evidence. What would have seemed best to you would have been an exact record of Christ's teaching and acts, drawn up by one of the Apostles in the name of the Twelve, duly dated and signed by all, and circulated and received by the whole Church from the day after the Ascension down to the present time. And I quite agree with you. But then, as we have seen in the history of astronomy and in the history of the Old Testament, it has not pleased God to reveal Himself or His works to men in the way which men have thought best. Now you are not indeed obliged to infer that, because revelation in the Old Testament was accompanied by illusion, therefore revelation in the New Testament must have contained a similar alloy ; but you ought at least to be prepared for such a discovery. For me, it would be a terrible shock indeed if I were forced to suppose that a faithful Apostle of the Lord Jesus Christ had wilfully misrepresented the truth with a view to glorify His Master : but it is no shock at all to find that the highest revelation of God to man has been, like all other revelations, to some extent misinterpreted, obscured, materialized. I have learned to accept this as an inevitable law of our present nature. If it had been God's will to suspend this law of nature in favour of the New Testament, I think He would have consistently gone further, and miraculously prevented the scribes from making errors, or posterity from perpetuating them. But how can I think God has done this, when I know that even the words of the Lord's own Prayer are variously reported in the two Gospels of St. Matthew and St. Luke, and that every page of a critical edition of the New Testament teems with various readings between which the ablest commentators are perplexed to decide?

You must therefore make up your mind to believe that the earliest Gospel traditions—and even that triply attested tradition[1] which is common to the first three Gospels

---

[1] "Attested" is not the same as "originated." The tradition may (possibly) have been originated by a single author : but witness, or " attestation," was borne to its authoritative character by the three earliest Gospels, whose authors, or compilers, independently adopted it. It is therefore "triply attested."

and which runs through the three with a separate character of its own, like a distinguishable stream—passed through several phases before they assumed their present shape. In my next letter I shall probably ask you to consider what phases they passed through ; but you may perhaps expect me to say something at once about the Fourth Gospel ; for to that book many of the previous remarks do not apply. It was much later than the rest ; it has little in subject-matter, and nothing at all in style, in common with the rest ; it contains scarcely a word of the Common Tradition which pervades the first three Gospels ; it probably passed through no phases and suffered few accretions ; and it differs from the other Gospels, even from St. Luke's, in bearing a far more manifest impress of personal authorship. The three synoptic Gospels really agree with their titles in representing the Gospel "according to" their several authors ; but the Fourth Gospel (although, like the rest, preceded by "according to") is a Gospel written "by"—whoever wrote it.

The question is, who did write it? If it was written by an Apostle, an eye-witness of the life of Christ, then we have to face—I am not sure we have to accept—your alternative : "Either Jesus worked miracles, or the Apostles lied." But there is very little evidence (worth calling evidence) for the hypothesis that an Apostle wrote it, and much evidence against that hypothesis. St. John, the reputed author, is said, on the evidence of Justin Martyr, to have written the Apocalypse ; which, while it resembles in style what we might have expected from a Galilean fisherman, differs entirely from the style of the Fourth Gospel. Whoever wrote the Gospel, we may be sure that he did not reproduce the words of Jesus, but gave rather what appeared to him to be their latent and spiritual meaning. This can be proved as follows. Suppose three writers—say Boswell, Mrs.

Thrale, and Goldsmith—had composed accounts of the life and sayings of Dr. Johnson, widely differing in the subject-matter and style of the narrative, but closely agreeing in the character of Johnson's thoughts, as reported by them, and very often agreeing in the actual words imputed to Johnson ; and suppose a fourth writer, say Burke, had written his reminiscences of Dr. Johnson, which entirely differed in language, in thought, and in subject-matter from the first three: would you not say at once that this was strong proof, that Burke did not report Dr. Johnson's actual words, and that he had probably tinged them with his own style and thought? But if furthermore Burke reported Dr. Johnson's words and long discourses *in the same language as he reported Sheridan's, and in language indistinguishable from his own contextual narrative*, then you would, I am sure, find it difficult to be patient with any one who, through force of prejudice and pleasing associations, obstinately maintained that Burke's biography was equally faithful and exact with the three other concordant or synoptic biographies. Now this comparison exactly represents the facts. You will find several of the most learned and painstaking commentators differing as to where the introductory words of the author of the Fourth Gospel cease, and where John the Baptist's words begin ; and the style of our Lord's discourses in the Fourth Gospel is quite indistinguishable from the style of the author himself. As to the immense difference, in respect of style and thought and subject-matter, between the Synoptic Gospels, and the Fourth Gospel, you must have felt it, even as a child, reading them in English.

I must refer you to the article on "Gospels" in the *Encyclopædia Britannica* for what I believe to be the most probable explanation of the origin of this remarkable work. It is there shewn that there are extraordinary points of similarity between the emblematic language and emblematic acts attributed to Jesus in the Fourth Gospel, and the emblematic conceptions of the Alexandrine philosopher Philo, who flourished some sixty or seventy years before that Gospel was written. Dealing, for instance, with the dialogue between Jesus and the woman of Samaria near the well at Sychem, the writer of that article shews that, in the works of Philo, the well is an emblem of the search after knowledge; Sychem is an emblem of materialism; the "five husbands,"—or, as Philo calls them, "five seducers"—represent the five senses; so that the whole dialogue appears to contain a poetic appeal to the heathen world, to turn from the materialistic knowledge which can never satisfy, to the knowledge of the Word of God which is the "living water." Still more remarkable is Philo's emblematic use of Lazarus (or Eleazar, for the words are the same) as a type of dead humanity, helpless and lifeless till it has been raised up by the help of the Lord. But into this I have no space to enter. If you care to pursue the subject, I must refer you to the article above mentioned. Canon Westcott has pointed out that in arrangement and structure the Fourth Gospel has some distinct poetic features. I should go further and say that, in this Gospel, History is subordinated to poetic purpose, and that its narratives of incidents, resting sometimes on a basis of fact, but more often on a basis of metaphor, are intended not so much to describe incidents as to lead the reader to spiritual conclusions.

We have no account of the authorship of the Fourth Gospel till the year 170 A.D., and this we find to be "already legendary."[1] It is there said that, being requested by his fellow-disciples and bishops to write a Gospel, John desired them to fast for three days and then to relate to one another what revelation each had

---

[1] "The Fragment of Muratori," Westcott, *Introduction to the Gospels*, p. 255.

received. It was then revealed to the Apostle Andrew that "while all endeavoured to recall their experiences, John should write *everything in his own name*." No confidence can be placed in the exactness of testimony that comes so long after the event; but it points to some kind of joint contribution or revision such as is implied in John xxi. 24: "This is the disciple which testifieth of these things and *we know* that his testimony is true." That the Gospel was written "in the name of John" by some pupil of his—perhaps by some namesake—and revised and issued in the name of John by the Elders of the Ephesian Church, is by no means improbable. In some matters of fact, for example in distinguishing between the Passover and "the last supper," the Fourth Gospel corrects an (apparent) error of the Synoptic Gospels, a correction that possibly proceeded from the Apostle John; and perhaps the solemn asseveration as to the issue of blood and water from the side of Jesus ("And he that hath seen hath borne witness, and his witness is true: and he knoweth that he saith true, that ye also may believe") may be a reminiscence of some special testimony from the aged Apostle; but it is impossible to ascertain how far emblematic and historical narratives are blended in such passages as the dialogue with the Samaritan woman, the miracle at Cana, and the raising of Lazarus. The author was convinced (like every other believer, at that time) that Jesus *did* work many miracles, and *could* have worked any kind of miracle; but he had noted the unspiritual tendency to magnify the "mighty works" of Jesus as merely "mighty:" he therefore selected from the traditions before him those in which the spiritual and emblematic meaning was predominant. In doing this, he sometimes took a spiritual metaphor and expanded it into a spiritual history. Again, he had also noted an unspiritual tendency to lay undue stress upon the exact words of Jesus; and he therefore determined—besides giving prominence to the promise of Jesus concerning His Spirit, which was to guide the disciples into all truth —to exhibit, in his Gospel, the spiritual purport of Christ's doctrine rather than to repeat each saying as it was actually delivered.

As I write these words, with the pages of the Gospel open before me, my eye falls upon the story of the raising of Lazarus: "Jesus said unto her, I am the resurrection and the life: he that believeth on me, though he die, yet shall he live; and whosoever liveth and believeth on me shall never die." Is it possible, I say to myself, that Jesus did *not* say these entrancing words? And how often does the same question arise as one turns over the leaves: "Peace I leave with you; my peace I give unto you: not as the world giveth, give I unto you:" "Yet a little while and the world beholdeth me no more; but ye behold me: because I live, ye shall live also." Could any one at any time have invented such sayings? Still less, is it possible they could have been invented in the times of Trajan or Hadrian by any Asiatic Greek or Alexandrian Jew? But truth compels me to answer that, just as the Asiatic Jew St. Paul, although he never saw or heard Jesus, was inspired by the Spirit of Jesus to utter words of spiritual truth and beauty worthy of Jesus Himself, so an Asiatic Greek or Alexandrian Jew of the time of Trajan may have been prompted by the same Spirit to penetrate to the very depths of the meaning of Jesus and to express some of the conclusions to be derived from His sayings more clearly than we can see them even in the words of Jesus Himself, as they are recorded in the Synoptic Gospels. I do not see on what principle we can so limit the operation of the Holy Spirit as to say it could not extend, in its most perfect force, beyond the age of Domitian or Nerva or even Trajan. Having before me the doctrine of the Synoptic Gospels, I am forbidden by mere considerations of style and literary criticism from believing that Jesus used the exact words, " I am the true vine," " I am the good shepherd," " I am the light of the world," " I am the resurrection and the life ; " but I accept these sayings as divinely inspired, and as being far deeper and fuller expressions of the spiritual nature of Jesus than any of the inferences which I could draw for myself from the Synoptic doctrine. Do not then say that I "reject" the Fourth Gospel. I accept all that is essential in it ; and this I accept on far safer grounds than many who would accuse me of rejecting it. For their acceptance might be shaken to-morrow if some new piece of evidence appeared decisively shewing that the Gospel was not written by John the Apostle ; but my acceptance is independent of authorship, and is based upon the testimony of my conscience.

Surely you must feel that it would be absurd for one who tests religious doctrine to some extent by experience and by history, to reject the Fourth Gospel because it is in a great measure emblematic, and because it was not written by the man who was supposed to have written it. Be the author who he may, I shall never cease to feel grateful to him. The all-embracing sweep of view which enabled him to look on the Incarnation as the central incident of the world's history and to set forth Christ as the Eternal Word and Eternal Son, not dependent for this claim upon a mere Miraculous Conception ; the spiritual contempt for mere "mighty works," which leads him repeatedly to claim faith for Jesus Himself firstly, and for the "words" of Jesus secondly, and only as a last reserve to demand belief "for the works' sake ; " and the true intuition with which he fastens on the promise of Jesus (only hinted at in the Synoptic Gospels) that He would be present with His disciples at every time and place and that He would give them "a voice," and a Spirit not to be gainsaid—from which brief suggestion the author worked out in detail the promise of the Holy Spirit, and predicted the nobler and ampler future of the Church—these true, and profound, and spiritual intuitions will always excite my deepest gratitude and admiration. The doctrine of the Eternal Word had its origin perhaps in the schools of Alexandria, and certainly formed no part of the teaching of Jesus; but, Christianized as it is by the author of the Fourth Gospel, it commends itself as a key to many mysteries, and (like the Fourth Gospel itself) it appears to be but one among many illustrations of the divine development of Christian doctrine: "I have yet many things to say unto you, but ye cannot bear them now. Howbeit when he, the Spirit of Truth, is come, he will guide you into all truth." In a word, without the Fourth Gospel, Christendom might (it would seem) have failed for ever to appreciate the true nature of its Redeemer.

I cannot indeed repress some regret that this most marvellously endowed minister and prophet of Christ should have been allowed to select a poetic and even illusive form in order to publish his divine truths. Hitherto I have been able with pleasure and satisfaction to see the illusive integument being gradually separated from the inner truth, as in astronomy and in the history of the Old Testament. Now comes a point where I myself should like to recoil. But how puerile and faithless should I be if I assumed that God would give to the world along with His divine revelation precisely that modicum of illusion (and no more) which I myself personally am just able to receive with pleasure! Let us rather follow where, as Plato says, "the argument leads us." Or, if you prefer me to quote from the Fourth Gospel itself, let us follow the guidance of Him who is both "the Way and the Truth."

XVII

MY DEAR ——,

Once more I am compelled to digress: and, this time, it is in order to meet what you must let me call a preconception of yours. You say that it appears to you "impossible that Christ, if really divine, should have been permitted by God to be worshipped as a worker of miracles for eighteen centuries, although in reality he had no power to work them."

Is this much more than a repetition of your former objection that my views amount to "a new religion," and that illusion, although it may abound in the history of the thoughts of mankind, can never have been permitted to connect itself with a really divine revelation? I have already in part answered these prejudices—for they are nothing more—by shewing that illusion permeates what is called "natural religion," and by subsequently shewing that the inspired books of the Old Testament exhibit illusions in every page; not only the illusions of the chosen people, but illusions also on the part of the authors of the several books, who misinterpreted tradition so as to convert a non-miraculous into a miraculous history. But now let us deal more particularly with Christian illusions. Here I will try to shew you, first, how natural and (humanly speaking) how inevitable it was that illusions should gather round the earliest Christian traditions, and how easily there might have sprung up miraculous accounts in connection with them. Then, and not till then, having done my best to dispel your natural prejudice, I will take in detail the six or seven principal miracles attributed to Christ by all the three Synoptic Evangelists, and will endeavour to shew you that these accounts did actually spring up in a natural and inevitable way, after the manner of illusions, without any attempt to deceive on the part of the compilers of the Gospels. It will appear, I think, that the life and doctrine of Christ are independent of these miracles and can easily be separated from them.

For the present then I am to speak of the naturalness or inevitability of illusions gathering about Christ's acts and words in the minds of His disciples. Does any student of the Fourth Gospel need to be convinced of this? Perhaps the author of that work discerned the illusions of the early Church even too clearly, so that he slightly overshot the mark in the frequency of the false inferences and misunderstandings with which he delights to encompass the words and deeds of Jesus. Perhaps the composer of "the Spiritual Gospel" has been led even too far by his profound and true perception that this Incarnate Word—this Being from another sphere who was and is in the bosom of the Father—could not move on the earth, among earthly creatures, without being perpetually misunderstood by them. But is there not manifest truth in his conception of Jesus as of One having different thoughts from those of common men, different ways of regarding all things small or great, a spiritual dialect of His own, not at once to be comprehended by ordinary beings? Certain it is that, in the Fourth Gospel, Christ's discourses are one string of metaphors which are literally and falsely interpreted by those to whom they are addressed. " Flesh," " blood," " water," " sleep," " birth," " death," " life," " temple," " bread," " meat," " light," " night," " way,"—these and I know not how many more simple words present themselves, as we rapidly turn over the pages of that Gospel, always metaphorically used, and always misunderstood. Nor can it be said that they were misunderstood by enemies and unbelievers alone; His disciples constantly misunderstood them. The life of Christ in the Fourth Gospel is one continuous misunderstanding. I will not say that this represents the exact fact; but I doubt not that the inspired insight of the author, be he who he may, took in the full meaning of all the hints that are given by the Synoptists as to the misunderstanding of the disciples about their Master, and led him to the deliberate conclusion that the life of Christ in the flesh was one perpetual source of illusions to the Twelve—illusions through which, by the guidance of the Spirit, they were to be led to the truth: " What I do ye know not now, but ye shall know hereafter." I believe he went even further and perceived that Christ's life was in danger of becoming a total delusion to the earliest Christians through their tendency to the materialistic and the miraculous, and that the best means of preserving the Church from such a danger was to accustom the faithful to attach value to the words and deeds of Christ only so far as they could interpret them spiritually, trusting to the Spirit for continual guidance into new truth.

This then is my first proposition, that Christ was sure to be misunderstood by those around Him, owing to His manner of using the language of metaphor. You must know very well that this conjecture is confirmed by fact. Sometimes the Synoptists note the fact, as when He spoke of " leaven " and the Twelve misunderstood Him literally; and several other instances are on record. But it is of course possible that on many other occasions the misunderstanding may have existed, but may not have been noted by the Evangelists. Take one instance. In the discourse of Jesus to the Seventy Disciples (Luke x. 19) Jesus makes the following statement: " I have given you authority to tread upon *serpents and scorpions* and over all the power of the enemy, and nothing shall in any wise hurt (ἀδικήσει) you." How are we to understand this "*treading upon serpents and scorpions*"? Literally or metaphorically? Surely the text itself makes it evident that Jesus used the words metaphorically to refer to "the power of the Enemy," *i.e.* "the Serpent," or Satan, probably with a special reference to the casting out of devils. Moreover the passage is introduced by a statement that "the Seventy returned *with joy*, saying, Lord, *even the devils are subject unto us in thy name*. And he said, I beheld *Satan* fall as lightning from Heaven. Behold I have given you authority to tread *upon serpents......Howbeit* in this *rejoice not that the spirits are subject unto you;* but rejoice that your names are written in Heaven." As for the other part of the promise, " nothing shall hurt you," it surely does not seem to you that these words must imply literal " hurt "? If it does, let me direct your attention to a much more striking instance of Christ's extraordinary use of metaphor in a passage where the Disciples are told, almost in a breath, that *not a hair of their heads shall perish* and yet that some of them shall be "*put to death*" (Luke xxi. 16-18). I think then that you will agree with me that the "authority to tread upon *serpents*" mentioned in St. Luke contained not a literal, but a spiritual promise, to tread upon the power of "the Serpent." Nevertheless, that this promise about "serpents" was very early misinterpreted literally can be shewn, not indeed from a genuine passage of the Gospels, but from a very early interpolation in St. Mark's Gospel, xvi. 17, 18 : " These signs shall follow them that believe ; in my name shall they cast out devils ; they shall speak with new tongues ; they *shall take up serpents*, and if they drink any deadly thing, it shall in no wise hurt them ; they shall lay hands on the sick and they shall recover."

Here then we have a clear instance of misunderstanding

(not noted by the Evangelists) arising in very early if not in the very earliest times from the metaphorical language of Jesus. One more instance of probable misunderstanding must suffice for the present. You know how often in the Epistles of St. Paul the word "dead" is used to indicate spiritually "dead" *i.e.* "dead in sin." A similar use is attributed to Christ in the Fourth Gospel: "He that believeth in me, though he were *dead*, yet shall he live" (John xi. 25); but here the impending resurrection of Lazarus gives the reader the impression that it is literally used. However it is almost certainly metaphorical in John v. 24, 25, 28, "He that heareth my word and believeth him that sent me, hath eternal life, and cometh not unto judgment, but *is passed from death into life*. Verily, verily, I say unto you, the hour cometh and now is, when the *dead shall hear the voice of the Son of God, and they that hear shall live*. . . . Marvel not at this, for the hour cometh in which all that are in the tombs shall hear his voice, and shall come forth" &c. Here apparently the meaning is that the hour has already come ("now is") when the spiritually dead shall hear the voice, and the hour is on the point of coming when the literally dead ("all that are in the tombs") shall hear it. In any case, the metaphorical meaning is indisputable in the striking saying of Jesus (Luke ix. 60) "Let the *dead* bury their dead."

Now if Jesus was in the habit of describing those who were lost in sin as being "dead," and of bidding His disciples "raise the dead"—meaning that they were to restore sinners to spiritual life—we can easily see how such language might be misunderstood. It is probable that Jesus Himself had actually restored life to at least one person given over for dead, the daughter of Jairus, though by natural means. Of such revivification you may find an instance described in *Onesimus* (pp. 77—81) which is taken almost verbatim from the account of his own revivification given by the late Archbishop of Bordeaux to the late Dean Stanley, and sent me by the Dean as being taken down from the Archbishop's lips. If that was so, how natural for some of the Disciples to attach a literal meaning to the precept, "raise the dead"! They would argue thus, "Our Master healed diseases at a word, so can we; He once raised a child from the dead and bade us also raise the dead; some of the Disciples therefore ought to be able to do this." How natural, under the circumstances, such a confusion of the material and the spiritual! Yet I have little doubt that the diseases which were cured by the Twelve were almost always "possession," or paralysis, or nervous diseases. Compare the different accounts given by the Synoptists of the instructions of Jesus to the Twelve when He sent them forth on their first mission:

Mark vi. 7.	Matthew x. 1.	Luke ix. 1.
And he called unto him the twelve, and began to send them forth by two and two; and he gave them authority over the unclean spirits.	And he called unto him his twelve disciples and gave them authority over unclean spirits to cast them out, and to heal all manner of disease and all manner of sickness.	And he called the twelve together and gave them power and authority over all devils and to cure diseases.

Here you find that the first Gospel (St. Mark's) makes mention only of the "authority over unclean spirits," and this probably represents the fact. The third account is an amplification; and the second altogether exaggerates. Hence, when we read, in the context of the second version of these instructions, " Heal the sick, *raise the dead*, cleanse the lepers, cast out devils; freely ye received freely give" (Matthew x. 8), we cannot fail to see several arguments against the probability of the italicized words being literally intended by Jesus. First, the language of Christ habitually dealt in metaphor, and in metaphor habitually misunderstood by His disciples; secondly, there is no instance in which a single one of the Twelve carried out this precept during the life of their Master, and only one in which one of the Twelve (Peter) is said to have raised a woman from the dead (for St. Paul's incident with Eutychus can hardly be called a case in point); thirdly the precept is recorded by only one Evangelist;[1] fourthly that same Evangelist records only one case in which our Lord Himself raised any one from the dead, *i.e.* the revivified daughter of Jairus—and it seems absurd to represent Christ as commanding all the Apostles to do that which most of them probably never did, and He Himself (according to the First Gospel) only did once.

We pass now to another cause that may have originated miraculous narratives in the Gospels. Try to extricate yourself from our Western, cold-blooded, analytical, and critical way of looking at things. Sit down in the reign of Vespasian or Domitian in the midst of a congregation of Jewish and Græco-Oriental brethren, assembled for a sacred service, " singing a hymn " (as Pliny says, describing them a few years afterwards) " to Christ as to a God." What effect on the traditions of Christ's life and works would be produced by these " hymns and spiritual songs " which St. Paul's testimony (as well as Pliny's) shews to have been a common part of the earliest Christian ritual? Would they not inevitably tend, by poetic hyperbole and metaphor, to build up fresh traditions which, when literally interpreted, would—like the songs and psalms of the Chosen People—give rise to miraculous narratives? Part of the service indeed would not consist of hymns but of the reading of the " Scriptures " *i.e.* the Old Testament; but this also would tend in the same direction. For there you would hear, read out to

[1] Of course its omission by the other Evangelists might indicate that the words were not uttered by Jesus; but it might also indicate that the precept, being generally misunderstood, was considered so strange and at variance with facts that it had come to be discredited and considered spurious.

the congregation, marvellous prophecies how, in the day of the Lord the Redeemer, the eyes of the blind should be opened and the ears of the deaf unstopped, and the lame should leap as a hart; and the sole thought possessing you and every man in the congregation would be, " How far did all these things find fulfilment in the Lord Jesus Christ?" You would hear from the " Scriptures " narratives of marvellous miracles, how Moses gave water from the rock to Israel in the wilderness and fed them with food from heaven, how Elijah raised the widow's child from death, and how Jonah spent three days in the belly of the fish; and the sole thought possessing you would be, " How far were like wonders wrought by Christ?" Then would arise the hymn describing, in imagery borrowed from the Old Testament, how Christ *had* done all these things, and more besides, for the spiritual Israel; how He had spread a table for His people in the wilderness, and given to thousands to partake of His body and His blood; how Moses had merely given water to the people, but Jesus had changed the water of the Jews (*i.e.* the Law) into the wine which flowed from His side; how Jesus had fulfilled the predictions of the prophets by curing the halt, the maimed, the blind, the leper, the deaf; how He had even raised the dead and bidden His disciples to raise the dead; how He, like Jonah, had spent three days in the darkness of the grave. If you look at the earliest Christian paintings you will find that they represent Christ as the Fish (the emblem of food); others depict the Mosaic miracles of the manna and the water from the rock. These shew what a hold the notion of the miraculous food had taken on the mind of the earliest believers. How easy it would be to amplify a metaphor derived from the Eucharistic feeding on the Bread of Life and perhaps on the " honey-sweet fish " (as Christ is actually called in a poem written about the middle of the second century) into a miraculous account of the feeding of many thousands upon material bread and material fish! It is greatly to be regretted that we have not one left out of the many hymns and psalms of which St. Paul and Pliny make mention. The only vestige of one that I know is found in a verse of St. Paul's Epistle to the Ephesians. It is at all events printed by Westcott and Hort as poetry, and it is thought by many commentators to be an extract from some well-known hymn (Eph. v. 14):

"Wherefore (he) saith,
 Awake thou that sleepest
And arise from the dead
 And Christ shall shine upon thee."

This perhaps is our only specimen of the earliest Christian hymnals. Surely then it is noticeable that in three lines of this unique specimen there are three metaphors, and in the second line a metaphorical use of the word "dead" which — as I have pointed out above — has probably elsewhere resulted in serious misunderstanding.

After the hymn would come the sermon. The preacher would stand up like Apollos to "prove from the Scriptures," that is, from the Old Testament, that Jesus is the Christ. If you wish to know how some of the Christian Preachers would probably discharge their task you should look at the Dialogue with Trypho written (about a hundred years after Apollos) by Justin Martyr—who, I take it, was very much superior in judgment, learning, and ability, to the great mass of Christian Preachers in the first and second centuries. There—among many other instances of the adaptation of history to preconception—you will find Justin declaring that Jesus was born in a cave, and that the ass on which He rode into Jerusalem was tied to a vine, simply because certain prophecies of Isaiah mention a cave and a vine, and because he is determined to find fulfilments of

O

them in the life of Christ. But in the early times of Apollos, and during the next twenty or thirty years, before the Gospels had been committed to writing, there must have been a far stronger gravitation towards the Old Testament and a far more powerful tendency to find something in the life of Christ to fulfil every prediction about the Messiah and to correspond to every miracle wrought by Moses and the prophets. Judged in the light of these considerations, our present record of Christ's life ought to surprise us not by the number, but by the paucity, of the fulfilments of prophecy and the miracles contained in them.

Against these arguments for the antecedent probability that miracles would be baselessly imputed to Jesus (to be followed presently by a few instances to shew that they have been so imputed) I know nothing that has been recently urged except a consideration drawn from the life of John the Baptist: "To the Baptist no miracle has been imputed by the Gospels; to Christ miracles have been imputed; why not to both? What is the reason for this distinction except that the former did not perform miracles, while the latter did?" Two reasons can be given. In the first place Christ worked "mighty works," while John did not; and since many of these "mighty works" could not in the first century be distinguished from "miracles," they served as a nucleus round which a miraculous narrative might gather; in the history of the Baptist there would be no such nucleus. The second and perhaps more important reason is, that, as a counterpoise to the natural exaggerative tendency which might have led men to attribute miracles to the Baptist, there would be also a tendency to heighten the contrast between the Servant and the Master. This tendency appears to me to increase in the later Gospels till at last in the Fourth we come to the express statement, "John worked no miracle" (John x. 41). But whether I am right or not in this conjecture, it is quite certain that the attitude of the Christians towards the mere forerunner of the Messiah—about whom the Prophets had simply predicted that he would "turn the hearts of the children to the fathers"—would not be such as to render likely any imputations of miracles to him. At Ephesus, in the days of St. Paul, there were some quasi-Christians who had received none but "John's Baptism," and had "not so much as heard whether there is a Holy Ghost." That gives us a much stronger impression of the Prophet's influence, and a much weaker impression of the prevalence of the doctrine about the Holy Spirit in the earliest Christian teaching, than we should have inferred from what we read in the Fourth Gospel: was it likely, when the Baptist's influence seemed to the contemporaries of St. Paul still so powerful (perhaps too powerful) that they would be tempted unconsciously to magnify it by casting round him that halo of miraculous action which naturally gathered around the life of Christ?

Does it seem to you very hard, and almost cruelly unnatural, that the life of the Baptist—in whom the world takes comparatively little interest—should be handed down with historical accuracy (at least so far as miracles are concerned) while the life of Christ, the centre of the hopes and fears of the civilized world, has been permitted by Providence to become a nucleus for illusion and superstition as well as for the righteous faith and love of mankind? It is hard; it is not unnatural.

"When beggars die there are no comets seen;
The heavens themselves blaze forth the death of princes."

What does Shakespeare mean by this except to exemplify the universal, and natural, but illusive belief, that whatever affects the greatest man must also affect material nature? Therefore in proportion to the greatness of any man we must expect that the illusions about him will be great in the minds of posterity. How indeed could it be otherwise? Reflect for a moment. Jesus came into the world to be a spiritual Saviour, a spiritual Judge; but how few there were in those days who could fully appreciate even the meaning of these titles! Do you yourself, even at this date, after the lapse of eighteen centuries, grasp firmly this notion of spiritual judgment? Reverence can hardly restrain you from smiling at the Apostles for their unspiritual dreams of a "carnal" empire with twelve tangible thrones to be set up for their twelve selves in Palestine; but you yourself, have you never, at all events in younger days, dreamed sometimes of a visible white throne on material clouds, of a visible and perhaps tangible trumpet, of an audible verdict of "Guilty" or "Not guilty" externally pronounced on each soul? perhaps also of palpable palm branches, and of I know not what more sensuous apparatus, without which you can scarcely realize the notion of the Day of Judgment? And yet all these are adventitious and accidental accompaniments of the real and essential "judgment"—which is in Greek the "sifting" or "division" *i.e.* the division between good and evil in the heart of each one of us. But I doubt even now whether you understand the meaning of this spiritual "division" or judgment. Let me try to explain it. Have you not at any time suddenly, in a flash, been brought face to face with some revelation of goodness—some good person, or action, or book, or word, or thought—which in a moment, before you were aware, has lighted up all the black caverns of your nature and made your mind's eye realize them, and your conscience abhor them, setting your higher nature against your lower nature, so that, without your knowing it, this angelic visitant has taken hold of you, carried away the better part of you along with itself into higher regions of purer thought than yours, from whence your better nature is forced to look down upon, and condemn, your lower and grosser self? This "division" is the operation of the two-edged sword of the Spirit; and when a man's cheeks flush with shame, or his heart feels crushed with remorse, under this "dividing" power, and he *feels* the verdict "I am guilty," then he is being judged far more effectually than any earthly law court could judge him. Now it is this kind of judgment that Jesus had in mind when He spoke of the judgment of the world by the Son of Man. In this sense He has been judging, is judging, and will judge, till the Great Judgment consummates the story of such things as are to be judged. But how little has the world realized this!

Probably some would have realized less of the spiritual if they had imagined less of the material. You know how the English judges of our times still insist on much of the old pomp and ceremony which in the days of our forefathers was thought necessary in order to make justice venerable. The trumpets, and the javelin-men, and the sheriffs in the procession, the wig and gown and bands in court—they all seem a little ridiculous to most of us now; yet possibly the judges are right in retaining them. Possibly our brutal English nature will need for some decades longer these antique and now meaningless trappings before they will be able to respect the just judge for the sake of justice itself. And in the same way, from the days of Clovis to those of Napoleon, many a man who would have found it impossible to realize the righteous Judge as the invisible wielder of the two-edged sword of the Spirit, has felt a fear, which perhaps did more good than harm, at the thought of the opening graves, the unclothed trembling dead, the thunder-pealing verdict and the flames of a material hell. Who also can deny that the illusion which has represented Jesus as having possessed and exerted the power to cure every imaginable disease of the body, has led many to realize Him as the Healer of something more than material disease, in a manner otherwise impossible for masses of men living under an oppression which often scarcely left them the consciousness that they possessed anything but bodies wherewith to serve their masters?

Do not suppose, because I am forced by evidence to reject the miracles, that I am blind to the part that they once played in facilitating faith in Christ. A whole essay, a volume of essays might be written on that subject, without fear of exaggeration. The Miraculous Conception, the Miraculous Resurrection and Ascension, the miracles of the feeding of the four thousand and of the five thousand, —it would be quite possible to shew from Christian literature and history, how in times gone by, when laws of nature were unrecognized, these supposed incidents of Christ's life not only found their way into men's minds without hesitation and without a strain upon intellect or conscience, but also conveyed to the human heart, each in its own way, some deep spiritual truth satisfying some deep spiritual need. It is the old lesson once more repeated : the eyes take in, as a picture, what the ears fail to convey to the brain or heart, when expressed in mere words.

But now, there are abundant symptoms that the tempers and minds of men are greatly changed. Men's minds are more open than before to the need of some spiritual bond to keep society together ; and the character and spiritual claims of Christ, and the marvellous results that have followed from His life and death, are beginning (I think) to be recognized with more spontaneousness and with less of superstitious formalism. On the other hand, the vast regularity of Nature has so come home to our hearts that some believe in it as if it had a divine sanctity ;

the thought of praying that the sun or moon may stand still shocks us as a profanity; and boys and girls, as they stand opposite to some picture setting forth a Bible miracle, look puzzled and perplexed, or, if they are a little older, say with a sententious smile that "the age of miracles is past." In a word, that very element of inexplicable wonder which once strengthened the faith, now weakens it, by furnishing weapons to its assailants, and by inducing rash believers to take up and defend against sceptics a position that is indefensible.

In any case, it is the duty of each generation of Christians, to put aside, as far as it can, the illusions of the previous generation and to rise higher to the fuller knowledge of Christ: for the outworn and undiscarded illusions of one generation become the hypocrisies of the next. The illusions of the permanence of the Mosaic Law, of the speedy Consummation, of Transubstantiation, of the Infallible Church, of the Infallible Book, have all been in due course put away. A candid and modest Christian ought surely to argue that, where so many illusions have already been discarded—and all without injury to the worship of Christ—some may remain to be discarded still, and equally without injury to the Eternal Truth.

What if miraculous Christianity is to natural Christianity as the Ptolemaic astronomy is to the Newtonian? Both of these astronomical systems were of practical utility; both could predict eclipses; both revealed God as a God of order. But the former imputed to the unmoving sun the terrestrial motion which the latter correctly imputed to the earth; the former explained by a number of arbitrary, non-natural, and quasi-miraculous suppositions—spheres, and spirals, and epicycles, and the like—phenomena which the latter more simply explained by one celestial curve traced out in accordance with one fixed law. I believe that in religion also we have made a similar mistake and are being prepared for a similar correction. We have imputed to Christ some actions which have sprung from the promptings of our own imaginations—imaging forth what *our* ideal Deliverer would have done—and which have represented, not His motions, but the motions of our own hearts. By what we have euphemistically denominated "latent laws," that is to say by hypotheses as arbitrary and baseless as the old epicycles, unsupported by sufficient evidence and inconsistent with all that we see and hear and feel around us in God's world, we have endeavoured to explain a Redemption which no more needs such explanations than forgiveness needs them—a Redemption which is as natural (that is to say, as much in accordance with the laws of physical nature and the ordinary processes of human nature) as that Law of Love, or Spiritual gravitation, which may be illustrated in the microcosm of every human household. Now we are to learn the new truth: and as the God of Newton is greater (is He not?) than the God of Ptolemy, so let us not doubt that the God revealed in spiritual Christianity will be greater than the God revealed in material and miraculous Christianity. The new heavens will not cease to declare the glory of God; the new firmament will not fail to tell of His handiwork.

ARE THE MIRACLES INSEPARABLE FROM THE LIFE OF CHRIST?

XVIII

MY DEAR ——,

From the digressions concerning the growth of the Gospels and the possibility or probability that their truths would be conveyed through illusion I now return to our main subject, the question whether the life of Christ can be disentangled from miracles. And here you tell me that some of your agnostic and sceptical friends quote with great satisfaction the following sentence from Bishop Temple's recent *Bampton Lectures*[1]: "Many of our Lord's most characteristic sayings are so associated with narratives of miracles that the two cannot be torn apart." I can well believe what you tell me as to the advantage which they naturally take of this admission: "Here," they say, "is a statement made on high authority that, unless you can believe that Jesus worked *bonâ fide* miracles, such as the blasting of the fig-tree and the destruction of the swine, you must give up 'many of Christ's most characteristic sayings'—in other words, you must give up the hope of knowing what Jesus taught." I wish your friends, who quote this assertion with so much pleasure, would also have quoted the "characteristic sayings" alleged by Dr. Temple in proof of this assertion; for you would then have seen for yourself that many of these "characteristic sayings" are associated not with "miracles" but with "mighty works;" and I am sure you have not forgotten the difference between the two.[2]

[1] Page 153.   [2] See above, p. 158.

For example the first of the "characteristic sayings" is, "Son, thy sins be forgiven thee." Now these words were spoken to the paralytic man; and, as we have seen above, the cure of paralysis by appeal to the emotions—although a remarkable act, and although, if permanent, so remarkable as to deserve to be called "a mighty work"—cannot be called a miracle. But I need say no more of this, as I have treated of cures by "emotional shock" in a previous letter. Now all the other sayings quoted by Dr. Temple refer to "faith" or "believing;" and all, I think, are connected with acts of healing. There may be doubtless in some of our present accounts of the "mighty works" some inaccuracies or exaggerations as to the nature of the disease and the circumstances of the cure. For example, when the cure is said to have been performed at a distance from the patient, either (1) faith must have wrought in the patient by his knowledge that his friends were interceding with Christ, or (2) we must assume some very doubtful theory of "brain-wave" sympathy, or admit that (3) the story is exaggerated, or else that (4) there is a *bonâ fide* miracle. For my own part I waver, in such cases as that of the centurion's servant and the Syro-Phœnician's daughter, between the hypotheses which I have numbered (1) and (3), with a sentimental reserve in favour of (2); but any one of these seems to me so far more probable than the hypothesis of a suspension of the laws of nature that I do not feel in the least constrained by reason of such "characteristic sayings" concerning faith, to give in my adhesion to a narrative of miracle. On the contrary I say the mention of "faith," and Christ's "marvel" at faith, and His eulogy of the "greatness" of the "faith" in certain cases, all go to prove that these acts were not miracles, but simply acts of faith-healing on a colossal scale. I hope you will not feel inclined to sneer at the reservation in those last four words. You will surely admit that, if Christ did anything naturally, the result might be proportionate to His nature; and if His power of appealing to the emotions was colossal, the material result of that appeal might be proportionately colossal. I begin, therefore, the process of disentanglement between the historical and the miraculous in Christ's life by a protest against a hasty and blind confusion which refuses to discriminate between "miracles" and "mighty works," and calls on us to reject from the history not only the miraculous but the marvellous as well; and I assert that the acts of faith-healing with which, as Bishop Temple truly says, there are associated many of our Lord's most characteristic sayings, may be accepted as generally historical and natural.

This, however, would not apply to such a miracle as the restoration of the ear of the high priest's servant; and the reasons are obvious. The faith necessary for an act of emotional healing is not said to have existed, and is not likely to have existed, in a man who probably looked on Christ as an impostor. Even if it had existed, the case was not one where we have reason to think faith could have healed. Besides, the miracle is omitted by three out of the four Evangelists. It is possibly a mistaken inference from some tradition about an utterance of Jesus, "Suffer ye thus far;" which may have really had an entirely different meaning, but which led the third Evangelist to conclude that Jesus desired His captors to give Him so much liberty as would allow him to perform this act of mercy—a humane and picturesque thought, but not history. It is scarcely conceivable that the other three Evangelists should have mentioned the wound inflicted on the servant; that Matthew and John should have added a rebuke addressed by Jesus to Peter for inflicting it; and that John should have taken the pains to tell us the name of the high priest's servant—and yet that they should have omitted, if they actually knew, the fact that the wound was immediately and miraculously healed by Jesus. The irresistible conclusion is that St. Mark, St. Matthew, and St. John, knew nothing of this miracle.

When the acts of healing are set apart, and considered as "mighty works" but not "miracles," the *bonâ fide* miracles in the Synoptic Gospels will become few indeed: and I think it will be found that these few are susceptible of explanation on natural grounds. We will pass over the finding of the coin in the fish's mouth—which is found in St. Matthew's Gospel alone and can hardly be associated with any "characteristic saying" of Jesus—and come to a miracle common to the three Synoptists, the destruction of two thousand swine following on the exorcism of the Gadarene.

This is a very curious case of misunderstanding arising from literalism. It was a common belief in Palestine (as it was also in Europe during the middle ages), that the bodies of the "possessed," or insane, were tenanted by familiar demons in various shapes—toads, scorpions, swine, serpents, and the like. These demons were supposed to have as their normal home an "abyss" or "deep" (Luke viii. 31, ἄβυσσον); but this they abhorred, and were never so happy as when they found a home in some human body. The "possessed" believed that these demons were visible and material; and the juggling exorcist would sometimes (so Josephus tells us) place a bucket of water to be overturned by the demons in passing, as a proof that they were driven out. In a word, the "possessed" could hardly be convinced that he was cured, unless he saw, or thought he saw, the frogs, serpents, scorpions, or swine actually rushing from his mouth in some definite direction.

The explanation of the miracle will now readily suggest itself to you. Some man perhaps a patriotic Galilean, to whom nothing would be more hateful than a Roman army, conceived himself to be possessed by a whole "legion," two thousand "unclean swine." Identifying himself—as was the habit of those who were "possessed"—with the demons whom he supposed to have possession of him, the insane man declared that his name was "Legion, for we are many;" and they (or he) besought Jesus that He would not drive them into the "deep,"*i.e.* into the "abyss" above-mentioned. But by the voice of Jesus the man is instantaneously healed: he sees the legion of demons that had possessed him rushing forth in the shapes of two thousand swine and hurrying down into "the deep;" and what he sees, he loudly proclaims to the bystanders. It is easy to perceive how on some such a basis of fact there might be built the tradition that Jesus healed a demoniac whose name was Legion, and sent two thousand swine into the deep sea; and from thence by easy stages the tradition might arrive at its present shape.

So far, I think, you do not find it very difficult to separate the miraculous from the historical in the life of Christ, nor feel yourself forced to sacrifice any of the "most characteristic sayings of Jesus." Let us now come to a miracle of greater difficulty, the blasting of the barren fig-tree.

Even of those commentators who accept the miracle of the fig-tree as historical, most, I believe, see in it a kind of parable. The barren fig-tree, they say, which made a great show of leaves but bore no fruit, obviously represents, in the first place, the Pharisees, and in the second place, the nation, which, as a whole, identified itself with the Pharisees. Both the Prophets and the Psalms delight in similar metaphors. Israel is the vine; Jehovah, in Isaiah, is the Lord of the vine, who demands good fruit and finds it not, and consequently resolves to destroy the vine. So here, the Lord comes to the fig-tree of Phariseeism, the tree of degenerate Israel, seeking fruit ; and finding none, He curses it, and withers it with the breath of His mouth. Is it not easy to see how a parable, thus expressed in the hymns and earliest traditions of the Church, might speedily be literalized and give rise to a miraculous narrative?

Let me point out to you a curious fact confirmatory of this view. I dare say you may have noticed that St. Luke, although he agrees with St. Mark and St. Matthew in the context of this miracle, omits the miracle itself. Why so? Is it because he never heard of the miracle? Not quite so. It is because he had heard of it in a slightly different form, not as a miracle but as a parable, which he alone has preserved. St. Luke's version of the tradition is that the Lord, comes to the barren tree and, finding no fruit on it, gives orders that it is to be cut down : but the steward of the farm pleads for a respite ; let the ground be digged and manured, then, if there be no fruit, let it be cut down. A similar thought, you see, is here expressed in two different shapes, a miraculous and a non-miraculous ; and it is not difficult to understand how the former may have been developed from the latter.

But I see that your last letter has a remark on this very miracle, and on the difficulty of rejecting it. " It is associated," you say, " with one of the most characteristic sayings of Jesus : for it is in connection with the withering of the fig-tree that Jesus says (Matt. xxi. 21), ' If ye have faith, ye shall not only do *what is done to the fig-tree*, but even if ye shall say unto this mountain, Be thou taken up and cast into the sea, it shall be done.'" " Here," you say, " we have a characteristic saying of Jesus expressly referring to something done, and done miraculously."

Would it not have been wise, before making so

emphatic a statement, to consider how St. Mark, the earlier of the two narrators of this miracle, sets forth the comment of Jesus? The comments run thus in the first two Gospels, and I will add a parallel saying from the third Gospel, not attached to any miracle :

Mark xi. 21-23.	Matthew xxi. 20-21.	Luke xvii. 5-6.
And Peter, calling to remembrance, saith unto him, " Rabbi, behold the fig tree which thou cursedst is withered away." And Jesus answering saith unto them, '' Have faith in God. Verily I say unto you, Whosoever shall say unto this mountain, Be thou taken up and cast into the sea ; and shall not doubt in his heart, but shall believe that what he saith cometh to pass ; he shall have it."	And when the disciples saw it, they marvelled, saying, " How did the fig tree immediately wither away ?" And Jesus said unto them, " Verily I say unto you, If ye have faith, and doubt not, ye shall [*not only do what is done to the fig tree, but even if ye shall*] say unto this mountain, Be thou taken up and cast into the sea, it shall be done."	And the apostles said unto the Lord "Increase our faith." And the Lord said, "If ye have faith as a grain of mustard seed, ye would say unto this sycamine tree, Be thou rooted up, and be thou planted in the sea ; and it would have obeyed you."

You see then that the more authoritative (because earlier) of our two witnesses omits those very words on which you lay so much stress, the " express reference to something done, and done miraculously." And ought not this fact to make you pause and ask yourself " Am I really to suppose that the Lord Jesus encouraged His disciples to command material mountains to be cast into the sea, and material trees to be destroyed ? Did He Himself so habitually act thus that He could naturally urge His disciples to do the like ? Does it not seem, literally taken, advice contrary not only to common sense but also to a reverent appreciation of the law and order of nature ?" I would suggest to you that you might weigh the inherent improbability of the words in St. Matthew (literally taken), as well as the external probability—which I will now endeavour to shew—that the whole passage was metaphorical.

We know from St. Paul's works, as well as from Rabbinical literature, that "to move mountains" was a common metaphor to express intellectual or spiritual ability. St. Paul speaks of faith that would "move mountains;" and you will find in Lightfoot's *Horae Hebraicae* (ii. p. 285), "There was not such another *rooter up of mountains* as Ben Azzai." Now we know from St. Luke's Gospel (xvii. 6), that Jesus used a similar metaphor of trees, as well as of mountains, to exemplify the power of faith; and this without any reference to " something done and done miraculously: " "If ye have *faith* as a grain of mustard seed, ye would say unto this sycamine tree, Be thou *rooted up and planted in the sea;* and it would have obeyed." Planted in the sea! Can you dream that so preposterous a portent could have been prayed for by any sane and sober follower of Christ in compliance with his Master's suggestion? Bear in mind that these words in St. Luke's Gospel were uttered a long time before the blasting of the fig-tree is supposed to have happened, and at a different place. Does not then a comparison of this passage with the other two make it probable that Jesus was in the habit of encouraging His disciples to be " pluckers up of mountains " and "rooters up of trees," not literally but metaphorically, meaning thereby that they were to attempt and accomplish the greatest feats of faith?

You will, perhaps, be surprised when you find what it was that Jesus regarded as the greatest feat of faith in the passage of St. Luke just mentioned. It was a feat of which we are accustomed to think rather lightly; partly, perhaps, because we are often contented with the appearance of it without the reality: it was simply forgiveness. He had told the disciples they must forgive " till seventy times seven." The Apostles, in despair, replied " Increase our faith : " and then Jesus tells them that if they had but a germ of living trust, they could become "uprooters of sycamine trees," in other words they could perform forgiveness, the greatest feat of faith. But perhaps you will say, "At all events in St. Mark, the earliest authority for the miracle of the blasting of the fig-tree, there is no mention of forgiveness, and nothing that would indicate that his version of the words of Jesus referred to what you call ' the greatest feat of faith,' *i.e.* forgiveness." On the contrary, you will find that St. Mark, with some apparent confusion of different thoughts, retains the trace of the original spiritual signification of the words (Mark xi. 22—25): " Have *faith* in God. Verily I say unto you, whosoever shall say unto this mountain, Be thou taken up and cast into the sea, and shall not doubt in his heart but shall believe that what he saith cometh to pass, he shall have it. *Therefore* I say unto you, All things whatsoever ye pray and ask for, believe that ye have received them, and ye shall have them; *And whensoever ye stand praying, forgive, if ye have aught against any one;* that your Father which is in heaven may forgive your trespasses."

I contend that, upon the whole, an impartial critic must come to the conclusion that neither the miracle, nor the reference to the miracle, is historical; and that, in all probability, both the miracle and the reference to it arose from a misunderstanding, without any intention to deceive. We must remember that the " short sayings" of the Lord Jesus—as they are called by some early writer, Justin, I think—must have caused considerable difficulty to the compilers of the earliest Gospels in the attempt to arrange them in order. Pointed, pithy, and brief, pregnant with meaning, sometimes obscured by metaphor, many of these sayings, if taken out of their context, were very liable to be misunderstood. Some compilers might think it best, as the author of St. Matthew's Gospel has done in the Sermon on the Mount, to group a number of these sayings together without connection; others, as the author of St. Luke's Gospel, might object to this arrangement, and might make

P

it a main object to set forth these sayings "in order," attaching to each its appropriate and explanatory context. Now to apply this to the particular case of the legend of the fig-tree. It seems probable that the compilers had before them two traditions, one, a parable about a barren fig-tree destroyed by the Lord of the vine-yard because it bore no fruit; another, a precept about the power of faith in uprooting a mountain or a tree, *i.e.* in achieving the greatest of spiritual tasks, the task of forgiving. St. Luke interpreted both the parable and the precept spiritually, and kept the two distinct. St. Mark interpreted the parable literally and adopted the tradition which made it refer to an actual destruction of a tree; he also appended to it the saying on the power of faithful prayer to work any wonders soever, as being an appropriate comment on so startling a miracle; but he did not think fit to adapt the saying to the miracle by any insertion of the word "tree" ("Verily I say unto you, whosoever shall say unto this mountain, Be thou taken up" &c.); and he retained the old connection of the saying with forgiveness. St. Matthew—of course, when I say St. Matthew, I mean the unknown authors or compilers of the Gospel called by his name—is more consistent. He, like St. Mark interprets the parable literally, and he appends to it the saying on the power of faithful prayer; but he inserts in the latter an express reference to the miracle which, according to his hypothesis, had recently been worked before the eyes of the Disciples and could hardly therefore fail to be mentioned: "If ye have faith and doubt not, ye shall [*not only do what is done to the fig-tree, but even if ye shall*] say unto this mountain," &c. In order to complete the adaptation, he also omits the words that connect the saying with forgiveness, and relegates them to the Sermon on the Mount (vi. 14, 15) which he makes the receptacle for all those sayings of Jesus for which he can find no special time and place.

"All this is shadowy, barely possible, mere conjecture. I maintain that conjecture, fairly supported, is enough to give the finishing blow to all faith in a miracle so different from Christ's other "mighty works" as this of the fig-tree. Before finally and utterly rejecting a story found in a generally truthful narrative we wish not only to know that the story is improbable, but also to answer the question, "How may it have crept into the narrative?" The above conjecture supplies a fairly probable answer to that question; and the combined result of the evidence for the probability of some rational explanation, and against the probability of the miraculous occurrence, is so great that I can feel no hesitation in rejecting the miracle of the fig-tree and in declaring that the "characteristic sayings" of Jesus about the uprooting of mountains and trees were never intended to be literally understood.

And now, before going further, ask yourself once more, "What have I lost, so far, by giving up the miracles of Jesus? Does He sink in my estimation because He did not blast a fig-tree or destroy two thousand swine, or draw a fish with a stater in its mouth to the hook of Peter? Or have I lost a precious and 'characteristic saying' of Jesus because I no longer believe that He really encouraged His disciples to pray for the uprooting of material mountains and material trees?" I am quite sure your conscience must reply that you have hitherto lost nothing. If so, take courage, and follow on step by step where the argument leads you.

XIX

MY DEAR ——,

You remind me that I have omitted the most important of all those sayings of Christ which are associated with miracles—the passage in which he comments on the feeding of the Four Thousand and on that of the Five Thousand, as two separate acts, apparently implying their miraculous nature. I have not forgotten it; but I reserved it to the last because it is, as you justly say, the most important and the most difficult of all; but I believe it to be susceptible of explanation.

Let us first have the facts before us. In the Gospels of St. Matthew (viii. 15) and St. Mark (xvi. 6) Jesus is introduced as bidding the Disciples "beware of the leaven of the Pharisees and the leaven of Herod" (or, as Matthew, "the Sadducees.") Upon this the disciples, as usual, interpret the words of Jesus literally; they suppose that, since they have forgotten to bring bread with them (for they had but one loaf) their Master wishes to warn them to beware of leaven during the approaching feast of Passover or unleavened bread. Hereupon Jesus, in order to shew them that He was not speaking literally, rebukes their dull and literalizing minds as follows :—

Mark viii. 17-21.	Matthew xvi. 8-12.
"Why reason ye because ye have no bread? Do ye not yet perceive? . . . . . When I brake the five loaves among the five thousand, how many baskets full of broken pieces took ye up?" They say unto him, "Twelve." "And when the seven among the four thousand, how many baskets full of broken pieces took ye up?" And they say unto him, "Seven." And he said unto them, "Do ye not yet understand?"	"Why reason ye among yourselves because ye have no bread? Do ye not yet perceive neither remember the five loaves of the five thousand and how many baskets took ye up? Neither the seven loaves of the four thousand and how many baskets ye took up? How is it that ye do not perceive that I spake not to you concerning bread? But beware of the leaven of the Pharisees and Sadducees." Then understood they how that he bade them not beware of the leaven of bread, but of the teaching of the Pharisees and Sadducees.

Now before I proceed further I must point out to you that these words are not found in St. Luke's Gospel. For my own part I am disposed to believe them to be genuine, though not quite in the exact form in which we now find them. I think St. Luke may have omitted them because he found some difficulty or obscurity in them; or because he did not know of them; or perhaps because he did not know of, or did not accept, the feeding of the Four Thousand, to which they refer. But suppose we are forced to give them up as altogether spurious, that is to say, as not being genuine words of Jesus, though genuine parts of the first and second Gospels; what is the consequence? Simply that we shall be reduced to St. Luke's version of the words, which is as follows (Luke xii. 1): "Beware ye of the leaven of the Pharisees which is hypocrisy." Can we say that St. Luke has herein omitted words that are essential to the life of Christ, or that we have lost anything of the highest importance, or even that we have lost a very "characteristic saying" of Jesus in omitting the statistical comparison which St. Luke omits? I think not.

But now let us assume that Jesus uttered these words or something like them. I think you would perceive that they could be interpreted metaphorically, if you could only comprehend how the accounts of the miraculous feeding of the Four Thousand and of the Five Thousand (obviously literal as they now stand in our Gospels) could be referred to as spiritual incidents. In order to answer this question we must now pass to the narratives of the two miracles themselves. I suppose even those who accept them literally would admit that they are emblematic, and that they represent Jesus, the Bread of Life, giving Himself for the world. The Fourth Gospel manifests this in the subsequent discourse where the feeding on the bread and fishes introduces the subject of the feeding on the flesh and blood of Christ. The notion that we feed on the Word of God, first found in Deuteronomy (viii. 3), pervades all Jewish literature. It is found in Philo (i. 119): "The soul is nourished not on earthly and corruptible food, but on the *words* which Gods rains down out of His sublime and pure nature which He calls heaven." It reappears in the account of our Lord's temptation, when He replies to Satan, quoting Deut. viii. 3, "Man shall not live by bread alone but by every *word* that proceedeth out of the mouth of God;" and again (John iv. 32), "I have *meat* to eat that ye know not."

On that last occasion the Fourth Gospel tells us that the disciples actually misunderstood the metaphor and interpreted it literally; and to this day I dare say many would give a literal interpretation to the "daily bread" of the Lord's prayer; but there can be little doubt that Jesus meant by "bread" every gift and blessing that constitutes life, and primarily the spiritual sustenance of the soul. As to the emblematic use of the "fish," it cannot be traced to the Old Testament; but in a very early period of the existence of the Church, as early as the reign of Vespasian, we find the Fish in rude paintings representing the Eucharistic food of the faithful; and it is said that this appellation was given to Jesus from the initial letters of the Greek title I(esous) Ch(ristos) Th(eou) U(ios) S(oter) [Jesus Christ, Son of God, Saviour] because they made up the Greek word *Ichthus,* fish. About the middle of the second century we find one of the earliest extant Christian poems describing how the Church everywhere presented to the faithful, as their food, "the Fish, great and pure, which the Holy Virgin had caught." The poet evidently did not invent this metaphor; it was established, intelligible, and inherited, at the time when he used it, and must have been in use much earlier. To speak of "crumbs" metaphorically may perhaps seem to us a bold metaphor, but it may be illustrated by the dialogue between Jesus and the Syro-Phœnician woman: "It is not meet to take the children's food and cast it unto dogs:" "Truth, Lord; yet even the dogs eat of the *crumbs* which fall from the master's table." Now it was a common-place in the doctrine of Jesus that every disciple who ministered the Word or Bread of Life invariably received it back in ample measure: "Freely ye have received, freely give." Give what? Certainly not material bread, but the truth or bread of life. And again, "Give, and it shall be given unto you: good measure pressed down and running over shall THEY[1] give into your bosom." Again, I ask, give what? What but the spiritual Bread, which, by the laws of spiritual nature, cannot be freely given without a yet more rich return into the giver's heart? It was this Bread that Christ ministered to His disciples and bade them set before the people; it was this Bread which the disciples found multiplied in their hands so that it sufficed for all, and they themselves were fed from the crumbs that fell from the food.

In course of time the story of this spiritual banquet finding its way into Christian hymns and traditions would

[1] *i.e.* the Powers of Heaven

be literalized and amplified with variations. As Moses
" spread a table" for Israel " in the wilderness," so also,
it would be said, did Jesus of Nazareth when he fed
thousands of His followers on divine Bread. The Fish,
*which is not mentioned in our Lord's dialogue with the
Disciples*, might naturally be added to the Bread, in the
narrative, as a Eucharistic emblem. If the Fish had
been mentioned by our Lord in the dialogue under question, my explanation would at once fall to the ground ;
but it is not mentioned ; and the only difficulty is in explaining how Jesus could have spoken metaphorically of
the "seven" as well as the "twelve" baskets. We can understand the "twelve"—each one of the twelve Apostles
who ministered, receiving a return of spiritual "crumbs"—
but whence the "seven"? Here I can but conjecture.
You know that seven is what is called "a sacred number."
I find in the Fourth Gospel, xxi. 2-14, a story (evidently
emblematic) of a miraculous meal of bread and fishes in
which "seven" apostles took part. This may have been
based upon some tradition in which seven apostles were
recorded as having taken part in a spiritual Eucharistic
feeding of the multitude. If that was so, it would follow
that in the latter case there would be "seven baskets" of
fragments, as in the former case there were "twelve," corresponding to the number of the ministering apostles : and
Jesus, in the dialogue under consideration, would remind
His disciples how on two occasions where the bread of
life was multiplied for the hungry, the twelve Apostles
received the twelve baskets of crumbs, and the seven
received the seven.

What is the argument in the words under consideration,
according to your interpretation? I presume you would
take them thus : "Why do you suppose I am talking
about literal bread? Can I not make bread as I please?
Do you not remember my two miracles, and how from

five loaves for five thousand people there came twelve baskets of fragments, while from seven loaves for four thousand people there came seven baskets?[1] How then can I (or you while you are with me) be in need of literal bread?" But this interpretation is open to one serious objection. It is opposed to the whole tenour of Christ's life. Nowhere else in the Gospels do we find that Jesus used any miraculous power to exempt Himself and His disciples from hunger. We are even taught that on one occasion He resisted a prompting to turn stones into bread, as being a temptation from the Evil One. For His disciples he might undoubtedly have been willing to do what He would not do for Himself; but that Jesus (like Elisha) so habitually used miraculous powers to shelter His disciples from the inconveniences and hardships of a wandering life, that he could encourage them to believe that he would do so on the present occasion, is a hypothesis quite inconsistent with the Gospel history. Moreover, plausible although this interpretation may appear to us—because we are familiar with the literalizing interpretation of the miracles of the Four Thousand and Five Thousand—it does not, if I may so say, bring out the proportion of the sentence. Surely it does not sound logical to say, " Did I not once supply you with bread for four and five thousand people (literally)? Why then do you not understand that I now speak of 'leaven' metaphorically?" Instead of this, should we not rather expect : " Do you not remember how on two previous occasions 'bread' was used spiritually? Why then do you not understand that 'leaven' is here used spiritually?" Now this is what I believe to have been the original meaning of the words if genuine. I believe that Jesus intended to remind the

---

[1] Two different kinds of baskets appear to be denoted by the two different Greek words. A similar difference is also found in the narratives of the feeding of the Four Thousand and the Five Thousand: but it would be easy to shew that no inference of importance can be drawn from this distinction.

Disciples how on two previous occasions the multitude had been fed with the spiritual Bread, the Bread of Life: "You know that that was what I meant before, when I spoke of Bread; how is it then that you do not understand my meaning now when I speak similarly of leaven?"

I do not pretend to say that this explanation is completely satisfactory even to me, much less to claim that it should completely satisfy others. Some may prefer to rationalize the miracle as an exaggeration with a substratum of fact; others may reject the dialogue as a late interpolation. Yet even then I think the considerations above alleged—which I have put forward, on the supposition that the dialogue is genuine—may go a long way toward shewing how these miraculous stories may have sprung up without any real basis of miracle, and how, in the elaboration of these narratives, words that cannot be accepted as historical may have been attributed to Jesus *without any fraudulent purpose*. Although I am unwilling to admit (and do not feel called upon by evidence to admit) that the words and doctrine of Jesus have been seriously modified to suit the miraculous interpolations of early Christian times, yet of course (on my hypothesis) some slight occasional modifications cannot be denied. For example, in the miracle of the Four Thousand, Jesus is introduced as saying, "How many loaves have ye?" These words must necessarily be rejected by any one taking my view of the narrative, as the addition of some later tradition which, interpreting a metaphor literally, endeavoured to set forth the literal fact dramatically as it was supposed to have occurred. In the same way it is possible that the dialogue now under consideration may be an amplification of a simple rebuke from Jesus to the disciples for misunderstanding His precept as to leaven, the early tradition having run somewhat after this fashion: "The Lord spread a table for the hungry in the wilderness : He gave them bread from heaven to eat. The Lord gave food unto the multitude through the hands of the Twelve; and in their hands the Bread of Life was multiplied so that a few loaves satisfied many thousands. Then did the Lord warn His disciples that they should *beware of leaven and feed on nought save the one true Bread. But they understood not His words, and remembered not the mighty works of His hands.*" It seems to me quite possible, I say, that the dialogue under discussion may have arisen from an amplification of some such words as those above italicized ; and I am somewhat the more inclined to take this view because St. Mark's narrative (the earliest) contains a curious little detail which looks like a trace of some old hymn about " the one true Bread " *i.e.* Jesus : " They had not in the boat with them more than *one loaf* (Gr. *bread*)."

If these suggested solutions seem improbable, let me once more remind you that you have to choose between them and greater improbabilities. Either the miraculous narrative must be historically true ; or it must have been deliberately fabricated ; or it must have sprung into existence without intention to deceive. As to the improbability of the first of these solutions, I say nothing, because you have rejected it. Certainly it would be difficult for a painter to depict in detail the processes necessitated by this miracle without producing a grotesque impression: but on this point I am silent, as it is beside my purpose. It remains therefore for you to decide whether the theory of deliberate falsehood, or of the unconscious accretions of tradition and misunderstanding of metaphor, supplies the least improbable explanation. For my part, having regard to the character of Christ's disciples, the abundant evidence that they misunderstood the teaching of their Master, and the frequent instances of miraculous narrative arising from misunderstanding in other cases, I have no hesitation in saying that, in this case also, the hypothesis of deceit is far more improbable than that of misunderstanding.

I had not intended to touch on any other miracle; but one more can be so briefly discussed that I will not omit it. I dare say you have anticipated (though you have not read *Onesimus*[1]) that I should explain the "walking on the waves" and the "stilling of the sea" as narratives derived from early Christian hymns representing the Son of God as stilling the storms that threaten the bark of the Church. Nevertheless you may not have perceived how easily a historical and authentic tradition of the deeds and words of Christ would lend itself to amplification so as to be elaborated into the full miraculous narrative as we now find it in the Gospels. Well then, open your Greek Testament at St. Mark's narrative (i. 25-27, or Luke iv. 35, 36) of the exorcism of an unclean spirit. You will there find it stated that Jesus "rebuked an unclean spirit;" and a somewhat rare word is used to express the rebuke, "Be thou *muzzled* (φιμώθητι)." It is further added that the disciples, in their astonishment, said to one another "What is this? *With authority he commandeth even the unclean spirits and they obey him.*" Now you know very well that the same Greek word (πνεῦμα) expresses two totally distinct English words "spirit" and "wind;" but you may not so well know that the same ambiguity is found in Hebrew. Look at Psalm civ. 4 in the Old Version, and you will find "Who maketh his angels (*i.e.* messengers) *spirits;*" but the New Version gives, more correctly, "Who maketh *winds* his messengers," or, "Who maketh his angels *winds.*" Now suppose that in some cases where the above tradition was circulated in the Church, either in Greek or Aramaic, the word "unclean" was omitted, as it easily might be for

[1] Pp. 275-6.

brevity. It would follow that, without the change of a single word, the hearers might interpret the story as follows : "Jesus *rebuked the wind*, saying to it, *Be thou muzzled.* His disciples marvelled, saying, What is this? *With authority he commandeth even the winds* and they *obey* him."

But you may say perhaps, "Jesus could not use such an extraordinary phrase as 'Be thou muzzled,' in addressing the wind. To a human being it would be applicable, or even to a spirit, but not to the wind." Well, it certainly would be rather unusual: but turn to St. Mark iv. 39, and you will there find a passage telling you how, in a storm at sea, Jesus awoke and "*rebuked the wind*" with the words " *Be thou muzzled* (φιμώθητι)," and how the wondering disciples said to one another, "*Who is this that even the wind* (Matthew and Luke, 'the *winds*') and sea *obey him ?* " It appears to me by no means unlikely that we have here two versions of the same tradition ; the one in the earlier chapter of St. Mark representing the facts ; the other in the later chapter resulting from a misunderstanding of the facts, whence there sprang up the amplified and beautiful tradition of the Stilling of the Storm—a story which must have in all ages commended itself to the Church, and may still commend itself, by reason of its deep spiritual truth, but which ought, in this age, to be recognized as in all probability, not historically true.

Neither of the above-mentioned explanations of this miraculous narrative appears to me by any means certain ; but either seems to me decidedly more likely than that Jesus so far raised Himself above the conditions of humanity as to rebuke and check the winds and the seas. If I interpret the life of Christ aright, He neither did, nor wished to do, any such thing, and would have regarded the suggestion to do it as a temptation from

Satan. I say this with reverence, almost with fear and trembling, knowing that I must give account of these words hereafter before Him. But what can a man do more to shew his homage for the Truth than follow where the Truth appears to lead?

In any case I am sure we cannot rightly understand the life and mind of Jesus until, by a great effort, we have divested ourselves of our inveterate and vulgar belief that He wrought His mighty works as mere demonstrations of His divine mission, and that He had power to perform any works whatever, quite regardless of the laws of nature. Had that been the case, I do not see how He could have blamed the Pharisees for asking Him to work a sign in heaven. Why should they not have asked it, and why should not He have worked it? Jugglers and impostors were very common in the East: Galilee and Samaria were thronged with professional exorcists: in miracles performed on men there was always the possibility of collusion; any act on earth was open to suspicion of imposture, but in heaven—this was the general belief—there could be certainty; no mere magician could work a sign in heaven. " Let but the sun stand still for half a day, and we will believe," surely this, from the demonstration-point-of-view of miracles, was a very natural request; and if Jesus really had the power of stopping the sun for half a day, and if He felt that His wonder-working faculty was given to Him for the mere purpose of demonstrating His divine power, I cannot understand how He could have refused, much less rebuked, the request of the Pharisees.

But in truth His mighty works or signs were not wrought in this deliberate way for the mere purpose of demonstration. They were the results of an irrepressible pity, appealing to an instinct of power. He could not see a demoniac or a paralytic look trustfully upon Him without longing to help, and in many cases feeling that it was God's will that He should help. To suppose that He cured all who were brought to Him is absurd, and is contrary (as we have seen above) to the evidence of the earliest Evangelist. He had the power of distinguishing between faith and not faith; had He an equal power of discerning physiological possibilities from impossibilities? Did a kind of instinct tell Him that the restoration of a lost limb was not like the cure of a paralytic, not one of the works "prepared for Him by His Father?" I do not suppose that such physiological distinctions were intellectually known by Christ in His human nature, any more than the modern discoveries of geology, astronomy, or history. But experience and some kind of intuition may have enabled Him to distinguish those cases which He could heal from those (a far more numerous class) which He could not. In performing these "mighty works" of healing, Jesus appears on many occasions to have studiously avoided that very publicity which—on the theory of their being intended as demonstrations—ought to have been a condition of their performance. He takes the patient apart, or expressly warns him to be silent about his cure—acts quite inconsistent with the demonstration-hypothesis. Probably He felt that these works, although they came to Him fresh from His Father's hands, were not without a danger. Men crowded round Him, not to hear the truth but to see "the miracles." Instead of recognizing that He did only such works as "the Father had prepared for Him to do," they thought that He could do "anything He pleased." I think we ought to feel that the very notion of such a power as this was absolutely revolting to Jesus: "To stop the sun, to call down fire or bread from heaven, to stay the course of rivers, and cast down the walls of cities —doubtless Joshua and Elijah had done these works; but they were not the works that the Father had prepared for the Son to do." Joshua and Elijah were but servants. He was the Son: and, being the Son, He felt bound to conform Himself each moment to that heavenly Will which He ever felt within Him and saw before Him, which dictated "mighty works" indeed, but always works of love and healing. In one sense He was entirely free; He could do all things because all things were possible with the Father, and the Father and He were one; in another sense He felt Himself less free than any being that had ever assumed the shape of man, because all other human creatures had deviated, but He alone could never deviate, no, not by a hair's breadth, from the indwelling Will of the Father.

It is for these reasons then that I reject miracles, not because they are impossible, not even because they are *a priori* improbable, not because they were once useless and are now harmful; but because the facts are against them. If the evidence shewed that miracles had actually occurred, I should be prepared to learn from these materialized parables as reverently as from word-parables, and to believe that God—in order to break down men's excessive faith in the machine-like order of the visible world, and in order to divert their attention from Sequence to Will—fore-ordained these divergences from the monotonous routine of things. But the evidence does not shew this. The criticism of the Old Testament, and the criticism of the New Testament, and the researches of science, and the closer study of the life of Christ Himself, all converge to this conclusion—that Christ conquered the world, not by working miracles, but by living such a life and dying such a death as might be lived and died by the Son of God, incarnate as a Son of man, and self-subjected to all the physical limitations of humanity; and by bequeathing to mankind, after His death, such a Spirit as was correspondent to His own nature.

XX

MY DEAR ——,

You wish to draw my attention to the Resurrection of Christ. "That," you say, "is either miraculous or nothing. The arguments by which you appear to be driving miracles into non-existence—expelling them first from profane history, then from the Old Testament, then step by step from every part of the New—cannot make a stand at your convenience, so as to except the Resurrection. Yet even St. Paul makes the Resurrection of Jesus the basis of his own belief and Gospel. If, therefore, that final miracle falls to the ground, the Pauline Gospel falls with it: and to that downfall I fear your arguments all tend, although you yourself do not see it or wish it."

I entirely deny the quiet assumption of your first sentence; which, as it stands (but I am sure you cannot mean it), affirms that the Resurrection of Christ "is either miraculous or nothing." I assert, without fear of contradiction, that if the phenomena which convinced the earliest disciples and St. Paul of the reality of the Resurrection of Christ, were not miraculous but natural, they constitute the most wonderful event in the history of the world. But what you wish to say, I suspect, is this: "By the Resurrection of Christ I mean the Resurrection of the body; now if Christ's body was raised again, the act must have been miraculous." But how if the Resurrection was spiritual? St. Paul himself speaks of a "spiritual body," not a material body, as rising in the

Resurrection. Do you suppose that a "spiritual body" can be touched? Or that St. Paul could have touched the presence that appeared to him when he heard the words, "Saul, Saul, why persecutest thou me?" Now if the Resurrection of Christ was spiritual and not material, there may have been no suspension at all of the laws of material nature, but simply a real, spiritual fact, manifested to the world according to certain laws by which spiritual facts are manifested to the senses.

But this theory, you will reply, although possibly consistent with the Pauline narrative, is inconsistent with the Gospel accounts of the Resurrection. It certainly is. But it is quite certain—however unprepared you may possibly be for the statement—that the Gospel accounts of the Resurrection, taken altogether, cannot be compared, for weight, with the Pauline evidence. You know that the oldest Gospel (St. Mark xvi. 8) terminates (probably because it was left incomplete) with a vision of angels who speak of the tomb as empty and of Christ as risen; but not a word about Christ's resurrection itself. The next Gospel in chronological order (St. Matthew's) mentions one appearance of Christ to some women, and another to some disciples in Galilee; but as to the last it is said that "some doubted." Not till we come to St. Luke's Gospel do we find detailed appearances of Jesus to disciples in or near Jerusalem, in the course of which Jesus is present at a meal and offers to eat, as evidence that He is no mere spirit. In the last Gospel of all (St. John's) there is added an appeal to the sense of touch; and in an Appendix to that Gospel, Jesus is represented as inviting the disciples to a repast of fish and bread, apparently miraculously supplied and prepared ("they see a fire of coals there and fish laid thereon, and bread," John xxi. 9), which He distributes to the disciples. Afterwards he holds a long discourse with them. Similarly long discourses between the risen Saviour and the disciples are recorded in the first chapter of the Acts of the Apostles, which we know to have been written after the Gospel of St. Luke. You see how unsatisfactory all this is. The further back we go, and the nearer to the event, the more meagre and shadowy does the evidence become. It does not appear in a form ample and cogent until a period so late as to throw irresistible doubt upon its truth. How can we possibly answer the doubter's natural question, " If there was this unanswerable evidence of the material resurrection of Jesus, why was it suppressed for two generations?" Moreover, some of these later accounts, which relate the handling of the body of Jesus, or the presence of Jesus at the breaking of bread, might be literal misinterpretations of some traditions concerning visions of Christ accompanying the " handling of the body of the Lord Jesus" in the Lord's Supper. It is very significant that St. Peter—whose allusions in the Acts of the Apostles to his personal evidence concerning the Resurrection of Christ are of the briefest kind—is introduced by St. Luke as mentioning only one definite kind of manifestation of Jesus; and that is one in which the Apostles "did *eat and drink with him* after he rose from the dead" (Acts x. 41). Lastly, there are traces of interpolations, or additions, at a very early date in the post-resurrection chapters of St. Luke, and probably of St. Matthew and St. John; and in dealing with the post-resurrection narrative of the life of Christ some of the earliest Fathers quote passages not found in our Gospels but agreeing somewhat with the suspected additions in the third and fourth Gospel. The sum of all is, so far as my own experience goes, that after a patient and prolonged study of the evidence, with every desire, and indeed I may say with an intense anxiety (at one period of my life), to justify myself in continuing to believe all that I once believed, I now rise from the perusal of the last chapters of the Gospels and the first chapter of the Acts of the Apostles, with the conviction that *something* certainly happened to persuade the Apostles that their Master had verily risen from the dead, but what that *something* was, the evidence, so far as it can be obtained from the Gospels, does not enable us to determine.

But we have not yet touched on the evidence of St. Paul and to this we now pass. Here at last we stand on firm ground. Here for the first time we find (in St. Paul's first Epistle to the Corinthians xv. 8), the unquestionable evidence of an eye-witness, probably recorded several years before the appearance of any Gospel now extant. No one who is competent to form an opinion on the question can for a moment doubt St. Paul's assertion that Christ "appeared" to him, and that some such appearance as that recorded thrice in the Acts, converted him from a persecutor into an apostle of Christianity. We have just been asking, "What was that unknown something—possibly some manifestation of Jesus after death—which inspired the Twelve with the conviction and the faculties necessary to overcome the world?" Now we seem to have found the answer. An appearance that overcame and converted a recalcitrant enemy might well satisfy and imbue with confidence loving disciples, longing to believe. Especially might this be the case if Jesus had predicted, as I believe He did predict, that His work would not be cut short by death, but that in Him would be fulfilled the saying of Hosea: " In the third day he shall raise us up and we shall live in his sight." Although these words may have been neglected or not understood at the time when they were uttered, they may have well recurred to the minds of the Disciples, after their Master's death, with a powerful effect. To urge that the despair of the Twelve could be a greater obstacle than the vehement and bigoted antagonism of Saul, in the way of their receiving a vision of their beloved Master, is a paradox so pedantical that it is scarcely worth mentioning. You cannot have forgotten, too, how St. Paul himself assumes that the appearances of the Saviour to himself, and to the original Apostles, were of the same kind and on the same footing : " He *appeared* unto Cephas, he *appeared* unto James, he *appeared* unto five hundred brethren . . . and last of all he *appeared* unto *me* also." In the two latest Gospels these " appearances " have been magnified into accounts that represented Jesus as possessed of flesh and bones, as capable of eating, as reclining at a meal, and as entering into long and familiar discourses : naturally we ask as to St. Paul's, the indisputably earliest account of a manifestation of Christ, what traces it exhibits of similar distortions and exaggerations? You know the answer. There are no such traces. The manifestation to St. Paul is plainly admitted by the accounts in the Acts to be what is commonly called subjective. The "subjectivity" of some of the earlier manifestations of Jesus to the disciples is dimly suggested by some passages in the Gospels which describe how " some doubted " and others failed to recognize Him ; but it is not merely suggested, it is plainly expressed, in the accounts of the manifestation to St. Paul. The Apostle is clearly stated to have seen a sight and heard words, which other people, his companions, with the same opportunities for seeing and hearing, did not see and did not hear. Putting aside some slight discrepancies in the three accounts given in the Acts [1]—

---

[1] "And the men that journeyed with him stood speechless hearing the voice but beholding no man," Acts ix. 7 ; "And they that were with me beheld indeed the light, but they heard not the voice of him that spake to me," *ib.* xxii. 9. Whether Saul's companions saw and heard nothing except subjectively, through force of sympathy, or whether (comp. John xii. 29) some natural phenomenon may have been interpreted in one way by Saul and in another way by his companions, cannot now be determined : but I

discrepancies easily and naturally explicable, and valuable as shewing that the accounts have not been arbitrarily harmonized—we may say that this is the substantial result: the Lord Jesus appeared to St. Paul in what is called a vision. I myself firmly believe that there was a spiritual act of Jesus simultaneous with the conveyance of the manifestation to the brain of the Apostle. But none the less,—however coincident it may have been with a spiritual reality, if there was no presence of a material body, the manifestation of Jesus to St. Paul must be placed in the class of visions: and if it was not seen by others who had the same physical means of seeing, it must be called, in some sense, "subjective."

Yet this vision sufficed for him and for the world. In the strength of this vision, (followed, no doubt, by subsequent visions and communings with the Lord Jesus), the Thirteenth Apostle, the intruder, as he might be called—not "chosen of men," like Matthias, not called by Christ in the flesh—did the great work of which you and I, with millions of others, are now joint inheritors. Think of it! Is it not a remarkable instance of "men working one thing while God worketh another" to see the Apostles with due form and ceremony electing their substitute for the Traitor to be the solemnly ordained Twelfth Apostle, (henceforth unnamed in Holy Writ) and all the while the Holy Spirit preparing a Thirteenth! And for this Thirteenth Apostle, who never looked on the face of Christ, never heard a single word of His doctrine, it has been reserved to tell us perhaps more about the meaning of Christ's teaching and certainly to give us more cogent proof of His Resurrection than all the other Apostles and Evangelists put together! Truly the last has been first!

---

have confined myself to indisputable fact in stating that Saul "saw a sight and heard words which other people, his companions, with the same opportunities for seeing and hearing, did not see and did not hear."

And in the strength of his proof of Christ's Resurrection —mere vision though we may call it—this Thirteenth Apostle, in the face of persecutions outside the Church, and discouragements and jealousies inside the Church, first converted the Roman empire to the Christian faith; then, fifteen centuries afterwards, reconverted and purified a large section of the Church from mediæval corruptions; and now, as I believe, some nineteen centuries afterwards, is on the point of still further purifying the Church from antique superstition and from modern materialism!

What shall we say of the mighty vision that originated these stupendous results? Shall we take the view of the modern scientific young man, and lecture the great Apostle on the folly of that indiscreet journey to Damascus at noon-tide, when his nerves were a little over-wrought after that unpleasant incident of poor Stephen? Shall we say it was all ophthalmia and indigestion—that flash of blinding light, those unforgettable words, "Saul, Saul, why persecutest thou me?"—all a mere vision? Is a fact that changed the destinies of Europe to be put aside with the epithet "mere"? Would not even a materialist stonemason recognize that a vision which built St. Peter's and St. Paul's is of some tangible importance? You and I and your scientific young lecturer—do we not in some sort owe our existence to this "mere vision," but for which the earth might be a chaos of barbarism, England a forest scantly populated with tattooed bipeds, and our civilized selves non-existent? Patricidal creatures, let us not speak lightly of the "mere" author of our own important being!

To my mind the manifestation of the Resurrection of Christ appears, not as an isolated fact, but as a part, and the central part, of the great revelation of the immortality of the soul which has been conveyed by God to man, in accordance with the laws of human nature, from the beginning of the creation of the world by the medium of imaginative Faith. In the same way the laws of astronomy have been conveyed by God to man, in accordance with the laws of human nature, from the beginning of the creation of the world, by the medium of imaginative Reason. I have shewn in previous letters that Imagination has been the basis of all that is worth calling knowledge. To shew the bearing of this on the manifestations of the Resurrection of Christ shall be the object of my next letter.

XXI

My dear ——,

You are startled, and well you may be, "at the notion that the resurrection of Christ has been the mere offspring of the imagination." I am quoting your words, but you have not quoted mine. I never said, nor should I dream of saying, that the resurrection of Christ was "the offspring of the imagination," any more than I should say that the law of gravitation is "the offspring of the imagination," or that light is "the offspring of the eye." But this is just an ordinary specimen of the way in which people whose minds are blocked and choked with prejudice, misunderstand what is contrary to their preconceptions. You have made up your mind that the Imagination is a kind of excrescence on humanity, a faculty independent of the Creator, and incapable of being made by Him the medium of revelation; and so you pervert my words to suit your fancies. But what I said was that Imagination is the basis of all that is worth calling knowledge, and that, as God reveals the laws of astronomy through imaginative Reason, so He has revealed the Resurrection of Christ through imaginative Faith.

Before speaking of the special bearing of the Imagination upon the manifestation of Christ's Resurrection, let me say a word or two on the manner in which our human environment appears to have been adapted to foster the growth of this faculty. You will be better prepared to expect great things from the Imagination when you reflect on the great things that have been wrought by God for its development. You say that you do not understand the statement in the last paragraph of my last letter, that the Imagination has been made "the medium of conveying the revelation of the immortality of the soul," and still less do you comprehend how this revelation has been going on "from the creation of the world," especially since, during a large portion of this time, there must have been no men to receive any revelation at all.

I said deliberately "from the creation of the world," and not "from the creation of mankind," because inanimate creation itself appears to me to bear witness to a purpose, from the first, that this visible world should help its future tenants to imagine things invisible. Consider but one instance, the immense influence of Night upon the Imagination, and you will perhaps come to the conclusion that, but for the provision of darkness ("these orbs of light and shade"), men would never have been led to a faith in the light of immortality. In the first place by revealing to us the wonder-striking order of the infinite stars—which, but for darkness, would have remained for ever a closed book to men—Night leads us to dream, or to infer, that there may be other pages still unturned in the book of Nature's mysteries, and stimulates us, however far we may progress in thought, still to press on to something more beyond; and at the same time, throwing a temporary veil over all the sights of day, it persuades us to trust that on the morrow the veil will be removed, and that in the meantime all things will continue in their order.

Night is aided by sleep and dreams. Slumbering in the darkness, and bereft of the control of the understanding, Imagination has reproduced before the mind's eye the sights of daylight, blended together without thought of fitness, order, time, or place, so as to form quite new combinations which scarcely any deliberate daytime effort could have so vividly depicted : and in the long train of confused visionary images there have sometimes passed before the mental eye of the mourner or the murderer the very shapes, and even the voices of the dead, forcing the slumberer to start up and cry, " They live, they still live ; there is a life beyond the grave." This trans-sepulchral existence having been once discerned, the Imagination has set to work to formulate the laws of it, and to map out and people its regions, thus causing heaven and hell to become realities and (in course of time) ancestral traditions, and almost inherited instincts. Sometimes, Imagination has come with a special and rarely manifested force to the aid of a belief in a future life. Not in dreams, but in wakeful moments, though for the most part by night, there have appeared before the mind's eye such vivid images of the departed, as have convinced not only the seers of the visions but also their friends—and so, by a pervasive influence, all but a small minority of the human race—that something real has been seen, the spirit of the dead made visible : and to this day, in England, there are not wanting men of the highest ability, culture, and love of truth, who busy themselves with serious investigations into the reality of apparitions.

Does this seem to you fanciful? Surely it is the fact that Night and its phenomena have largely influenced the spiritual, or superstitious, side of human nature: and if you admit this to be the fact, the only difference between us is this, that to you this subtle but universal influence of Darker Nature on Man appears to have been the result of chance, whereas I think it came from God. To you, one half of Time appears to have been allowed by God to be spiritually barren, set apart for the mere repairing of the human material machine : I do not believe that the spiritual making of Man was foreordained on this "half-time" principle.

If however you ask me what amount of truth or reality there has been in these dreams and visions, I should reply, as about poetry and prophecy, that some of these imaginations have represented realities, some unrealities; but that the total result to which they have led men, the belief in the immortality of the soul, is a reality. But when I speak of a "real vision" of a spirit or ghost, I hope you will not misunderstand me so far as to suppose that I could mean a material, gas-like (though intangible) form, occupying so many cubical inches of space. A spirit, so far as I conceive it, does not occupy space; nor is it the object of sight, any more than of smell or touch; it is, to me, of the nature of a thought, only a thought personified, *i.e.* a thought capable of loving and being loved, of hating and being hated. But though it may not be the object of the senses in the same way in which external things are, it may be manifested to the Imagination, *i.e.* the mind's eye, in such a way as to produce the same effect as though it were an external object seen by the body's eye.

Every one who loves truth will tread with cautious steps in this mysterious province of phantasmal existence, and carefully measure his language, knowing that we are in a region of illusion, exaggeration, and (sometimes) of imposture. But there does seem evidence to shew that people (mostly perhaps twins), at a distance from one another, have in some at present inexplicable manner influenced one another so that the disease or death or calamity of one has been simultaneously made known to the other; and you have probably read of cases, fairly supported, which would shew that a passionate longing on the part of a dying man to see some distant friend may create a responsive emotion, if not an actual vision, in the mind of that friend. We are so completely in the dark as to the originating causes (for physiology tells us nothing but the instrumental causes) which produce our thoughts, that I see nothing at all absurd in the notion that every truthful and vivid conception of one human being in the mind of another upon earth, arises from some communion in the spirit-world between the spirits of the two.

So much for conjectures as to the possible reality or possible causes of some classes of apparitions. I do not often myself set much store on them, except so far as they are of use in reminding us how wide is the province of possibility, or how narrow the province of certainty, in the region of ultimate causation. I lay stress, not upon any conjectural explanation of ghost phenomena, but upon the following general considerations, most of which are of the nature, not of conjectures, but of facts : 1st, man is what he is, largely in virtue of the Imagination ; 2nd, one half of man's time and one half of the phenomena of Nature seem to have no other purpose (so far as man is concerned) than to stimulate the Imagination ; 3rd, if we suppose that this wonderful world is under the government of a good God, although opposed by an inferior Evil, we are led to infer that He has implanted in us this faculty of Imagination and that the noble aspirations and beliefs which have been developed by it have not been unmixed delusions ; 4th, among the noblest of the beliefs thus developed, has been the belief in the immortality of the soul, which, after being tested by the faith of many centuries, is at this day cherished by the majority of civilized mankind ; 5th, this belief has proved its truth, so far as imaginations can prove themselves true, by working well, *i.e.* it has raised and ennobled those who have entertained it, and has made them (on the whole) morally the better for it ; 6th, a part of the training of the Imagination, intimately connected with the production of the belief in the immortality of the soul, has been the development of a power to see mental visions, with all the vividness of material visions ; 7th, among these visions, some of the most common have been apparitions of the forms of the dead, and some of the best authenticated of these have occurred where a strong unfulfilled desire has possessed the departed in the moment of dying and where the seer of the apparition has been bound by close ties to the dead.

These are the considerations, mostly facts—you may dispute some of them, but not all I think—in the light of which I should endeavour to illustrate the manifestation of Christ to His disciples after death. To these facts I merely added the conjecture that possibly there may be something besides the mere movement of our brains that produces these images of the departed, something—I will not say external, for a spirit, if independent of place, can be neither external to us nor internal—but some act in the invisible world of spirits corresponding to every apparition upon the visible world. But I did not pledge myself to such a theory. I only insisted that the whole revelation of poetry and religion through the Imagination has been of such inestimable importance to man that we cannot put it all aside as false because imaginative ; we must regard it with reverence and be prepared to find that in the central event of the purest religion of all, the Imagination has been made the medium of the culminating revelation of spirit and truth. Indeed, if the spiritual world is real and near, it is difficult to conceive how God —without breaking the Laws of Nature and without unfitting us for life in a world of sense—could better give us glimpses of an invisible environment, than by causing it to press in, as it were, upon the Imagination, so that the mind's eye, thus stimulated by real invisibilities, may, for the time, supplant the bodily faculty of sight, and afterwards leave behind in us a permanent suggestion that, as there is a material world corresponding to the bodily eye, so there is a mind's world corresponding to the mind's eye. With this pre-conception I will ask you to approach the narrative of Christ's Resurrection as I shall endeavour to set it forth in my next letter from the natural point of view.

XXII

My dear ——,

My last letter broke off rather abruptly with a promise to do my best to set forth hereafter the Resurrection of Christ as it may be regarded from a natural point of view.

Looking at the facts in this light, we have in the first place to set before ourselves the short life of One of whom we must merely say that He was unique in the goodness and grandeur of His character, and that He died with the unfulfilled purpose of redeeming mankind from sin, deserted for the moment by the few disciples who had adhered to Him almost to the last. He died, for the time, the most pitiable, the most despair-inspiring death that the world has ever witnessed, asking in His last moments why He had been "forsaken" by God. But His death—pardon me if I deviate for one moment from material to celestial facts, provided that I never deviate into miracles—was really the triumph over death, and His Spirit had in reality (we speak in a metaphor) broken open the bars of the grave and ascended to the throne of the Father carrying with Himself the promise of the ultimate redemption of mankind. This was now to be revealed to the world as the culminating vision in that continuous Revelation through the Imagination by which the minds of men had been led to look beyond this life to a life that knows no end. Speaking terrestrially, we must say that the influence of Jesus, love, faith, remorse, were moulding the hearts of the disciples on earth to receive the truth; speaking celestially we may say that Jesus bent down from His throne by the right hand of God to prepare them for the manifestation of His victory. What in this crisis exactly befell on earth we shall never know. The tradition that Jesus appeared on the third day, or after three days, to His disciples, is so naturally derived from the prophecy of Hosea "on the third day he shall raise us up"—a prophecy probably applied by Jesus to Himself—that we can place no reliance on its numerical accuracy. Nor do we know exactly where Jesus first appeared to His disciples. The oldest tradition[1] declared that they were to "go to Galilee" after their Master's death, and that He had promised to guide them thither; but a subsequent account interpreted the words about "Galilee" quite differently.[2] In any case, before many days had elapsed, to some one disciple, perhaps to Mary Magdalene—out of whom there had been cast "seven devils"—it was given to see the Lord Jesus.

Here, by the way, we must note the remarkable prominence given in all the Gospels to the part played by women in receiving the first manifestations of Christ's Resurrection. Writers who were careful to avoid giving occasion for unbelief might naturally have desired to give less prominence to the testimony of highly imaginative and impressionable witnesses; and indeed St. Paul, in his brief list of the appearances of Jesus (possibly because writing as an Apostle who had seen Christ, he desired to confine himself almost entirely to manifestations witnessed by Apostles), makes no mention of the appearances to women: their prominence, therefore, in all the Gospels,

---

[1] Mark xvi. 7: Matthew xxviii. 7: "He goeth before you *into Galilee.*"
[2] Luke xxiv. 6: "Remember how he spake unto you *while he was yet in Galilee.*"

testifies strongly to the early and universal acceptance of the tradition that women were the first witnesses to the risen Saviour. But to resume. The news quickened the faith even of those disciples who had not seen and who could not yet believe; and presently apparitions were seen—a thing almost, though (I believe) not quite, unique in visions—by several disciples together. Probably the most frequent occasions for these manifestations were when they had met together to partake of the body and blood of their Master; and it was in the moment of the breaking of the bread that the image of the Living Bread was flashed before them, appearing in the form of Jesus giving Himself for them, and uttering words of blessing, comfort, or exhortation, audible to the ears of the faithful, who at the same moment were handling His body and touching the blood which flowed from His side. At other times he appeared before them with other messages; to the women he seemed to wave them off as if deprecating a too close approach, or as if bidding them go hence and carry the glad tidings to the Apostles; others He seemed to rebuke for their want of faith; in the sight of others, His hands, outstretched in the attitude of parting benediction, seemed to send forth His disciples to preach His word with promise of His presence; but how these messages were conveyed, whether by gesture simply, or by spiritual voice (as in the case of St. Paul), audible perhaps to one, and by him interpreted to the rest, or audible to all that were in the same faithful sympathy—these and other details cannot now be determined.

" Why did not the adversaries of Christ confront His followers by producing the body from the tomb, thus disproving the story that His body had risen from the dead?" The tomb was probably empty. That is probable for two reasons, first because the earliest traditions agree that the women going to the tomb found the stone rolled away; and secondly, because the adversaries of Jesus appear to have themselves subsequently circulated a story that the disciples had stolen away the body. This they would hardly have done if they had known that their own explanation could be at any moment refuted by opening the tomb, which would have shewn the body still lying there. Possibly some of the enemies of Jesus had themselves removed the body, influenced by some of those predictions of Jesus about Himself, which, though they had not the power to inspire the disciples with faith in the moment of His death, had power to inspire His enemies with a vague fear. Being almost surprised in the act, they may not have had time to replace the great stone at the entrance of the tomb, when the women arrived; if so, the action of Christ's own enemies prepared the way for the belief in His resurrection by exhibiting to the sorrowing disciples the stone rolled away and the empty sepulchre. First came the cry, " He is not here," and that prepared the way for " He is risen."

How long the visionary period lasted we cannot tell. It is almost certain that there were many more visions than the five recorded by St. Paul (1 Cor. xv. 6, 7). At least one of St. Paul's five visions, that to St. James, is not mentioned in any of our extant Gospels; on the other hand St. Paul omits some of those peculiar to the third or fourth Gospels, as well as the manifestations to the women. Perhaps the visions were so many, and all so like each other, that the Church found it difficult to select which to record; and each Evangelist chose those which appeared to him fittest, either because they were the earliest, or because the witnesses were numerous, or because they were apostolic, or because they contained the most striking proof of a veritable resurrection. We may therefore easily accept the statement that the period of visions lasted for forty days or even for a much longer time, probably till the disciples felt emboldened to take an active course in preaching the Gospel.

Concerning Christ's manifestation to St. Paul I have said enough in my last letter—if anything needed to be said—to shew that it must have been of the nature of a vision, and (in a sense) "subjective." But it differs from the rest in that it was made to an enemy while the other manifestations were made to devoted disciples. Love, remorse, faith, affection, stimulated the Apostles to cry, "He cannot have died," and prepared their souls to see the image of Jesus risen; but where, it may be asked, was the spiritual preparation in the heart of St. Paul to receive such a vision? You may trace it in the words which St. Paul heard from Jesus: "It is hard for thee to kick against the pricks." They shew that the future Apostle had been struggling, and struggling hard, against the compunctions of conscience. Being a lover of truth from his childhood, he was prepared to give up all for its sake; but recent events had made him ask whether he was not fighting against the truth instead of for the truth. He had been persecuting the Christians; but their faith and patience had made him doubt whether they might not be right and he wrong. When the first martyr Stephen looked up to heaven and there saw Jesus seated at the right hand of God, then or soon afterwards, the question must have arisen in the mind of the persecutor, "What if the follower of the Nazarene was speaking truth? What if the crucified Jesus whom I am now persecuting was really exalted to God's throne?" Such was the struggle through which Saul's mind was passing when the Spirit of Jesus, acting indirectly through the constancy and faith of His persecuted disciples, having first insensibly permeated and undermined the barriers of Pharisaic training and education, now swept all obstacles before it in an instantaneous deluge of conviction that this persecuted Jesus was the Messiah. At that same moment the Messiah Himself (who during these last months and weeks of spiritual conflict had been bending down closer and closer to the predestined Apostle from His throne in heaven) now burst upon the convert's sight on earth.

But I think I hear you saying, " All this sounds well ; but he has repeatedly described these visions of the risen Saviour as subjective : how then can he call them real ? What is real ? " Let me refer you to the paper of Definitions which I enclosed in a previous letter.[1]

1. *Absolute reality cannot be comprehended by men, and can only be apprehended as God, or in God, by Faith.*

2. *Among objects of sensation, those are (relatively) real which present similar sensations in similar circumstances.*

Now if you try to regard the manifestation of the risen Christ under the second head, as an "object of sensation," you must pronounce it "unreal," inasmuch as it would not " present similar sensations in similar circumstances ; " by which I mean that, with similar opportunities of observation, different persons (believers, for example, and unbelievers) would not have derived similar sensations from it. But your conclusion would be false because you started from a false premiss : these manifestations cannot be classed "among objects of sensation."

The movements of the risen Saviour appear to me to have been the movements of God ; His manifestations to the faith of the Apostles were divine acts, passing direct from God to the souls of men. Since therefore these manifestations belonged to the class of things which " can only be apprehended as God, or in God, by faith," I call them " absolute realities "—as much more real than flesh and blood, as God Himself is more real than the paper on which I am now writing.

[1] See *Definitions* at the end of the book.

XXIII

MY DEAR ——,

I am not surprised to hear that you consider the theory above described of Christ's resurrection, "vague, shadowy, and unsatisfying." But as in the very same letter you say that you are quite convinced of the unhistorical nature of the account of the resurrection of Christ's material body, I think you ought not to dismiss the subject without giving more attention than you have given as yet to it. As a student of history and as a young man bent on attaining such knowledge as can be attained concerning the certainties or probabilities that have the most important bearing on the life and conduct of myriads of your fellow-creatures, you ought at least to ask yourself what better explanation you have to offer of the marvellous phenomena of the Christian Church and in particular of St. Paul's part in spreading Christianity.

I sympathize with the " sense of bathos," as you call it, which comes over you when you hear that the phenomena of the Resurrection of Christ are to be explained by a study of the growth and development of the revelation given to mankind through the Imagination. I sympathize with you; but I sympathize with you as I should with a child who might be standing by Elijah's side at the time when the prophet saw his never-to-be-forgotten vision. That child would feel, no doubt, "a sense of bathos" because the Lord was not in the fire, nor in the whirlwind, nor in the earthquake, but in the still small voice.

You are in the childish stage of susceptibility to anything that is noisy and big; you have not been taught by experience and thought to appreciate the divineness of things obvious, ordinary, and quiet; above all you have not yet learned to revere your own nature nor to acknowledge (except with your lips) that you are made in the image of God. Retaining still a keen recollection of the pain with which I passed through that stage myself, I have neither the inclination, nor the right, to despise your present condition of mind; but I believe, if you will still keep the question open in your mind, and if you will meditate a little now and then on the frequency, or I may say the universality, of illusion in the conveyance of all the highest truth, you will gradually come, as I came, to perceive that the essence of the resurrection of Christ is that His Spirit should have really triumphed over death, and not that His body should have risen from the grave.

No doubt you would be much more impressed if the tangible body of some dead friend of yours, after being buried in the earth, had appeared to certain witnesses and touched them, and eaten in their company, than if a vivid apparition of the friend had appeared to the same witnesses; but I think you would much more easily believe the latter than the former; and you might be more impressed by a strong conviction of the latter than by a doubtful, timid, clinging to the former. I can hardly think that if you had received several accounts from independent witnesses, of apparitions of this kind resulting in a marvellous change of character in all who had seen them, you would at once put them aside simply because they might be called in some sense natural. The very fact of their being natural would lead you to consider how strange must have been the causes that had produced such strange results; how powerful must have been the personality that had thus forced itself on the mental retina of the seers of the apparition; and if something important had followed from such a vision, say, for example, the writing of a great poem, or the foundation of a noble empire, I cannot think that you would set down the vision as a negligible trifle.

But you feel, I dare say, that, though you might be impressed by the stories of such an apparition, you could not feel certain that the apparition represented any reality; there would be no definite proof that the witnesses of the apparition were not under the influence of a delusion. Well, I will admit that there would be no proof of the ordinary kind, that is to say, no proof such as is conveyed through the senses about ordinary terrestrial phenomena; but I think you might feel certain; only it would be that kind of certainty which is largely bred from Faith and Hope. And this sort of certainty, and no other, appears to me that which was intended to be produced by the Resurrection of Christ. His manifestations were unseen and unheard save by the eye and ear of Faith. If the proof of His resurrection had not depended upon Faith, then the Roman soldiers would have seen His material body miraculously issuing from the shattered sepulchre, and the companions of Saul would have both seen Christ and understood the voice that cried, "Saul, Saul, why persecutest thou me?" If we could ascertain exactly the historical basis for the account in the Fourth Gospel of Christ's manifestation to the doubting Thomas, we should probably find—supposing that we were really justified in treating the account as historical—that there was in Thomas a strong desire to believe, combined with a strong sense of the impossibility of attaining adequate proof. As in the life of Christ, so in the resurrection of Christ, conviction appears never to have been forced on any entirely unwilling unbeliever.

In order to believe in the resurrection of Christ, it is not enough to be convinced that the evidence is honest and genuine, and that the witnesses could not be deceived; that kind of belief savours of the law-court, and there is nothing spiritual in it; but the man who truly and spiritually accepts Christ's resurrection is he who says to himself as he reviews the life of Christ and the history of the Church: " Being what He was, and having done the work that He has done, this Jesus of Nazareth ought not to have succumbed to death. If there is any evidence to shew that the veil of the invisible has been so far thrown back, be it for a moment, as to shew me Jesus in the spiritual world still living and triumphant over death, my conscience opens its arms at once to embrace that belief." And there is this advantage in basing your faith on the spiritual resurrection of Jesus, that you keep the region of faith distinct from the region of disputable testimony. If you rest your hopes on the material resurrection, that is a question of doubtful evidence. Your heart says, "Oh that it might be true!" Your brain says, "I cannot honestly say that I think it is true." Hence a constant conflict between heart and brain, while you are forced again and again to ask yourself, " Must I be dishonest in order that I may persuade myself that I am happy? And even if I can honestly believe in the material resurrection to-day, how do I know that some new evidence —the discovery of some new Gospel for example—may not overturn my belief to-morrow?"

But the life and doctrine of Christ, the conversion and letters of St. Paul, the growth and victories of the Church, and the present power of Christ's Spirit are facts that can never be overthrown; and if you say, " On the basis of these indisputable facts, considered as a part of the evolution and training of mankind I rest my hope and my faith that Jesus has conquered death and still lives and works among us and for us "—why then you rest on a basis that cannot be shaken. And surely such a faith is more strong, more spiritual, more comforting, yes, and more certain too, than a "knowledge" which you know in your own heart to be no knowledge! How long will mankind be content to be ignorant that the HALF which constitutes truth is worth more than the WHOLE which is made up of truth and truth's integumentary illusion! How many there are to whom the saying of old Hesiod is still unmeaning:—

> *Alas thou know'st not, silly soul,*
> *How much the half exceeds the whole!*

You cannot obtain, and must not expect to obtain, any demonstrative proof of the Resurrection of Christ, any more than you can obtain a demonstrative proof of the existence of a God: yet you can feel as strong and as sincere a conviction of the former fact as of the latter.

It is curious that St. Paul's parallel between the Resurrection of Christ and that of men should be so habitually overlooked. He assumes, as a matter of course, a similarity, almost an identity, between the Resurrection of men and the Resurrection of Christ: "If there is no resurrection of the dead neither hath Christ been raised," and again: "Now hath Christ been raised from the dead, the first fruits of them that are asleep." This reasoning holds excellently, if the Resurrection is to be the same for us as it was for our Saviour, a spiritual Resurrection, and if the Resurrection of Christ visibly revealed the universal law which shall apply to all who are animated by the Spirit of God. But if Christ's Resurrection was of a quite different kind, if it was a bodily stepping out of the tomb three days after burial, how can this be called the "first fruits" of the Resurrection of men whose bodies will all decay and for whom therefore no such stepping out from the tomb can ever be anticipated? The best, the truest, the most comforting belief in the end will be found to be that Jesus was "put to death in the flesh but *quickened* (not in the flesh but) *in the spirit.*" And as it was with Him, so we believe it will be with us.

But perhaps you will remind me that one of the Creeds mentions "the Resurrection of the *body*," and that St. Paul anticipates the Resurrection, not of a "spirit," but of "a spiritual *body;*" and you may ask me what I infer from this. I for my part infer that St. Paul desired to guard against the notion that the dead lose their identity and are merged in God or in some other essence; he wished to convey to his hearers that they would still retain their individuality, the power of loving and of being loved; possibly also he wished to suggest a life of continued activity in the service of God; and in order to express this he used such language (metaphorical of course) as would unmistakeably imply that identity would be preserved, and activity would be possible. But he took care to guard his language against materialistic misinterpretation by insisting that the body would be "spiritual" and therefore invisible to the earthly eye and cognizable only by the spirit. The new body, he says, is "a building from God," "a house not made with hands, *eternal;*" and he prefaces this by saying "the things which are seen are temporal; but the things *which are not seen* are *eternal.*" Hereby he clearly implies that the new body will be "not seen." Elsewhere he tells us that "the things prepared by God" for them that love Him (and of course he includes in these the "building from God, the house not made with hands") are such as eye "*hath not seen* nor ear heard, nor have they entered into the heart of man; but God hath revealed them unto us *by the Spirit;*" and again, "the things of God none knoweth *save the Spirit of God*," which has been imparted to the faithful.

To speak honestly, I must add that, even if I found St.

Paul had committed himself repeatedly to any theory of a material or semi-material Resurrection, consonant with the feelings of his times, I should not have felt bound to place a belief in a materialistic detail of this kind upon the same high and authoritative level as the belief in the Father, the Son, and the Holy Spirit, or any other general and spiritual article of faith. But I find no such materialism in St. Paul. He appears to me to say consistently, 1st, that Christ's Resurrection was a type of ("the first fruits of") the Resurrection of mankind; 2nd, that in contrast to the first man Adam, the earthy, who became a living soul, the last Adam, the heavenly, became a "life-giving spirit;" 3rd, that, as we have borne the image of the earthy, so we shall also bear the image of the heavenly; 4th, that the " body " of the faithful after death will be " spiritual," just as the Church of God is " a *spiritual house*," and the sacrifices of the saints are "*spiritual* sacrifices." There is no more ground for thinking that St. Paul supposed that we should hereafter have spiritual hands, or be spiritual bipeds, than for thinking that he supposed the sacrifices of the Church to be spiritual sheep, or the temple of the Church to be composed of celestial stones. After our Resurrection, we are still to be conscious of God's past love, still to rejoice in His present and never-ending love, still to be capable of glorifying and serving God, of loving as well as of being loved—this St. Paul's theory of the " spiritual body" certainly implies; and it need not imply more. And what our Resurrection will be, that Christ's Resurrection was.

The ordinary fancies about the Resurrection teem with absurdities, and are redeemed from being ridiculous, only because they all spring from the natural and reasonable desire that we may hereafter preserve our identity. But they ought to be suppressed if they create, as I fear they create, additional difficulties in the way of conceiving, and believing in, a future life. I do not wish to scoff at the popular views; but it is important that those who adopt the materialistic theory of the Resurrection should realize the unnecessary and grotesque inconsistencies with which they obscure the Christian faith. Popular Christianity appears generally to accept a sensuous paradise, only excluding what some may deem the coarser senses, the smell, touch, and taste. But what is the special merit of the other two senses, hearing and seeing, that they alone should be allowed places in Paradise? And this visible, semi-spiritual body upon which the vulgar fancy so insists—what purpose will it serve? "The purposes of recognition between friends." Then it will be like the old material body of the departed—at what period of his existence? Shall he be represented as a youth of twenty or a man of forty, or of fifty, or as a child of ten? And how as to the body of one who was deformed, maimed, or hideously misshapen and ugly? " It would be a purified likeness, summarizing, as it were, every period of life, so that it would be recognizable, not indeed by our eyes but by those of spiritual beings." That is conceivable : but why all this trouble to obtain a visible body that shall make recognition difficult, when recognition can be conceived so much more easily as the result of mere spiritual communion? Keep by all means the language of the *Apocalypse* and of the *Pilgrim's Progress* in order to describe in poetry the condition of the blessed dead ; but remember that it is the language of poetry ; and let every such use of words be concluded (as with a doxology) by the thought, " Thus will it be, only far better, infinitely better ; for God is love ; and our future communion with the love of God will be a height of happiness such as no power of sense can reveal, and only the spirit-guided soul can faintly apprehend."

But perhaps you will say " You are ready enough to

attack other people's notions about the semi-material resurrection; but you are not equally ready to explain your own notions about a spiritual resurrection. You cannot even tell us what a spiritual body is, except that it has the power of loving and being loved." Precisely so; I am quite ignorant. Yet in my knowledge of this matter I am superior to a very great number of other theologians. For they think they know, whereas I know that neither I nor they know. Let me go a little further in my confession of ignorance and admit that I do not really possess knowledge about a number of other matters about which many profess with great glibness to know everything. I am certain that I exist; but I doubt whether I can analyse and explain the reasons for my certainty, and I am quite sure I cannot prove my existence by logic. If I am pressed for a proof, I should say (as I have stated in a previous letter) that my belief in my existence was largely due to the Imagination. *Cogito, ergo sum,* " I think, therefore I am,"—if intended as a serious proof, and if there is any real meaning in the " *ergo* "—appears to me to be the most babyish of arguments. I respect the gigantic intellect of the arguer, but not even a giant can make ropes of sand; and it needs but a little grammar to dissolve this reasoning to nothing. " I think " means " I am one thinking." In some languages, in Hebrew for example, you might have no other way of expressing the proposition than in this form : " I am one thinking." What sort of reasoning then is this ! " I *am* one thinking, therefore I *am*." " This *is* white paper, therefore it *is !* " Surely a ridiculous offspring to issue from great logical travail ! And besides, what infinite assumptions are presupposed in that monosyllable " I " ! How do I know that " *I* think," and that it is not the great world-spirit who thinks in me, as well as rains outside me? Why ought I not to say "*it* thinks," just as I say "*it* rains"? What do you mean by " I " ? Tell us what " I " is. And how can the desperate logician set about telling us what " I " is, without assuming that his own " I " is, which is equivalent to assuming " I *am* " ? Surely this is altogether a hopeless muddle, and we ought to give up reasoning about " I " and " am ; " yes, and I would add not only about " I " and " am," but also about a number of other fundamental conceptions, which are far more profitably assumed as axioms. For my part, whenever I use the words " mind," " matter," " substance," " spirit," " soul," " intellect," and the like, and make any serious statement about them, I hardly ever do so without a mental reservation, saying to myself—" but ˋof course there may be no such things precisely as these, but some other things quite different, producing the results which we ascribe to these ; so that all these statements may be only proportionately true."

I do not object to the use of the materialistic language where it is recognized as metaphor by those who use and those who hear it ; but the mischief is that it is often not so recognized. Once make yourself the slave of the popular language about " spirit," and " substance," and what not—and you are in danger of being manacled intellectually as well as theologically. The popular belief is that a man's spirit is inside him, like his qualities ; the latter like peas in a box, the former like gas in a bladder. Drive a hole through a man's left side or the middle of his head, and—out goes the spirit ; that is the common materialistic creed. Now I have a strong desire to declare that this creed is ridiculously false. But I will be consistent and simply say that I know nothing whatever about it. My spirit may possibly be inside me; but it may possibly be outside me ; say at a point six feet, or six miles, above me ; or away in Jupiter, or Saturn, or down at the earth's centre ; or it may be incapable of occupying space. What does it matter to you or to me, theologically or intellectually, whether that part of us which we call our "spirit" has its local habitation inside us, or outside, or in no locality at all? Is it not enough to recognize that we have powers of acting, loving, trusting, and believing, and to feel certain that God intends these powers to be developed and never to perish? Yet I remember that a friend of mine was shocked, and almost appalled, when I avowed ignorance as to the locality of my spirit. He seemed to think I might as well have no spirit at all, if it could not prove its respectability by giving its name and address!

For my part I am now quite certain of Christ's spiritual Resurrection, and in that conviction I am far happier and far more trustful than when I at first mechanically accepted upon authority and evidence the belief in the Resurrection of Christ's body, and subsequently strove to retain that belief, against the testimony of my intelligence and my conscience. I think you also will find, as years go on, when it becomes your lot to stand by the grave into which friend after friend is lowered, that a heartfelt conviction of the spiritual Resurrection of Christ affords more comfort to you at such moments than your old belief—based largely upon historical evidence, and brain-felt rather than heart-felt—in His physical Resurrection. For the former unites us with Christ, the latter separates us from Christ. We none of us expect that the material and tangible bodies of our friends will rise from the dead in the flesh without "seeing corruption;" but we do trust that they shall rise as "spiritual bodies" over whom death shall have no power. This trust is confirmed by the belief that Christ rose as we trust they shall hereafter rise. If, therefore, Christ rose a material body from the grave—that stirs no hope in us. But if, while His body remained in the grave, His spirit rose triumphant to the throne of God, then we see a hope indeed that may suit our case and give us some gleam of consolation. The bodies of the dead may lie there and decay; but what of that? Even so was it with the Saviour: but the spiritual body is independent of the flesh and shall rise superior to death.

Do not imagine that the spiritual body is one whit less real than the material body; only, as the material body belongs to the time-world, so the spiritual body belongs to the eternal world. Each is suited to its own environment, but each of them is a real body. As to the relation between the material and the spiritual body we know nothing, and we need know nothing.

When will men learn to be less greedy of shams and bubbles of pretended material knowledge, and more earnest and patient in their sober aspirations after spiritual truth? When will they realize that an unhesitating faith in a few elementary principles is better than a tremulous quasi-knowledge of a whole globe of dogmas?

XXIV

MY DEAR ―――,

You take me to task for the abrupt termination of my last letter. I broke off, you say, just when you thought I was on the point of explaining what I meant by a spirit: "Surely you have some theory of your own and are not content with disbelieving other people's theories." Well, I thought I had said before that I am content to know merely this about a spirit, that it possesses capabilities for loving and serving God, or other nobler capabilities corresponding to these. But if you press me to set up some theory of my own that you may have the pleasure of pulling it to pieces, I will confess to you that my nearest conception of a spirit is a personified virtue. This cannot very well be quite right; any more than a carpenter can be like a door, or like anything else that he has constructed. But it is the nearest I can come to any conception that is not too repulsively material. And sometimes, when I try to conceive of the causes of terrestrial thoughts, and emotions, and spiritual movements, I find myself recurring to the antique notion, hinted at in one or two passages of the Bible, and I believe encouraged by some of the old Rabbis, that there are two worlds; one visible, terrestrial, and material, the other invisible, celestial, and spiritual; and that whatsoever takes place down here takes place first (or simultaneously but causatively) up there; here, the mere outsides of things ; there, the causes and springs of action ; the bodies down on earth, the spirits up in heaven.

This is but a harmless fancy. Let me give you another. You know—or might know if you would read a little book recently published called *Flatland*, and still better, if you would study a very able and original work by Mr. C. H. Hinton [1]—that a being of Four Dimensions, if such there were, could come into our closed rooms without opening door or window, nay, could even penetrate into, and inhabit, our bodies ; that he could simultaneously see the insides of all things and the interior of the whole earth thrown open to his vision : he would also have the power of making himself visible and invisible at pleasure ; and could address words to us from an invisible position outside us, or inside our own person. Why then might not spirits be beings of the Fourth Dimension? Well, I will tell you why. Although we cannot hope ever to comprehend what a spirit is—just as we can never comprehend what God is—yet St. Paul teaches us that the deep things of the spirit are in some degree made known to us by our own spirits. Now when does the spirit seem most active in us ? or when do we seem nearest to the apprehension of "the deep things of God"? Is it not when we are exercising those virtues which, as St. Paul says, " abide "—I mean faith, hope and love ? Now there is obviously no connection between these virtues and the Fourth Dimension. Even if we could conceive of space of Four Dimensions—which we cannot do, although we can perhaps describe what some of its phenomena would be if it existed—we should not be a whit the better morally or spiritually. It seems to me rather a moral than an intellectual process, to approximate to the conception of a spirit : and toward this no knowledge of Quadridimensional space can guide us.

[1] "*A Romance of the Fourth Dimension*," Swan Sonnenschein.

What, for example, do we mean when we speak of the Holy Spirit, and describe Him as the Third Person in the Trinity? I hope you will not suppose— because I happen to be a rationalist as regards the historical interpretation of certain parts of the Bible, or because I have not disguised my dislike of the formal and quasi-arithmetical propositions in which the Athanasian creed sets forth the doctrine of the Trinity—that I reject the teaching of the New Testament on the nature and functions of the Holy Spirit. Literary criticism may oblige us to regard the long discourses on the functions of the Paraclete or Advocate in the Fourth Gospel as being in the style of the author and not the language of Christ; but it is difficult to suppose that the sublime thoughts in those passages are the mere inventions of a disciple of Jesus; and the characteristic sayings of Christ in the Synoptic Gospels bear cogent though terse witness to His acknowledgment of a Holy Spirit who should "speak" in His disciples, and "teach" His disciples what to say, when they were summoned before the bar of princes: "it is not ye that speak, but the Holy Spirit," Mark xiii. 11; "it is not ye that speak, but the Spirit of your Father which speaketh in you," Matth. x. 20; "the Holy Spirit shall teach you in that very hour what ye ought to say," Luke xii. 12. I need not remind you how large a space "the Spirit" claims in St. Paul's Epistles, and especially of the use which the Apostle makes of the triple combination of the Father, the Son, and the Holy Spirit. Even, therefore, if I could give no explanation of the whole of it, nor so much as put into words the faint glimpse I may have gained into the meaning of a part of this doctrine, I should be inclined to accept the existence of the Holy Spirit on the authority of Christ or St. Paul, as being a doctrine that does not enter into the domain of evidence, a conception of the divine nature from which I might hope to learn much, if I would reverently keep it before me and try to apprehend it. But I seem to have a glimpse of it. That influence or "idea" of the dead which, as Shakespeare says, "creeps into our study of imagination," and which reproduces all the best and essential characteristics of the departed—when this has once taken possession of us, do we not naturally say that we now realize "the spirit" of the dead, feeling that it guides us for the first time to the appreciation of his words and deeds? Now as God, the initial Thought, needed to be revealed to us by means of the Word of God, so the Word needed to be revealed to us by means of the Influence of the Word. Or, to put it more personally, as the Father needed to be revealed by the Son, so the Son needed to be revealed by the Spirit. Those who knew Christ merely in the flesh knew but little of Him, and had little understanding of His words. It was the Spirit of Christ that guided, and still guides, His disciples into the fuller knowledge of the meaning of His past life on earth and His present purposes in heaven.

I own, however, that I have sometimes felt at a loss when I have asked myself, "How is this Spirit a Person? And do I love Him or It? And if Jesus and the Spirit of Jesus are two Persons, then must I also infer two personalities for myself, one for my mortal terrestrial humanity, another for my immortal celestial spirit?" These questions are extremely difficult for me to answer with confidence : yet I feel instinctively that they have a profound and satisfying answer to which I have not yet attained ; but I suggest some answer of this kind, "When we endeavour to form a conception of God we ought to put aside the limitations of human individuality. Now we cannot do this while we conceive of God simply as the Father, and still less while we conceive of Him simply as the Son ; but we can do it when we conceive of Him as being an all-pervasive Power, the source of order and harmony and light, sometimes as a Breath breathing life into all things good and beautiful, sometimes as a Bond, or Law, linking or attracting together all things material and spiritual so as to make up the Kosmos or Order of the Universe. The traditions of the Church have taught us that there has been such a Power, subsisting from the first with the Father and the Eternal Son, in whom the Father and the Son were, and are, united; and by whom the whole human race is bound together in brotherhood to one another and in sonship to the Eternal Father. What is this Being but the Personification of that Power which, in the material world, we call Attraction and in the immaterial, Love? Is it not conceivable that this Being which breathes good thoughts into every human breast should love those whom It inspires? And we—can we love our country, and love Goodness, Purity, Honour, Faith, Hope, and yet must we find it impossible to love this personified Love, this Holy Spirit? But if we love the Spirit of God, and the Spirit loves us, then we can understand how it may be called a Person."

I foresee the answer that might be given to these—I will not call them reasonings, say meditations. "All this is the mere play of fancy: you personify England, Virtue, Goodness, Hope, Faith, and the like; and such personifications are tolerable in poetry; but you do not surely maintain that such personifications have any real existence: in the same way, you may find a certain conception of the Supreme Being useful for the encouragement of devotion, but you have no right hence to infer that this conception represents an objective reality, much less God Himself." My reply is that in the region of theological contemplation where demonstration, and proof of the ordinary kind, are both impossible, I conceive I "have a right" to do this on the authority of Christ and

St. Paul and the Fourth Gospel, and the general tradition of the Church. I would sooner believe that myself and my spirit have a dual personality; I would sooner recognize the presence of the Angels of England and France and the other great nations of the world about the heavenly throne, like the Angels of the seven churches of Asia or the Angel of the Chosen People; I would sooner acknowledge the actual personality of Hope, Faith, and I know not what other celestial ministers between God and man; I would sooner, in a word, believe that personality depends upon some subtle combination such as only poets have dimly guessed at, than I would give up the belief that there is beside the Eternal Father, and the Eternal Son, an Eternal Spirit, to the description of whom we can best approximate by calling Him personified Love.

Looking at the Spirit of God in this way I sometimes seem to discern a closer connection than is generally recognized between the Resurrection and the power of loving. You will remember that St. Paul constantly connects the Resurrection of Christ with the "Spirit;" Christ was "raised from the dead *in*, or *by*, *the Spirit*; and St. Peter says that Christ was "put to death in the flesh, but quickened *in the Spirit*." Now this Spirit is the Power of Love. Do we ask for an explanation of this connection? It is surely obvious that the Resurrection of Christ would not have directly availed men (so far as we can see) unless it had been manifested to them. But how was it manifested? We think it was by love: on the one hand by the unsatisfied and longing love of the sorrowing disciples, creating a blank in the heart which could only be filled by the image of the risen Saviour; on the other hand by the unsatisfied and longing love of the Lord Jesus Christ, dying with a purpose as yet unfulfilled. Thus—so far as concerns the influence of the Resurrection of Jesus upon humanity—it was the Spirit of Love that raised Jesus from the abyss of inert oblivion and exalted Him to the right hand of God in the souls of men. I dare not say that, if Jesus had failed to root Himself in the hearts of men He could never have been raised from the dead; just as I dare not say that, if St. Peter had not been inspired to say "Thou art the Christ," the Church could never have been founded on the rock of heaven-imparted faith. Let us avoid this way of looking at things, as being repulsive and preposterous, putting things terrestrial before things celestial. Let us rather say that, because the rock of faith was being set up by the hand of God in heaven, therefore at that same instant the Apostle received the strength to utter his confession of faith; and because Christ's Spirit had soared up after death to the heaven of heavens and thence was bending down lovingly to look upon His despairing followers, therefore they received power to see Him again, living for them on earth.

Yet as regards ordinary men, I cannot help occasionally reviving that same preposterous method which I would discard in the case of Christ. And starting from terrestrial phenomena first, I sometimes ask myself, Is it possible that the resurrection of each human soul may depend upon the degree to which it has rooted itself in the affection of others? The Roman Catholic Church teaches that the condition of the dead may be affected by the prayers of survivors; and many abuses have resulted from a perverted and mechanical misinterpretation of that doctrine; but how if the spirit of a dead man actually owes its spiritual resurrection, not indeed to formally uttered petitions, but to the silent prayers, the loving wishes, the irrepressible desires, of fellow-spirits on earth and in heaven? How if a man lives in heaven and in the second life so far as his spirit has imprinted itself on the loving memories of others above and below? "Has the dead man kindled in the heart of one single human being a spark of genuine unselfish affection? To that extent, then, he receives a proportional germ of expansive and eternal life—might it not be so? And if it were so, then we could better understand how both the Lord Jesus Christ, and we mortal men, die in the flesh but are raised to a life eternal after death " in the Spirit " and "by the Spirit"—that great pervasive spiritual Power of Love which links all things in heaven and earth together.

I trust I have theorized enough to please you. I have done so because on the whole I think it best that you should see all the weakness, as well as all the strength, of my position—the credulous and fanciful side of it, as well as its breadth, its naturalness, its reasonableness, its spiritual comfort, its dependence on moral effort, its recognition of Law, its consistency with facts, and its absolute freedom from intellectual difficulties. Regarded in the ordinary way, as being the revivification of the material body, the Resurrection of Christ becomes an isolated portent in history; regarded naturally, it becomes the triumph of the Spirit over the fear of death, the central event of our earthly history. Central I say, but not isolated; because there are seen converging towards it, as it were predictively, all the phenomena of the evolution and training of the Imagination ; all instances of true poetic and prophetic vision ; the stars of heaven and all the creative provisions of night and darkness and sleep and dreams, nay even death itself. And what higher tribute (short of actual worship) can be paid to the personality of Christ than to say that " the phenomena of His resurrection are natural." I think if I were depressed and shaken in faith—as one is liable to be at times, not by intellectual but by moral considerations, when one feels that evil is stronger than it should be, both in oneself and outside oneself—it would be a great help to go and hear some agnostic saying with vehement conviction, "The resurrection of Christ was natural, purely natural." I should bid him say it again, and again ; and I would go home and say it over and over again to myself by way of comfort, to strengthen my faith : "The manifestations of the Resurrection of Christ were purely natural. So they were. Things could not be otherwise. Being what He was, Christ could not but thus be manifested to His followers after death. It was the natural effect of Christ's personality upon the disciples ; and through the disciples upon St. Paul. Then what a Person have we here ! A Person consciously superior to death, and, after His death, fulfilling a promise which He made to His disciples that He would still be present with them ! What wonder if He is even now present with us, influencing us with something of the power with which He moved the last of the Apostles ! What wonder if He is destined yet for future ages to be a present Power among men until the establishment of that Kingdom which He proclaimed upon earth, the Fatherhood of God and brotherhood of man ! "

XXV

MY DEAR ——,

I had not forgotten that, in order to complete the brief discussion of the miraculous element in the New Testament, it is necessary to give some explanation of the origin of the accounts of the birth of Christ. Your last letter reminds me of this necessity, and you put before me two alternatives. "If," you say, "Christ was born of a Virgin, then a miracle is conceded so stupendous that it is absurd to object to the other miracles: but if Christ was not born of a Virgin, then, unless the honesty of the Gospel narratives is to be impeached, some account is needed of the way in which the miraculous legend found its way into the Gospels;" and you add that you would like to know what meaning, if any, I attach to the statement in the Creed, that Jesus was "born of a Virgin."

As you probably anticipate, I accept the latter of your alternatives, and I will therefore endeavour briefly to shew how the story of the Miraculous Conception "found its way into the Gospels." But first I must protest against your expression as inexact. The story of the Miraculous Conception, so far from having "found its way into *the Gospels*," found its way into only two out of the four, namely, St. Matthew's and St. Luke's. And this fact, strong as it is, does not represent the strength of the negative argument from omission. Of the *nine* authors, or thereabouts, of the different books in the New Testament, only two contain any account, reference, or allusion to the Miraculous Conception. No mention is made of it in any of the numerous Epistles of St. Paul ; nor in any of his speeches, nor in those of St. Peter, recorded in the Acts of the Apostles, nor in any part of that book ; nor in the Epistles of St. John, St./James, St. Peter, St. Jude ; nor in the Apocalypse ; nor in the Gospels of St. Mark and St. John ! Even the two Gospels that mention it contain no evidence that it was known to any of the disciples during the life-time of Jesus, and one of these (Luke iii. 23) traces the genealogy of Jesus from Joseph and expressly declares that He " was supposed " to be " the Son of Joseph."[1] This negative evidence becomes all the more weighty if you consider how very natural it was, and I may almost say inevitable, that the story of a Miraculous Conception should speedily find its way into the traditions of the early Church. The causes that worked toward this result were, first, Old Testament prophecy ; secondly, traditions and expressions current among a certain section of the Jews ; thirdly, the preconceptions of pagan converts.

Recall to mind what was said in a previous letter concerning the importance attached by the earliest Christians to the argument from prophecy. Now there is a prophecy in Isaiah which, *if separated from its context*, might seem to point to nothing but the Miraculous Conception of the Messiah : " The Lord himself shall give you a sign : behold a virgin shall conceive and bear a son and shall call his name Immanuel." But a careful study of the context puts the matter in a quite different light. Isaiah (vii. 10—viii. 4) is promising to King Ahaz

[1] Yet I have heard it said, "*So far as evidence goes,* you have no more reason for rejecting the Miraculous Conception than for rejecting the story that Jesus washed the feet of the Apostles : for two witnesses attest the former ; but only one, the latter. Your objection is *a priori*." Such arguments seem to me to fail to recognize the first principles of evidence. The omission of a stupendous marvel, an integral part (and is not the parentage an integral part?) of a biography, by biographers who have no motive for omitting it and every motive for inserting it, is a *strong proof that they did not know it.* For a similar instance, see above, p. 167.

deliverance from the kings of Syria and Samaria. As the king will not ask for a sign, the prophet promises that the Lord will give him one ; a virgin shall conceive and bring forth a child and shall call his name Immanuel (" God with us ") : he shall " eat butter and honey " when he arrives at the age of distinction between good and evil ; for before he arrives at that age, the land abhorred by Ahaz shall be "forsaken by both her kings." The meaning appears to be that, within the time necessary for the conception and birth of a child, that is to say, in less than a year, the prospects of deliverance for Judah from her present enemies (Syria and Samaria) shall so brighten that a child shall be born and called by a name implying the favour of God ; afterwards, before that child shall grow up to childhood, the two aggressive countries of Syria and Samaria shall be themselves desolated, as well as Judah, by the " razor " of Assyria which shall shave the country clean from all cultivated crops. Amid the general desolation, the fruit trees will be cut down, the corn will not be sown ; bread there will be none ; there will be nothing to eat but " butter and honey ; " it is not the new-born child alone who shall eat " butter and honey ; " " butter and honey shall *every one eat that is left in the land*" (vii. 22).

In all this, even though we may suppose that there may have been some Messianic reference, there is no prediction at all of a conception from a virgin or of a miracle of any kind. Indeed, the prophecy appears to find some sort of fulfilment in what happens immediately afterwards (Isaiah viii. 1-4), when the prophet contracts a marriage, and calls the son who springs from it by a name implying the vengeance imminent on Samaria and Assyria : " Call his name Maher-shalal-hash-baz (*i.e.* booty, quick, spoil, speedy) : for before the boy shall have knowledge to cry my father ! my mother ! the riches of Damascus and the spoil of Samaria shall be taken away before the king of

Assyria." No doubt it may be said that this son was not called "Immanuel," so that the prophecy was not fulfilled in him. But the same argument might be urged against the application to our Lord; for He also was not called "Immanuel," but received the old national name of "Joshua," "Jeshua," or "Jesus." Reviewing all the circumstances of the prophecy, I think we may say, without exaggeration, first, that there are no grounds for seeing in it any reference to a Miraculous Conception; secondly, that, when isolated, it might easily be misinterpreted so as to convey such a reference.[1]

Even if no such prophecy had existed, the language and preconceptions of the earliest Christians and their converts would almost necessarily have introduced a belief in the Miraculous Conception. The language of Philo—who represents not a mere individual eccentricity but the current phraseology of the Alexandrine school of thought, and whose influence may be traced in almost every page

---

[1] You remember that the two accounts of the Miraculous Conception differ in respect of the "annunciation"; which St. Matthew describes as being made to Joseph. St. Luke as being made to Mary. It is interesting to note how these two variations correspond to two variations in the ancient prophecy.

In the LXX the name is to be given to the child, not by the mother, but by the future *husband*: "The virgin shall be with child and bring forth a son, and *thou shalt* call his name Immanuel". In the Hebrew, the "virgin," or "maiden," is *herself* to name the child: "A *virgin* shall ... bring forth and *shall* call, &c." Adopting the former version, a narrator would infer that the announcement of the birth was to be made to Joseph, as the first Gospel does: "She shall bring forth a child and *thou* (Joseph) shalt call his name Jesus." Adopting the latter version, and changing the third into the second person for the purpose of an "annunciation," the narrator would infer that since the name was to be given *by the mother*, the announcement was made *to the mother*, as the third Gospel does: "*Thou shalt* be with child, and shalt bring forth a son, and *shalt* call his name Jesus."

Note also that afterwards, when St. Matthew actually quotes the whole prophecy with the name "Immanuel" (i. 23), he alters the verb into the *third person plural*: "That it might be fulfilled which was spoken of the Lord by the prophet, saying, Behold the virgin shall be with child, and shall bring forth a child, and *they shall* call his name Immanuel." The reason is obvious. It would not be true to say that *Mary* called her son "Immanuel;" it would only be possible to suggest that *men in general* ("they"), looking on the Child as the token of God's presence among them, might bestow on him some such title (not name) as "God with us." Consequently St. Matthew here alters "thou" into "they."

of the Fourth Gospel—consistently affirms that, whenever a child is mentioned in the Old Testament as having been born to be a deliverer in fulfilment of a divine promise, that child is "begotten of God." The words of Sarah, he says, indicate that, in reality, "The *Lord begot* Isaac." God is also spoken of as "the *husband of Leah.*" Zipporah is described as being "pregnant by *no mortal.*" Samuel, in words that contain an implied belief that only his maternal parentage was mortal, is declared to be "perhaps a man," and "born of a human mother." I have already quoted one passage about Isaac ; but another asserts that he is to be considered "*not the result of generation* but the work of *the unbegotten.*" Sometimes the language of Philo is so worded as to convey even to a careful reader the impression that he believed in a literally Miraculous Conception, as for example when he says that " Moses introduces Sarah as being *pregnant when alone*, and as being *visited by God.*" Elsewhere, he removes the possibility of misunderstanding by saying that "the Scripture is cautious, and describes God as the husband, not of a virgin, but of virginity." None the less, you can easily see how expressions of this kind, current among Jewish philosophers a generation before the time of St. Paul, might be very easily interpreted literally by ordinary people unskilled in these metaphorical subtleties, and especially by Gentile converts asking for a plain answer to a plain question, "What was the parentage of this man whom you call the Son of God ?"

In truth the preconceptions of the Gentile converts must have played no small part in preparing the way for the doctrine of the literal Miraculous Conception. The Greeks and Romans who worshipped or honoured Æsculapius son of Apollo, Romulus son of Mars, Hercules son of Jupiter, and a score of other demi-gods, would be quite familiar with the notion of a god or hero born of a human mother and of a divine father; they would not only be prepared for it in the case of Jesus, whom they were called on to adore as the Son of God, they would even demand and assume it. They would argue much as Tertullian argued: "If he was the son of a man, he was not the son of God; and if he was the son of God, he was not the son of a man." This argument ought to have been met by a flat denial, thus: "The mere physical and carnal union by which, according to your legends, the gods, assuming the forms of men, generated Æsculapius, Romulus, and Hercules, is not to be thought of here. When we speak of Jesus being the Son of God, we do not mean that His body was formed by God descending from heaven and assuming human shape or functions, but that His Spirit was spiritually begotten of God. It is therefore quite possible that Jesus may have been the Son of God according to the Spirit and yet the son of man according to the flesh." But instead of that, the whole truth, there came back this half-true answer. "The parentage was divine, but not of the materialistic nature you suppose: God did not assume human shape: the generation was spiritual." By these words there may have been meant at first, simply what Philo meant, that while the spiritual parentage was divine, the material parentage was human: but such an answer would leave many under the impression that the body as well as the spirit of Jesus resulted from a spiritual generation in which no human father participated. The Gentiles would naturally interpret the Philonian doctrine literally and say of Mary, as Philo had said of Sarah, that she was "pregnant when alone, and visited by God."

From a very different point of view, the ritual and hymnals of some of the Jews might facilitate the growth of the belief that Jesus was born of a virgin. For they might naturally speak of their Messiah as being a child of the virgin daughter of Sion, whose only husband was Jehovah. And hence in the Apocalypse, a book imbued with Jewish feeling, we find Jesus described (xii. 1—6) as the child of a woman who evidently represents Israel: "A woman arrayed with the sun, and the moon under her feet, and upon her head a crown of twelve stars; and she was *with child*. . . . And she was delivered of a *son, a man child, who is to rule all the nations with a rod of iron.*" This personification of the daughter of Israel or of Jerusalem as representing the nation, the bride of Jehovah, is very common in the prophets. You may find similar personifications in the New Testament. The Apocalypse describes the Church as the Holy City, the New Jerusalem, descending from Heaven "*as a bride* adorned for her husband." St. Paul speaks of the New Jerusalem, which is above (*i.e.* the spiritual Jerusalem, free from the law), as being " the *mother* of us all." Sometimes the personification of the Church is liable to be misinterpreted literally, as in St. Peter's and St. John's Epistles, where "the elect lady" "thine elect sister" and "the (lady) in Babylon" have been supposed by some to refer to individuals, but are believed by Bishop Lightfoot to represent the Churches of the places from which, and to which, the epistles were written. The whole of St. Paul's Epistles presuppose the metaphor of a Virgin Church, and toward the end of the second century (177 A.D.) we find a very curious passage (in an epistle from the Church of Lyons) in which the repentance and martyrdom of some previous apostates are described as a restoration to "the Virgin Mother" of her children, " raised from the dead." You see then how this personification runs through all Jewish and all early Christian literature, so that the Church, old or new, might be described as a woman; and I ought perhaps

T

not to have omitted the strange dream in the second book of Esdras (x. 44-46) where Israel is a woman and the Temple is the son : " This woman whom thou sawest is Sion . . . she hath been thirty years barren, but after thirty years Solomon builded the city and offered offerings, and then bare the barren a son." Does not this continuous stream of thought shew how natural it would be for the earliest Jewish Christians to adore Christ in their hymns as the son of the daughter of Zion, the son of the Virgin Mother? Add to this the prejudice among the Gentile converts against a human paternity for the Son of God, the influence of the Alexandrine Jewish philosophy and the still more powerful influence of Isaiah's prophecy about " the virgin," and I think you will see that the causes at work to produce the belief in the Miraculous Conception were so strong that I may almost say a miracle would have been needed to prevent it.

But it has been urged that St. Luke was a historian and a physician ; that he had great power of careful description—as may be seen from his exact account of St. Paul's shipwreck ;—that he describes the circumstances of the miraculous birth in a plain and simple manner : and that he assures us that he had taken every pains to make himself acquainted with the truth of the things which he records.[1] All this may be : but because a man can describe exactly a comparatively recent shipwreck, which he may have himself witnessed, or which at all events may have been witnessed by some who told him the story, it does not follow that he has exact information about a miraculous birth which occurred (if at all) upwards of sixty years—more probably upwards of seventy—before he wrote. The mother of Jesus had, in all probability, passed away when St. Luke was writing. Such obscurities and variations by this time attended the stories concerning

[1] *Contemporary Review*, Feb. 1886, p. 193.

the infancy of Jesus, that we find even the compiler of St. Matthew's Gospel apparently ignorant that the home of the parents of Jesus was (if St. Luke is correct on this point) not Bethlehem, but Nazareth. It is hardly possible to deny his ignorance when we find in the First Gospel these words : " Now when Jesus was born in Bethlehem of Judæa.... And he arose and took the young child and his mother and came into the land of Israel. *But when he heard that Archelaus was reigning over Judæa, he was afraid to go thither; and being warned [of God] in a dream, he withdrew into the parts of Galilee and came and dwelt in a city called Nazareth.*" Obviously the writer is ignorant that "a city called Nazareth" was the original home of the parents of Jesus, and that they had no reason for returning to "Judæa ;" his whole narrative assumes that Bethlehem in Judæa was the home, and that the parents of Jesus were only prevented from returning thither by the fear of Archelaus, which forced them to leave their native city and to take up their abode in "*a city* called Nazareth." Now it is probable that St. Luke's account is here the correct one, and that the erroneous tradition found in the First Gospel was a mere inference from the prophecy that " from Bethlehem " there should " come forth a governor." But what a light does this discrepancy throw upon the uncertainty of the very earliest traditions about the infancy of Jesus when we find *the only two Evangelists who say anything about it, differing as to the place where the parents of Jesus lived at the time when they were married!* I have no doubt that St. Luke did his best, in the paucity, or more probably in the variety, of conflicting traditions, to select those which seemed to him most authoritative and most spiritual. Even the most careless reader of the English text must feel, without knowing a word of Greek, that St. Luke's first two chapters —which contain the stories of the infancy—are entirely different from the style of the preface (i. 1-4), and from that of the rest of the Gospel. The two chapters sound, even in English, like a bit out of the Old Testament; and any Greek scholar, accustomed to the LXX, would recognize that they were either a close translation from the Aramaic, or written by some one who wrote in Greek, modelling his style on the LXX. It is probable that they represent some traditions of Aramaic origin, the best that St. Luke could find when he began to write of the wonders that had happened more than sixty or seventy years ago. To those who can form the least conception of the extent to which Oriental tradition in the villages of Galilee might be transmuted after an interval of sixty or seventy years, it must seem quite beside the mark to assert the historical accuracy of the tradition concerning the Miraculous Conception which St. Luke has incorporated in his Gospel, on the ground that he was a physician; that he took pains to get at the truth; and that he has written a masterly and exact account of a shipwreck which he, or some friends of his, may have witnessed in person.

The very sobriety of his own preface ought to put us on our guard against attaching to St. Luke's history such weight, for example, as we attach to the history of Thucydides. He says, it is true, that he had "traced the course of all things accurately from the first, *i.e.* from the commencement of Christ's life:" but this amounts to much less than the statement of Thucydides, who tells us that he had personally inquired from those who knew the facts, besides having seen some of the facts himself (Thuc. i. 22). He does not say that "the eye-witnesses and ministers of the word" had given *him* any special information: on the contrary he mentions himself only as one of many who had received "traditions" from eye-witnesses, and he implies that a good many of the existing narratives, *based upon these very traditions*, were at least so far unsatisfactory that they did not dispense with an additional narrative from him. The emphasis which St. Luke lays on the fact that he has traced things "from the first," and that he writes "in order,"—combined with the mention of "many" predecessors who have "taken in hand" the work which he intends to do over again—makes it almost certain that some of these Evangelists had omitted all account of our Lord's birth; others had not regarded chronological order; others had not written "accurately." All these deficiencies indicate a great and general difficulty in obtaining exact information; and the mere honesty of a new attempt, under circumstance so disadvantageous, cannot justify us in attaching a very high authority to a tradition in this new Gospel, of a miraculous character, and in a style that appears to be not St. Luke's own, referring to an incident supposed to have occurred upwards of sixty years before. This digression about St. Luke's Gospel will not be without its use if it leads you to perceive that history, and experience, and criticism, while they tend to make us believe more, tend also to make us know less, about Christ's life and doctrine; I mean, that we find we know a little less about the historical facts of Christ's life than we supposed we knew, while we are led to believe a great deal more in the divine depth and wisdom of His ideas.

I pass to the second question which you put to me, "What sense, if any, do you yourself attach to the statement in the Creed that Christ was born of a Virgin?" Before I tell you what sense I attach to it, or rather what sense seems to me the only one compatible with the facts, I must honestly express my doubt whether any sense that is compatible with the facts, is also compatible with the words. To speak plainly, the statement appears to be so obviously literal that I shrink from interpreting it metaphorically; and yet, if taken literally, it appears to me to be false. The word "Virgin" is perhaps the only word in the service and ritual of the Church of England (if the Athanasian Creed be left out of consideration, owing to the non-natural and humane interpretations of it which have been sanctioned by high authority) which has made me doubt at times whether I ought to do official work as a minister in that Church. As regards the "resurrection of the body," asserted in one of the Creeds, I feel little or no difficulty: for St. Paul's use of the term "spiritual body" allows great latitude to those who would give a spiritual interpretation to the phrase in the Creed; and I trust that I have made it clear to you that I accept Christ's Resurrection as a reality, though a spiritual reality.[1] But the words implying the birth from the Virgin stand on a different footing. In the Resurrection of Jesus I believe that there was a unique vision of the buried Saviour, apparent to several disciples at a time ; but in the conception and birth of Jesus I have no reason for thinking that there was anything unusual apparent to the senses. What can I mean then by saying that Jesus is "born of a Virgin"?

All that I can mean is this. Human generation does not by any means account for the birth of a new human spirit. So far as we are righteous, we all owe our righteousness to a spiritual seed within us; "we are not," as Philo would say, "the result of generation but the work of the Unbegotten." So far as we are righteous, we are "born not of blood, nor of the will of the flesh, nor of the will of man, but of God" (John i. 13). But of the Lord Jesus Christ we are in the habit of saying and believing

[1] I must admit that a more serious difficulty is presented to Sponsors by the interrogative form of the Creed in the Baptismal service, to which they are expected to reply in the affirmative: "Dost thou believe .. in the Resurrection of the *flesh?*" But I can hardly think that many clergymen would wish to reject an otherwise eligible Sponsor who confided to them that he could only accept "flesh" in the sense of "body," and that too in the Pauline sense of "spiritual body."

that He was uniquely and entirely righteous; and therefore we say that He was uniquely and entirely born of God. In all human generation there must be some congenital divine act, if a righteous soul is to be produced; and in the generation of Christ there was a unique congenital act of the Holy Spirit. That Word of God which in various degrees inspires every righteous human soul (none can say how soon in its existence) did not inspire Jesus, but was (to speak in metaphor) totally present in Jesus from the first so as to exclude all imperfection of humanity. Human unrighteousness—such as we are in the habit of attributing to human generation—there was, in this case, none. Therefore we say that the generation of Jesus was not human but divine.

So much I can honestly say because I heartily believe it. How far one is justified in putting so strained an interpretation on the words "born of the Virgin Mary"— even in the Church of England, where simultaneous conservatism and progress have been bought at the cost of many strained interpretations—is a question on which I may perhaps hereafter say a word or two, but not now. Meantime let me merely add my conviction that there may have been a time when this illusion of the Miraculous Conception did more good than harm. In former days, that spiritual truth which we can now disentangle from the story of the Miraculous Conception may have been conveyed by means of it to hearts which would have otherwise never recognized that Jesus was the Son of God. It was surely better then, and it is better now, that men should believe the great truth that Jesus is the Son of God, at the cost of believing (provided they can honestly believe) the untruth that Jesus was not the son of Joseph, than that they should altogether fail to recognize His divine Sonship, because they were alive to the fact that He was born of human parents in accordance with the laws of humanity. But in these days the doctrine of the Miraculous Conception seems to me fraught with evil ; partly because the weakness of the evidence makes the narrative a stumbling-block for many who are taught to consider this doctrine essential and who cannot bring themselves to believe it ; partly because it tends to sanction a false and monastic ideal of life ; to separate Jesus from common humanity and from human love and sympathy ; and to encourage false notions about a material Resurrection of the body of Jesus, which naturally result in a false, bewildering, and disorderly expectation of a material Resurrection for ourselves.

XXVI

MY DEAR ———,

You ask me whether one who has seceded from miraculous to non-miraculous Christianity still finds himself able to pray as before. But towards the end of your letter you amend your question. You are "quite sure," you are pleased to say, from what you know of me, that I shall "answer this question affirmatively, though in defiance of all logic:" and therefore, anticipating my answer, you state your objection to it beforehand, and ask me how I can meet your objection, which is to this effect: "If the laws of nature are never suspended, then it is absurd, or perhaps impious, to pray for that which implies their suspension. For example, a friend of mine may be in a stage of disease so fatally advanced that, without a suspension of the laws of nature, it is no more possible that he should recover from the disease than that his body should rise from the grave. According to the tenets of your non-miraculous Christianity, must I not abstain from praying that he may recover?"

I do not see any great difficulty here. Change the hypothesis for a moment. Suppose your friend to be no longer living, but dead. Are you willing—would you be willing, even were you the most orthodox believer in miraculous Christianity—to pray that the body of your dead friend might arise revivified from the grave a week after he had been laid in it? You know you would not be willing. Why not? You cannot say "Because it is impossible," for you would admit (on the supposition of your being a believer in the miraculous) not only that it is possible, but that it has actually been done in times past. But you would feel, I am sure, that you dare not, and ought not, to pray for this object, because such a prayer would be a revolt against that established order of things which you recognize to be a manifestation of God's present will. I say "God's present will," because you do not (if you agree with me) regard death as being in accordance with God's future will : it is an evil, sprung, not from God, but from evil, out of which God is working good. But He bids us acquiesce in it during our present imperfect state of existence ; and hence, though you believe He will ultimately destroy death, you do not feel justified in praying that its present operation may be neutralized by a suspension of the laws of nature.

Now to return to your own supposition that your friend is not dead, but merely in danger of death. Health and life are dependent upon many complex causes, among which (it will be admitted by all) are those mysterious fluctuations of the thoughts and emotions, which I believe in many cases to proceed—I speak in a metaphor— straight from God Himself. To one who believes that the spirits of men are in constant communion with the all-sustaining Spirit of the Creator, the thoughts of men may well seem to be as dependent upon their divine Origin as the air in my little room is at this moment dependent upon the changes of the circumambient atmosphere. Of course, if you are a thorough-going, scientific hope-nothing and trust-nothing, such a belief as this appears to you an idle dream. From your point of view, you are a machine ; your friend is a machine ; all men are machines ; the world is a machine ; the action and inter-action of all these animate and inanimate machines is predetermined, even to the minutest movement of a limb, or most fleeting shade of thought, in each one of the myriads of human mechanisms called men.

The thorough-going materialist, when he rebukes his son and tells him that he "ought not to have" told a lie, knows perfectly well that his son could not possibly help telling that lie, and that he was bound by all the laws of nature to tell it. The materialist father is, in fact, telling a lie himself; only more deliberately than the little son. He is using words which have no true meaning for him, as a kind of oil to grease the wheels of the little machine before him, having learned by accumulated experience that this lying phrase, "You *ought* to have," has for many thousands of years proved a very effective kind of oil, and that the true and scientific phrase, "It would have been better if you could have, but you could not," would be wholly inefficacious. But since it is obvious that this view of existence converts all moral language, and almost all the higher relations of life, into one gigantic lie, I make no apology at all for putting it by with contempt as being beneath the consideration of a child of ten—at which age, as far as I remember I grappled with this question of predestination, and settled it (so far as I was concerned, for ever) by coming to the conclusion that "it does not *work.*" Now when you have once given up, as unworkable, the theory that all our thoughts and emotions spring necessarily from antecedent material causes, you have bidden good-bye to Knowledge, so far as concerns the origin of human thought, and you are thrown back upon Faith. I believe therefore, and I make no apology for my belief, that the mysterious fluctuations of human thought and will may sometimes proceed from God without the intervention of material causes, perhaps in virtue of the existence of some invisible law of union by which the souls of men are united to God and to one another.

This being my belief—which at all events does not contain so many and such perpetually-recurring inconsistencies as the belief of your thorough-going materialist—you will understand, without much further explanation, when and why I should pray even for those of whom the physician is inclined to despair. Faith and hope, have, before now, worked such wonders in healing, that "while there is life there is hope" has passed into a proverb. I cannot be sure that my prayers might not have some kind of direct power—by a kind of brain-wave such as we have heard of lately—in affecting the emotions and spirits of the sufferer. It is seldom that even a physician can speak with certainty about the immediate issue of a disease: and whatsoever is uncertain is (if it be also right) a reasonable subject for prayer. But if I were myself absolutely convinced that there was no chance of my friend's recovery without a suspension of the laws of nature, I should feel that prayer rightly and naturally gave way to resignation.

No one however who is in the habit of praying will think it necessary to spend much time or thought in discriminating exactly between that which may be, and that which cannot possibly be. He must know that, very often, where his prayer trenches on the province of the material, the line cannot be drawn except by an expert in science, which he may not happen to be; and besides, in the mood of prayer, he will feel that the scientific and discriminating spirit is out of place. He is not thinking of things scientifically, but spiritually, putting his wishes before the Father in heaven, and content to couple each wish with an "If it be possible." Sometimes he learns, after constant repetition, that the prayer is an unfit one, and he discontinues it; in that case he has gained by his prayer a closer insight into, and conformity with, the will of God. In other cases he continues his prayer and receives an answer to it—either the answer that he himself desires, or some other perhaps, quite different from that which he expected, but one which he ultimately recognizes to be the best. But there will be cases where he will continue his prayer, feeling it to be right and natural, although he receives no answer to it at all, so far as he can discern. For he will feel quite certain that no genuine prayer is wasted. Our spirits, or our angels—to use the language of metaphor—are not on earth: they sit together in heaven, that is to say, in the heart of God; and whenever one of us can conceive a genuinely unselfish and righteous wish for a brother spirit and wing it with faith so that it flies up to heaven—a flight by no means so easy or so common as we suppose, and probably not often flown, unless the arrow is feathered by deeds and pains as well as words—then it not only brings back a blessing upon the wisher but also thrills through the spiritual assembly above and comes back as a special blessing to the person prayed for. But need I add that this is not a process to be performed mechanically? There is no recipe for effectual prayer.

But, to come down from metaphors, let me attempt to answer your question, " What difference of attitude in prayer will there be between the believer in natural, and the believer in miraculous, Christianity? " As far as my experience goes, there will be very little; except that the former will be rather more disposed to ask, before uttering a prayer, how far the granting of it might indirectly affect others. Logically and theoretically there ought to be a great deal of difference; for if the believer in the miraculous were consistent, he might naturally pray that a miracle might be performed for him, as it has been for others, for a good purpose. As a matter of fact, the prayers of children trained in orthodoxy are thus sometimes consistent. I dare say one might find a child who has prayed that the sun might stand still that he might have a longer holiday. And why not now—from the child's point of view—as well as formerly? But I suppose few men in England, now, even of the strictly orthodox, are in this puerile stage. Almost all full-grown English Protestants recognize that, although miracles were freely performed from the year 4004 B.C. to, say A.D. 61 or thereabouts—when St. Paul shook off the serpent and took no harm—yet "the age of miracles is now past." Yet I have heard of men of business who make a point of praying earnestly on the subject of commercial speculations, the rise and fall of consols, the price of sugar and the like. Will any one maintain that people are not the worse for such prayers as these, or that the believer in natural Christianity is not a gainer by losing the desire and the power to utter them? On the whole, I see but one subject of prayer mentioned in our English Prayer-book, as to which natural Christianity would probably dictate silence : I mean the weather. It might be argued that, " since the weather is affected by human action (by the clearing of forests, draining of marshes, and so on), and since prayers affect human action, therefore they *do* affect the weather *indirectly*, and *may* affect it *directly*." But from "indirect" to "direct" is a great leap ; and I am moved toward resignation rather than prayer, by the thought that, in revealing to us more and more of the extent of the causes and effects of meteorological phenomena, God seems to be shewing us that, in asking for weather that suits ourselves, we may be asking for weather that may not suit others. I should be sorry to see harvest prayers excluded from our Church service ; but I think they should express our hope and trust in God's orderly government of the seasons, beseeching Him to bestow on the husbandman patience and skill so as to meet and improve adversity, and on the nation thrift and frugality so as to avoid waste.

Since writing the last paragraph I was interrupted ; and now, returning to my letter, I feel strongly inclined to cancel the last two or three pages of apologetic argumentation ; arguing about prayer seems so absurdly useless. Yet perhaps my remarks may weigh for something with you in your present oscillation. They may possibly prevent you from giving up, in a moment of virtuous logic, a habit which, once discontinued, is not easily resumed. Let them pass then ; but let them not pass without a protest that they by no means express my sense of the vital necessity of prayer for a Christian. To me it seems the very breath of our spiritual life, as needful for peace and 'union with God as communion between children and parents is needful for domestic concord. Without it, faith must speedily vanish. Even a comparatively dull and lifeless petition at stated intervals has some value as a sign-post, indicating the road on which we ought to be travelling though our feet may be straying elsewhere. But in truth real Christian prayer (mostly silent) should be, as St. Paul says "without ceasing;" for prayer is but aspiration and desire, emerging into shape. When a man has reached such a height that he has ceased to wish to be something better than he is, then and then only may he cease to pray.

One kind of prayer at all events I have felt able to retain which seems to me of far more value than the prayer for fair weather—I mean prayer for the dead. I do not deny that, when coupled with superstitious views about heaven and hell, the custom of praying for the dead may result in superstition, and even in the encouragement of immorality ; and the hired and conventional prayers for the dead prevalent in the sixteenth century appear to me to have constituted an abuse against which our English Reformers did well to protest. But these abuses and corruptions seem to me accidental, and quite insufficient to deter us from use of the most helpful of spiritual habits. I do not propose to argue about it, but you may like to know the sort of accident by which I was led to form this habit, and the practical reasons for which I clung to it, and still cling to it, with the deepest conviction that it is not only spiritually useful, but also based on spiritual truth.

Many years ago a brother of mine was drowned at sea through the sudden capsizing of a vessel by night. When the news came, I was at first distracted between an intense desire to pray as before, and a kind of instinctive and general repugnance to all prayers for the dead as being "a Romanist practice." All the books I had read, and all the notions I had formed, about the fixed future of the dead, suggested that such prayers were useless, if not blasphemous. On the other side there was no argument at all, nothing but a vague strong desire to pray. The painful conflict of that night—a conflict, as it seems to me now, between true natural religion and the false appearance of revealed religion—is still present to my recollection. At last it occurred to me that more than a month had elapsed between the death and our knowledge of the death, and throughout all those thirty days my prayers had gone up to God for one whose soul was no longer upon earth. Were those prayers wasted? I could not believe it. Besides, we had not yet received full details of the loss of the vessel. It was just possible that my brother might have been saved in one of the ship's boats : he might be still living, and in sore need of help : how monstrous, if it were so, that I should in such a crisis cease to pray for him ! So with doubt and trembling I still continued my custom, fashioning some kind of prayer to suit the emergency. While I was in this oscillating state of mind, news came that a second boatful, and almost immediately afterwards that a third, had been picked up at sea. My brother was not in either : but why might there not be a fourth ? For some time, with less doubt than before, I continued to pray. Days, weeks, months rolled on, and now all hope had slipped away ; but the habit was now fixed. I could not, or would not, break it. Praying day and night for one who was possibly living ; just possibly living ; probably not living; certainly dead—I had learned to realize the presence of my brother's spirit, as very near and close to me, as one with whom I was still in some kind of communion ; and now to drop his name out of my prayers, simply because I should never touch his hand again in this world, seemed a faithless, a wicked, a cruel act. The prayer could not indeed remain the same in circumstances so completely changed ; I could of course no longer pray that the dead might be restored to me on earth : but it was still open to me to make mention of his name, and to beseech God that he and I might meet again in heaven : and thus, with a curious kind of compromise, worthy of a less youthful theologian, I circumvented my own orthodoxy by still praying in reality for my brother while I appeared to be praying for myself. More than seven-and-twenty years have now passed away, but not a night or morning has passed without the mention of that familiar name ; and I entreat you to believe me that, next to the power of Christ Himself upon the soul, I have not found, nor can I imagine, any influence so potent as this habit of praying for the dead, to detach the mind from petty and visible things, to unlock the spiritual world, to carry the soul up to the very source and centre of spiritual life, and to bring us into faithful communion with the Father of the spirits of all flesh.

You see I have kept my promise of not arguing on this matter. I have simply told you how I have longed and doubted ; how my doubts were dissipated by practice ; and what strength I have personally derived from the practice. Probably this will seem to you, if interesting, at all events inadequate. "Logically," you will perhaps say to yourself, "he ought to have attempted first to convince me that the eternal state of the dead is not finally determined at the moment of death; so that prayer may reasonably be expected to have some power to change their condition. He ought to have told me whether he believes in a Purgatory, or in a limited Hell; whether he is a Universalist; or whether he believes in the annihilation of all who are not to be saved. In a word, he ought to have given me a full account of his theory about the condition of the dead, before he commends to me the habit of praying for them."

Here I fear I shall terribly disappoint you; but, at the risk of whatever disappointment, I will confess to you the whole truth. This part of my Manual of Theology has large print, large margin, and several blank pages. I believe some things with such force and clearness that I prefer to say I do not believe them—I *see* them: but about many other things which most people believe, I know little or nothing. Do I believe in a Hell? Yes, as firmly as I believe in a Heaven; but not in your Hell perhaps, and certainly not in the ordinary guide-books to Hell and Heaven. Perhaps some would call my Hell "merely retribution," or "an illogical and ill-defined Purgatory;" and from their point of view they could be right in complaining of its indefiniteness; for they profess to know all about it and to be able to define it. But from my point of view I am equally right in speaking indefinitely; for I profess to have only a glimpse of it. Of the principles of Hell and Heaven I am certain, but of the details I am entirely ignorant. I know nothing whatever, and I know that no one else knows anything whatever, about the state of the dead; except that they are just as much in God's hand when dead as when living, and that

He will ultimately do the best thing for each; but what that "best thing" may be I cannot tell in detail, although I am very sure that it will be one thing for St. Francis and quite another for Nero. For the rest, all the elaborate structures and fancy-fabrics of Heaven and Hell, Purgatory, Paradise, Limbo, and other regions, whether theologians or poets be the architects, appear to me built upon the flimsiest foundations, tags of texts, fragments of words, quagmires of metaphor, quicksands of hyperbole. No; such real knowledge—or shall we say such conviction?—as we have about the eternal future of the dead, is to be based, not upon argument or inference from minute and disputable interpretations of small portions of Scripture, but mainly upon our faith in the divine righteousness and power. You will not, I hope, misunderstand my words that "God will do the best thing for each," or draw from them the inference, "Then he is a Universalist after all." I took for granted—I hope I was not wrong—that you would remember the definition of justice which you have read in Plato. In fact therefore I merely expressed in those words my conviction that God would be "just" to us after death.[1] Might we not also define the highest mercy, in the same terms in which we define the highest justice, as being the feeling that prompts us to "do what is best for each"? And, if so, does it not seem to follow that in Hell God will not cease to be merciful, and in Heaven God will not cease to be just? And hence are we not brought close to the conclusion that Heaven and Hell are not really places, but the diverse results of the operation of the Eternal—the just Mercy, the merciful Justice—upon the diverse dead? But here the question widens and deepens into expanses and depths altogether too vast

---

[1] Has not some confusion of thought arisen from a habit of confusing "just" with "severe"? I believe some men would feel more reverently towards God, if they would speak, not of His "justice," but of His "fairness."

and profound for me, and I give up the problem. All that I know is, that there will be hereafter a just retribution.

Yet if I am to tell you my own conjectural imaginations —for who can help at times imagining what the infinite unknown may be, however loth he may be to insist or dogmatize about it, or even to bestow much attention on it, when the urgent present presses its superior claims? —I will say for myself that I cannot believe I shall have served all my apprenticeship to righteousness in my brief life upon this earth, or that I shall be fit immediately after death, for that closest communion with God which appears to me the Heaven of Heavens. Some cleansing retribution, some further purification, seems to me necessary and likely for myself—and, I must add, for the greater number of those human beings with whom I have had to do—before we attain to that blessed consummation.

"So you believe in a Purgatory then?" How do I know? Say rather, I conjecture there may be many heavens. In any case, I find it very easy to imagine a retribution and a purification that shall be purely spiritual, without having recourse to any material flames or physical horrors. Some people find a difficulty in this notion: they consider it, but deliberately put it aside; as if mere remorse, sorrow, and self-condemnation, could never be bitter enough to constitute a just Hell. I do not think they have ever realized—perhaps they have never tried to realize—the pain that may be felt by a spirit sitting alone, away from this familiar world and every well-known face, and quietly judging and condemning itself. A mere accident, a ludicrous accident, once gave me a moment's experience of this feeling, and I have never been able to forget it, never been able to put aside the conviction that that feeling, intensified, might constitute Hell.

It happened in this way. Some years ago, before

nitrous oxide had come into very general use among dentists, I went to have a tooth extracted, and determined to try the gas. Perhaps I had some misgivings that it was a little cowardly; perhaps I was a little nervous; in any case I remember at the last moment thinking that I should like to be conscious of the precise moment when unconsciousness came; I remember struggling to retain consciousness—even when a tell-tale throbbing in the temples shewed that something new was going on—protesting to myself that the gas had "no power," "no power at all yet," "I don't believe it's going to have any power"—till the portcullis came down. I suppose the consequence was that I inhaled rather more than was usual; and when I came to myself I heard the voices of the dentist and the physician—a long way off, as it seemed to me, but with perfect distinctness—saying that "he was a long time coming to" and they did not "quite like the look of things," and so on. Meantime I lay motionless and without power either to move or speak, but perfectly conscious. I took in the whole situation at once. I was dead. I had passed into another state of existence. I could think more clearly than before. I was a spirit. And then the thought came pressing in upon me, as I reviewed my whole life and the manner of my death, that to avoid a little pain I had done a wrong thing and had deserted those who needed me and would miss me. No fear possessed me, not the slightest fear, of any external punishment for the fault which I thought I had committed: but in a detached solitude I seemed to be quietly and coldly sitting in judgment upon myself, impartially hearing what I had to say in self-defence, rejecting it as inadequate, and passing against myself the verdict of Guilty. Painful, increasingly painful, the burden of this self-condemnation seemed to press and crush me down more and more past power of bearing, so that at last, when in one moment I recovered both power of motion and knowledge that I was alive again, I leapt up from the dentist's arm-chair, and, without taking the least notice of the two operators, I gave vent to my feelings by shouting aloud the well-known words from Clarence's dream—

"—and for a space
Could not believe but that I was in hell."

I shall not easily forget the look of mingled humour and horror with which the dentist replied, "Well, sir, considering you are a clergyman, I should have hoped it might have been the other place." I tried to explain. I assured him that it was a quotation from Shakespeare; that I had not really believed that I was in the place commonly called Hell; and so on. But I am quite sure my explanations were utterly ineffectual; and to this day I probably labour under the suspicion, in the minds of at least two worthy persons, of having committed some horrible crime by which my conscience is racked with agony. In reality, however, it was a small offence, if any, for which I suffered that bad quarter of a minute; and I have often since thought that, if the mind is capable of inflicting such pain upon itself for a venial error, those pangs must be terrible indeed with which our sinful souls may be forced to scourge themselves when we judicially review the actions of a selfish life with a compulsory knowledge of all the evil, direct and indirect, which we have wrought, and when we realize at last—ah, how differently from the dull, decorous, conventional contrition with which we droned out the words on earth, kneeling on the hassocks in the family pew—that "we have left undone those things which we ought to have done, and done those things which we ought not to have done."

But why do I thus discourse in detail upon a subject

about which I have admitted that I know no details? It is in order to shew you that though I do not know much, the little I do know greatly influences me. The thought of a material Hell has probably contributed largely to insanity, and has exercised a baneful influence upon many women and children; but the majority of healthy men who profess to believe in a pit of flame are little influenced by it. It is so horrible, so unnatural, so unjust, that in their heart of hearts they feel sure the good God cannot mean it; He will let them off; or they will get off somehow—by absolution, by forensic justification, by baptism, by uncovenanted mercies, or what not. This is but natural. How can it not be natural to believe that an unnatural and arbitrary Hell may be dispensed with by an unnatural and arbitrary indulgence? I have no such consolations. With me, Hell is a different thing altogether: it is natural, it is inevitable, it is just, it is merciful. Not a day passes but I think of it and anticipate it in some sort for myself and my friends. *Tout se payera:* this act, I say, or this neglect, was wrong, and must have been injurious: the doers cannot escape from the consequences of it; I do not wish to escape from the consequences of it. God will work good out of evil; but He will be just, not indulgent. I do not want Him to be indulgent. Thus Heaven and Hell, impending over the routine of my every-day life, become to me practical and potent realities; but they are real to me because the conceptions I have formed of them are in accordance with the profound laws of spiritual nature, and quite independent of the conflicting fancies of theologians.

Ask me what I trust to be in Heaven, and I can give you no answer save that one which I have often given you before—a being capable of loving and of serving God. Ask me the nature of Hell and Heaven, and my only reply is that they will be God's retribution. Ask me whether all will be hereafter " saved," and I am silent, or merely answer that God is good, and that I believe a time will come when we, in Him, shall look back, and around, and forward, and shall see that His work has been "very good." Enough for me to work and fight on the side of God and against Evil, that His righteous Kingdom may come and bring with it the time when His work will be seen to have been "very good." As for other details, I know nothing and delight in knowing nothing. I do not know whether I shall live again on earth or elsewhere; whether I shall be a being of three dimensions, or four, or of no dimensions at all; whether I shall be in space or out of space. It is far better to give up speculations about accidental trifles such as these: for accidents they are, as compared with the essence of the second life, which consists in Love. Do not give up the belief in that, at any cost; least of all, at the cost of a little banter. " But surely it is possible that our very highest and purest conceptions of Heaven may fall short of the reality." Granted: but we must hold fast to the belief that there is at all events a proportion between our best terrestrial aspirations and their celestial equivalents. We must reject, as from Satan, the suggestion (was it Spinoza's?) that there is no more likeness between God and our conception of God than between the constellation Canis and a dog. "God may not be Love:" I do not believe you: but if He is not Love, He will be some celestial form of Love, corresponding to our Love, only infinitely better. "You will not retain your individuality:" possibly not, but certainly we shall have something corresponding to individuality, only better. And so of the rest. We shall talk humbly, as beseems our microcosmic faculties; we are but the transitory tenants of a little world, which is to the Universe but as a dew-drop to the ocean: yet even a dew-drop exhibits the same infrangible laws of light and the same divine glories that are manifested in the rainbow and the sunset. So it is with a human soul: there are laws in it of righteousness and justice and retribution—laws which cannot be broken by the fictions and illusions of theology, but must be manifested in all places and in all time, now and for all eternity, on earth, in Heaven, in Hell.

XXVII

My dear ——,

I will begin this letter by quoting the end of your last. For when you have thought over the matter I am sure your mind will be so completely changed that unless I send you an exact copy of your own words you will hardly believe you could ever have written them. You are speaking about the theology of St. Paul, and this is what you say: "I presume that Natural Christianity, however glad it may be to shelter itself under Pauline authority in the low estimate it sets on miracles, will find it difficult to digest or swallow Pauline theology. The abstruse and artificial doctrines of the imputation of righteousness, justification by faith, and the atonement, must surely stand at the very antipodes of any religion, Christian, or other, that can claim the name of *natural*."

I do not believe you can ever have given five minutes of attention to these subjects: or if you have, you must have attended, not to St. Paul, but to some voluminous commentator who has buried St. Paul's text under his own and other people's annotations. Cast your commentaries away. Read St. Paul for yourself in the light of his own works and the Old Testament (especially the Septuagint version), and I will guarantee that his general drift shall come out clear and definite enough; and, what is more, you shall acknowledge that his religion is perfectly natural, so natural that you meet exemplifications of it every day of your life, in every family, in your own home, in your own heart. It would be tedious if I were to give you a scheme of Pauline theology and then shew you the naturalness of each part of the scheme. For me it would be long and wearisome; and you too would be inclined to stop me at the end of every other sentence and say "I know that St. Paul says this or that, but how is it natural?" I will therefore begin at the other end, that is to say, with Nature, and endeavour to shew you that the natural history of a child, under favourable circumstances, exhibits the general features of St. Paul's theology, the scheme of Redemption by which the Apostle believed mankind to have been led to God.

We begin then with a baby—a creature wholly selfish (in no bad sense), say, "self-regarding." He is of course "in the flesh," or "walks according to the flesh;" that is to say, he obeys every impulse of the moment, and these impulses are what we call animal impulses. He is conscious of no Law, and therefore of no error: being "without the Law" he "knows not sin." As he grows up, he finds himself making mistakes, trespassing against Nature's rules, playing with fire, for example: and Nature's punishment makes him conscious of mistake, and desirous of avoiding mistake for fear of being punished; that is to say, he learns to avoid playing with fire because he has been burned for it. This is his first introduction to "the Law;" and if he obeys Nature's Law, through fear of Nature's punishment, or hope of Nature's reward, so much the better for him. Hitherto, however, there is no question of sin, only of mistake. But now comes in the parental Law, saying "Do this," "Do not do that." Sometimes he obeys: sometimes, when "the flesh" is too strong, he disobeys. In the latter case he is punished. This new kind of Law is not a machine-like reward or punishment like that of Nature: it is connected with a Will, which is dimly felt by the child to be higher and better than his own, yet constantly opposed to his own. Here then arises a conflict between his strong animal impulses, *i.e.* "the flesh," and a weak nascent impulse of conscience, *i.e.* "the spirit ;" the former bidding him disobey the higher Will, the latter bidding him obey. Even when he disobeys, the spirit has at least the power to make him uneasy in his disobedience, and this uneasiness for the first time reveals in him the nature of sin. Until the Law of the higher Will was thus placed side by side with his own will, and until the deflections of his own will from the higher Will were thus made manifest and rebuked by conscience, the child had no notion of sin. Now he knows it : " by Law has come the knowledge of sin."

As long as he is thus "under the Law" he cannot possibly be righteous ; he can neither be "justified" nor feel "justified." When he is disobedient under the Law, he is conscious of sin ; but when he is obedient under the Law, he is not conscious of peace or inward harmony : the Law stands up, for ever antagonistic to his natural impulses, and he cannot but dislike it, although he acknowledges its claims upon him : consequently, even when he obeys it, he obeys it with a sense of servitude, obeying in the fear of punishment or in the hope of reward. Such actions as are performed in this spirit have no spontaneousness or grace ; they are the tasks of a hireling, mere piece-work—" works," as St. Paul more shortly calls them, or "the works of the Law ; " and "by the works of the Law shall no flesh be justified." During this period he finds no guidance from the spirit of loving obedience, but has to trust in formularies and prescriptions, "do this," "avoid that ;" he fears lest he may do too little, and grudges lest he may do too much : he is in the condition, not of a son, but of a servant working for wages. Just as the Stoic said of the man who was not "wise," that whatever he did, even to the moving of his little finger, was sure to be wrong, so St. Paul taught—and it is the truth—that our every action, as long as we are "under the Law," is void of harmony, beauty, freedom, and spiritual life: it is but obedience to a dead rule; such actions are of the nature of sin and tend to spiritual destruction: "the wages of sin are death."

During this state the raw, half-developed, ungraceful, unharmonized, and ever-erring boy of fifteen appears to have retrograded from the perfectly graceful and unconscious selfishness of the innocent child of four. But it is not so. The knowledge of sin is the stepping-stone to a higher righteousness than could have been obtained by perpetuating the innocence of childhood. Even during the period of the "bondage to the Law" there were occasional intervals of freedom, prophetic of a higher state. Duty, sometimes, shining out before the child as something purer and nobler than a mere inevitable debt, appeared "sweet and honourable;"[1] and whenever Duty thus revealed herself, the child, in freely and ungrudgingly obeying her, was obeying no unworthy emblem of the Father in heaven; and by such obedience his character was strengthened and matured. But now the time has come for another step upwards. The boy disobeys and is forgiven. At first, forgiveness makes no impression on him. He does not understand it, does not believe in it, because he does not quite believe in the author of it; he regards his father as one too far above him to be able to sympathize entirely with his boyish desires and impatience of restraint, too much like a Law to be capable of feeling real pain at his faults. As long as he is in this condition, forgiveness comes to him as the mere remission of penalty; he is glad to "get off," but his heart is not yet touched, and there is therefore no real remission of sin, partly because he has no sufficient

[1] "Dulce et decorum *est pro patria mori.*"

sense of sin, partly because he has no faith in the forgiver.

But at last comes the revelation of the meaning of forgiveness. Some outward sign, a mother's tear, the mere expression of the father's face—it may be this, or it may be something of much longer duration and far more complex— but something at last brings home to him the fact that his sin weighs like a crushing burden upon the heart of some one else, who, in spite of his sin, still loves him and still trusts in him. His parents, he finds—or it may be some brother, sister, or friend—are bearing his sin and carrying his iniquity as if it were their own: the shame and the pain of it, which he feels as a mere unpleasant uneasiness, are causing to others an acute sorrow of which he had not dreamed before. Instead of being savagely angry with him, furious at the mischief he has done, and at the disgrace which he has brought upon them, instead of visiting upon him all the consequences of his fault, his parents are themselves suffering some part of it, themselves crushed down by it: if they punish him, they are not punishing him vindictively but for his good—it is hard indeed to believe this, but he believes it at last—the chastisement of his peace falls upon them as well as upon him; their heart is broken and contrite for his sake; their souls are a sacrifice for his; they feel his sin as if it were their own; they have appropriated his sin; have been identified with his sin; they are "made sin" for him.

Now if the youth has not in him the germ of faith or trust whereby he can believe in the sincerity of these (to him) mysterious and at first inexplicable feelings, why then the parental forgiveness is worse than nothing to him. If he resists its influence and calls it cant or humbug, it hardens instead of softening the boy's heart; and then the little spiritual sensitiveness that he once had, dies rapidly away. In this case "from him that hath not there hath been taken away even that which he seemed to have," and the good-tidings or Gospel of forgiveness has proved, in this case, "a savour of death unto death." But if he has the germ of faith to begin with, then the Gospel works its natural result: "to him that hath there is added, and he hath more abundantly." " Proceeding from faith" the message of forgiveness tends "to the increase of faith."[1] Insensibly he finds himself raised up from his former position to the level of those who have forgiven him ; he is identified with his forgivers in spirit, so that he now sees things as they see them, and for the first time discerns the hatefulness of sin, and hates it as they hate it, and longs to shake it off as a burden alien to his nature. At the same time, finding himself trusted by those in whose truth as well as goodness he himself places trust, he learns a new self-respect even in the moment when he awakens to his past degradation ; he has (he feels it to be true) something within him that may be trusted, some possibility of better things which at once springs up into the reality of fulfilment under the warm breath of affectionate and trustful forgiveness. In other words, righteousness is "imputed to him," and he becomes righteous. The gulf between the parental will and himself is now bridged over by a kind of atonement. The relations which he imagined and created for himself before between his parents and himself, were angry justice on the one side, sullen obedience or open disobedience on the other side : all this is now exchanged for an entirely different relationship, love on both sides, kind control from the one, willing, zealous obedience from the other, resulting in perfect peace and in an atmosphere of mutual goodwill, happiness, joy, favour. For this kind of "favour" we have no exact word in English, but in the Greek Testament it is called by a word which we must translate

[1] Rom. i. 17.

"grace:" the youth then is "no more under the law but under grace." No longer now is he a servant, performing "works;" a community of feeling unites him with those above him, whom he had once regarded as hostile and despotic. No longer the slave of rules and orders, no longer fearing punishment nor drudging for reward, he is quickened by a spirit within him which guides him naturally to do, and to anticipate, not only the bidding, but even the unexpressed wishes, of that higher Will. His whole life is now a service devoted to this new Master; yet he is not a servant, but free, because he serves willingly in a service which is the noblest freedom. The simplest actions are performed in a fresh spirit; all things have become new; the life of the flesh is ended, the life of the spirit has begun. Looking back upon his former self he finds that it is dead; he has died unto sin and risen from the dead that he may live again to righteousness.

Is it necessary for me to trace the parallelism between these phenomena in the life of the individual and the Pauline scheme of the redemption of man? You must have recognized in each step of the development sketched above some feature of the Pauline doctrine. My fear is, not so much that you may fail to acknowledge this, as that you may doubt whether the individual always passes through these phases. But I am confident that it must be so for all who are to be saved: there is no royal road of privilege or miracle by which a man can pass from the innocent selfishness of childhood to the practised righteousness of manhood, without passing through the narrow defiles of the flesh and fighting his battle with sin; nor do I believe that any man has ever been "saved," that is to say, has passed through that struggle so far safely as to attain some thoughtfulness for others, some love of righteousness for its own sake, unless he has received through the Word of God some such revelation as I have described.

The typical revelation of this kind, which sums up all others, is the revelation made by the atonement of Jesus Christ: but that revelation has been a silence for the myriads who have died in ignorance of the very name of Jesus : is there no other way then in which the Word of God has taught them, redeemed them, forgiven them, made atonement for them ? Yes, assuredly the Word of God has been mediating between God and men since men first existed—long before the time when the children of Israel " drank of that Rock which followed them, and that Rock was Christ "—and the chief vehicle of His mediation has been the influence of the righteous on the unrighteous, especially of parents on children. In this influence, the bright and central point has been the power which each man has, in some poor degree, of forgiving, and making atonement for, the sins of others—a power so weak and small, compared with the same power in Christ, that it may be easily ignored by superficial observers ; and some may think to do God honour by ignoring it. But in reality whoso ignores it is ignoring the best gift of God to man. This undeveloped power of forgiving has been that uneffaced likeness of God in which He created us ; and every act of forgiveness, from Adam down to John the Baptist, has been inspired by the Word of God to be a type and prophecy of that great and unique act which sums up and explains all forgiveness, the Atonement made by the Word's own sacrifice. I said above that the mother's tear might for the first time reveal to a child the meaning and power of forgiveness. What the tear of a mother may be to her child, that the Cross of Christ has been to mankind ; the expression as it were, of the Father's pitifulness for His sinful children, revealing to them the meaning, and the pain, of forgiveness.

St. Paul (you will find) in all his epistles recognizes the analogy between the human race and the individual ; and

X

all that he teaches about mankind corresponds to the development I have tried to sketch above. You will be told indeed that the attempt to trace such a parallelism as I have traced above, is an attempt to "read modern thoughts into an ancient author." But do not be in haste to call St. Paul an "ancient author," not at least in any disparaging sense, as if we had outgrown the antiquated limits of his thoughts. Being a man of realities St. Paul dived deep down below the surface of language, cant, and formularies ; he reached the very source and centre of the human heart where righteousness is made. He realized the making of righteousness as a visible process. Others, who have not realized it, think his writings misguided, antique, occasionally untrue. But do not you fail to distinguish between St. Paul's style and St. Paul's thought. He wrote in a hurry ; he did not think in a hurry. The general scheme of his theology needs no excuse, nor allowance, nor patronage. His illustrations of it, arguments in defence of it, even his expressions of it, are, from our point of view, often inadequate ; but his spiritual truths are the deepest truths of human nature, as it may be seen ascending through illusion and frailty to divine knowledge and divine righteousness. St. Paul has been wonderfully obscured by formularizing commentators. The best commentary on him that I know is an ordinary home ; but for a young man, away from home, and in danger of forgetting his childhood, the next best commentary is Shakespeare, and the next to that is Wordsworth, or, from a different point of view, the *In Memoriam*.

Tell me now ; was I wrong in saying that the Pauline scheme of salvation is eminently natural? I do not of course mean materialistic, but natural in the sense of orderly. Where, in the whole of this doctrine, is there any necessity for believing that the Son of God—"born of a woman" and manifested "in the flesh that he might destroy the works of the devil"—did or said anything that involves a suspension of the laws of nature? I have already shewn that the "miracles" wrought by St. Paul himself were in all probability works of healing, and natural; and the manifestations in which Christ "appeared" to him and to the other disciples have been shewn to be, in all probability, visions in accordance with the laws of nature, though representing an objective reality. There is no reference in St. Paul's works to the Miraculous Conception, nor to any of those miracles of Jesus which, if historical, must be admitted to be real miracles. On the other hand there runs through all his epistles an acknowledgment of a continuous spiritual Law, predetermined and inviolable. What else does St. Paul mean by the continual assertion that the calling of the Gentiles, and the "election" of all men, are "predestined?" Perhaps you have never yet appreciated the circumstances which led the Apostle to lay so much stress on the "predestination" apparent in history. I do not think you can ever understand St. Paul's teaching on this subject, as long as you fasten your attention on two or three isolated texts which appear to set it forth. You must look at it as a whole, and have regard to the motive of the author; and then you will find that it is to be understood negatively rather than positively. When St. Paul says "God predestined this, or that," he means, "God did not make a mistake, or change his mind, about this or that: *the gifts and calling of God are without repentance.*"

In setting forth Predestination, St. Paul is always mentally protesting against two tendencies already perceptible to him in the Church, the tendency of the Jews to regard the admission of the Gentiles into the Church as an after-thought, perhaps as a mistake; and the tendency of the Gentiles to regard the Law of

Moses as a complete and useless failure. It was one of St. Paul's main objects to shew that the history of Israel and of the Gentile world revealed a thread of immutable purpose of salvation running through the whole —a purpose to subordinate evil to good, the flesh to the spirit, the Law to the Gospel; so that there has been no mistake, no dislocation of the divine scheme, nor change of the divine will. Although the Apostle always refers things to a Will and not a Law as their ultimate origin, yet the whole tenour of his argument exhibits that Will as being not liable to caprice or accidental shifting, but a Will of predestination, a Law, so to speak, tinged with emotion. No doubt St. Paul, sometimes, in the attempt to shew the immutability of the divine purposes, puts forward somewhat baldly and repellently the insoluble problem of the origin of evil, as if God Himself predestined not only rejection but also the sin that was the cause of rejection. But it was not his intention to exhibit God as originating evil ; and the cause that leads him so to do, or so to appear to do, is his intense desire to exhibit God's mysterious plan of not at once annihilating evil but of utilizing it and subordinating it to good. The foreordained purpose of God before the foundation of the world is the redemption of mankind ; and in order to help men to attain to this height, the flesh, the law, death, yes, even sin itself, are forced to serve as stepping-stones. Hence even in rejection, as well as in election, the Apostle cannot fail to discern the hand of God. There is a Law in all God's doing, and especially in His election. God hath chosen the weak things of this world to confound the strong and the foolish things of this world to confound the wise ; the first-born is rejected, the younger son is chosen. This is not accident ; it is a type of the general law exemplified in the vision of Elijah. Not by the whirlwind or the fire or the earthquake but by the quiet and neglected processes of nature does God perform His mightiest works. This deep truth pervades the doctrine of St. Paul. Pierce through the antique and Oriental integument of his expression, and you will find no other Christian writer who so clearly brings out that the Christian religion is not according to caprice but according to Law.

XXVIII

MY DEAR ——,

You tell me that you have been shewing my letters to some of your young friends, and that they have expressed various objections to non-miraculous Christianity. Some say that I am an "optimist;" others that it is a compromise between faith and reason, and that compromises are always to be rejected; one says that I am for introducing "a new religion;" others that a Gospel of illusion must, by its own shewing, be itself illusive; others, that "these new notions are so vague that they can never be put into a definite shape, and they are so mixed up with theories and fancies and suppositions of error in every period of the Church, that they can never commend themselves to the masses."

Do you know what "cant" means, and why it was so called? "Cant" is the sort of language used (not always deceitfully) when a man "chants," or utters in a kind of sing-song, words that he has not felt himself, or, if he has ever felt, has ceased to feel, through the too frequent use of them. Hence he cannot speak them, but "sing-songs" them, "chants" or "cants" them. Now I take leave to think that two or three of the objections above-mentioned come under this head of "cant." I mean that your young objectors, not knowing exactly at the moment what to say about opinions that are new and require some thought to understand or criticise, and being desirous of saying something at the moment, and something, if possible, that shall be brief and smart, say what they have heard other people say about other sets of opinions which have some affinity of sound with mine. This is a very common habit with inferior professional reviewers, who are bound to say something readable and epigrammatic for limited remuneration and consequently in limited time : but your friends have not come to that yet, and are therefore not to be so easily excused.

"Optimist!" How can a man who believes in a real Satan be an optimist? I thought an optimist was one who believed the world to be the best of all possible worlds. This I do not, and cannot, believe. I trust indeed that a time may come when we may be optimists after a fashion ; when we shall look back, in God, upon the universal sum of things and find that it has been the best possible under the circumstances, and that evil has been marvellously subordinated to good : but I never can believe that a Universe in which God defeats Satan is better than a Universe in which God reigns unresisted ; and therefore, as to this "best of all possible worlds," I rest always humbly silent. Some people may believe, if they can, that evil is another form of good ; that the world is like one of those spectroscopes—I think they call them—where several different pictures on a round card, each meaningless by itself, are converted into one significant picture by whirling the card round too quickly for the eye to follow. In the same way they seem to suppose they can take little pictures of oppression, adultery, murder, and the other myriad shapes of sin, spin them round fast enough along with other little pictures of temperance, purity, peace, and all the virtues ; and the whole becomes a panorama of moral perfection ! Argue thus who will ; I cannot.

If I am not an optimist in my view of this world, you will surely not accuse me of optimism in my views of the next. Do my notions of heaven and hell encourage any one to be selfish and luxurious or idle now, in the hope that he will be let off easily hereafter? Have I not said that there will be no "letting off"? That God will do the best thing for Nero—is that do you think likely to make Nero altogether an optimist in the life to come? I think He will do the best thing for me ; but I sometimes shiver when I say it ; awe possesses me, awe mingled with trust, but certainly not without a touch of fear. Assuredly the certainty of retribution in heaven makes me no optimist for myself or others, as to the life after death. In one sense only am I an optimist, that I believe that the best will ultimately prevail, and that faith, hope, and love, will prove the dominant powers in the Universe. This I believe, and to this belief I cling as a most precious hope, to be cherished by action as well as by meditation ; but this is not, I think, what is ordinarily meant by optimism ; and certainly it does not encourage the spirit of *laissez faire* which optimism is supposed to breed.

Next as to "compromise." The ordinary cant about "compromise" is sometimes the lazy expedient of those who wish to avoid the trouble of coming to a decision, and to shelter their indolence under a noble censoriousness What they mean by "compromise" is any theory that attributes results to more than one cause. It is generally very easy to elaborate some extreme theory which shall explain almost everything by some single cause, by Faith, for example, on the one side, or by Reason on the other ; and it is equally easy for the advocates on either side to demolish the theory of their adversaries ; but it is far from easy afterwards to shew how, and to what extent, *both* causes are accountable for the result which has been fictitiously attributed to a single cause. Now the two extreme parties, in their contests, afford us fine cut-and-thrust exhibitions ; the via media exhibits an organized campaign. The theatrical multitude, which does not care in the least about truth, but delights in intellectual slashers, soon finds it dull work, after clapping an exciting *mêlée*, to have to sit still and listen to a dispassionate and impartial discussion ; so they cry " compromise " and hiss. But the term is a misnomer. " Compromise," or " mutual promise," cannot describe a legitimate conclusion that hits the mark missed by two previously divergent shots. It is as if A were to hit the top of the target, and B the bottom, and then both A and B were to fall foul of C, and accuse him of " compromising," because he pierces the bull's eye half way between the two. " Compromise " often implies a failure of exact justice ; as when Smith thinks Jones owes him 50*l*., and Jones thinks he owes Smith only 40*l*. ; and they " split the difference " and make it 45*l*. ; both of them thinking that the arrangement is unjust, but both preferring the injustice to the expensive formalities of legal justice. This is " compromise," and illogical ; but there is none of this illogicality in a fair impartial discussion avoiding previous bias.

So in the present instance. Some have been biassed in favour of Faith, others in favour of Reason ; some have accepted as historical all the miracles and mighty works in the Old and New Testament indiscriminately, others have rejected all indiscriminately ; some have declared that every word in the Old and New Testament (I don't quite know how they have got rid of the difficulty of various readings) is exactly inspired and every detail historically true ; others, that there are so many errors and illusions that the books may be put aside as no better than myths : some have said that, since we cannot worship an unknown Being, we must worship the human race ; others that, since we cannot worship our very degraded selves, we must worship some being altogether different from ourselves : some have said that Christ is

God, and have ignored His humanity ; others have said
that He was a "mere man," and therefore not divine.
Now in all these cases the truth lies between the two
extremes. Man derives religious truth from Faith, but
Faith assisted by Reason ; Christ did not perform
miracles, but He did perform mighty works ; the Old and
New Testament, like all other vehicles of revelation,
contain illusion, but illusion preserving and protecting
truth ; we must not worship ourselves, and yet we cannot
worship one who is altogether different from ourselves ;
Christ is a man, and yet Christ is God. But to all these
conclusions we are not led by "mutual promise," give
and take of any kind, but by full and unbiassed consideration of all sides of the subject, knowing that (for the
present at all events) we shall displease all, both the
orthodox and heterodox alike.

So far from suggesting any compromise between Faith
and Reason, I have merely pointed out that the provinces
of the two are, to a very large extent, distinct, so that
many of their operations can be performed altogether
independently. I have never said, "Do not follow out
the conclusions of your Reason in this or that instance
because you would be led to inconvenient results," but,
"Follow out the conclusions of your Reason in every
instance and presently acknowledge that you are led, in
some cases, to results so absurd and unpractical that you
must infer Reason to be out of its province in these cases.
Reason your utmost for example about a First Cause and
Predestination and the Origin of Evil and the like ; but
then, when you have come to the conclusion that, logically
speaking, it is equally absurd to suppose that the world
had no cause, and that the First Cause had no cause, give
the subject up as being beyond the syllogistic powers."
Surely there is no unworthy compromise here, nothing
but common sense ! Wherever historical facts are affirmed

in religion, I have said that the accounts of those facts are to be judged upon evidence and by Reason alone ; here Faith and Hope have no place; history in the New Testament is to be judged like history in Thucydides.

In reality it is not I with my via media that am guilty of compromise; it is the Hyper-orthodox (if I may use a term that is nominally meaningless but really quite intelligible) and the Agnostic. For the Hyper-orthodox say " Accept the Scriptures in a lump." Why ? " Because it would be so very inconvenient not to have an infallible guide." Of course they do not say so in these precise words : but this is what their replies ultimately amount to. Again the Agnostics say, " Reject the Scriptures *in toto.*" Why ? " Because it would be so very inconvenient to weigh evidence and discriminate the true from the false." It is these, not I, who are calling in emotion to do the work of Reason, and who (partly, I think, to avoid facing unpalatable facts) force Reason to make a compromise with prejudice. " Convenience," as I have pointed out in a previous letter, may be a legitimate basis for accepting as a Law of Nature the tried and tested suggestions of the Imagination ; but it is not a legitimate basis on which to construct a belief in the genuineness of the Book of Daniel or the Second Epistle of St. Peter.

Let me mention one point where, in appearance, but not in reality, my theory is liable to the charge of compromise : I mean the discussion of the Miraculous Conception and the Supernatural Incarnation. In discussing the Miraculous Conception I have advised you to trust to your Reason alone, because here you have to deal with a statement of physical facts, true or untrue, and to be proved or disproved by evidence ; but as regards the Supernatural Incarnation and the statement that the Word of God became a human spirit, I have pointed out that here we have a statement that cannot be proved or disproved by simple historical evidence, nor even by miracle, because even if an archangel descended from heaven to trumpet forth a "Yes" or "No" to the world, the message might be from the Devil. If then we are to believe in the Incarnation we must have a twofold testimony. First must come the historical evidence indicating the words, and deeds, and character, and results, of the life of Christ, the truth of which must be judged by the Reason; and then there must come the witness of the conscience exclaiming "This life is divine; this man is one with God." Consequently it is quite possible to accept the Supernatural Incarnation while denying the Miraculous Conception; and this I have felt obliged to do. But where is the compromise or inconsistency? I am compelled by evidence and Reason to deny the truth of the Miraculous Conception, on account of the very small amount of evidence for it and the very large amount of evidence against it; I am equally compelled by evidence and Faith to accept the Supernatural Incarnation, because the evidence convinces me that a certain life has been lived on earth, and my conscience convinces me that this life could not have been lived by any being who was not one with God.

Are my accusers equally free from confusion? I think not. Ask the Hyper-orthodox why they believe in the Miraculous Conception in spite of the silence of all the earliest documents; they will reply, (if you penetrate below their first superficial answers, such as, "Because it is in the Bible," "Because I have believed it from my youth upward," and the like), "Jesus must have been born miraculously, because He was the Son of God" —a confusion of things historical and spiritual, and a manifest expulsion of Reason from her rightful province. Again, ask the Agnostic why he does not believe that

Jesus was the Son of God ; he will reply that he sees no proof of the fact, nor even of the existence of a God ; and if you press him to define what he means by "proof" of the existence of a God, you will find that he wholly ignores the influence of Imagination as a means of arriving at truth, and that he requires some kind of evidence that shall entirely dispense with Faith. Thus the Hyperorthodox and the Agnostic are equally guilty, the one of dispossessing Reason, the other of dispossessing Faith, from their rightful provinces ; and they accuse me of "compromising," not because I really compromise, but because I pursue truth at the cost of some trouble, while they—partly perhaps to avoid the pain of thinking, and the prospect of colliding with hard unpleasing truths— pursue severally that form of untruth to which they are inclined by prejudice.

And now for the next objection, that "this is a new religion." How can men give the name of a new religion to that which proclaims as the one means of salvation the Eternal Word of God believed in of old by Jews as well as by Christians ? Or is it a mark of novelty to accept Jesus of Nazareth as that Word incarnate ? The one thing new about the opinions put forward in my letters is this—that it is not a necessary condition for believing in Christ, that men should accept a number of historical statements which are, and have been, doubted by many honest seekers after truth. I believe I might add, without any exaggeration, that the statements which I impugn are rejected by so large a number of those who are most competent to judge, that, in spite of many inducements—some richly substantial, some nobly spiritual—many of the ablest and best educated young men of England cannot in these days be persuaded to become ministers of the religion which appears to insist on them. Beyond this protest, there is nothing, or very little, that is new about the theory which

I have endeavoured to set forth. I do not protest against any moral abuse in the Church of England or the orthodox churches—such abuses as made a great gulf in the days of Luther between the Roman Catholic Church and the Protestants, when indulgences for sins were sold by the cart-load. Possibly indeed the protracted belief in the miraculous, when it has long outlived the conditions which made it natural or pardonable, may tend to produce some moral evil ; some over-estimation of ostentatious and, so to speak, theatrical force ; some depreciation of the quiet processes by which God has mostly taught and shaped mankind ; some latent trust in a capricious God, who will not "reward men according to their works" but will exercise a dispensing power at the Day of Judgment. I say this may possibly soon happen, if it has not already begun to happen ; but at all events it is at present latent, and it is not on any ground of this kind that I am advocating a new view of the Old and New Testament. My object has been not to destroy the old belief, but to remove certain obstacles which tend to prevent people from embracing the essence of the old belief. The existence of a God, the immortality of the soul, the conflict between God and Satan, the redemption of mankind through the sacrifice of the eternal Son of God incarnate in Jesus of Nazareth, the Resurrection of the Lord Jesus, the operation of the Holy Spirit, the certainty of a heaven and hell, the efficacy of prayer, the ultimate triumph of goodness and God—all these things I steadfastly believe. But I see not the slightest reason why, in order to hold fast these precious truths, I should be compelled to believe that Joshua stopped the sun (or the earth ?) or that an ass talked with a human voice, or that the incarnate Son of God drowned two thousand swine or destroyed a fig-tree with a word.

I am probably doing no more than give utterance to

thoughts which have been already expressed by others, or which, though unexpressed, are latent in thousands of doubtful and expectant souls. But even were it otherwise, even were it granted that the form of Christianity set forth in my letters has some points of novelty, is mere novelty to suffice for its condemnation?—and this in our century, when God has been teaching and is teaching His children so much that is new in every department of knowledge! Is it absolutely incredible that the same Supreme Teacher who allowed some nineteen centuries to elapse between the Promise and the promised Seed, should allow another nineteen centuries to elapse between the Seed and the Harvest? Is it inconsistent that He who has led men to the truths of science through mistakes and illusions should lead men by the same paths to spiritual truth? How often must the Law of Illusion be inculcated before we take it to heart? Illusions have encompassed spiritual truth for Israel, for the Jews, for the Twelve in their Master's lifetime, for the first generation of Christians, and for every subsequent generation down to the time of Luther. So much we Protestants are bound to admit. Are we not then intolerably presumptuous in assuming that illusions must have suddenly disappeared in the fifteenth century and have left the theological atmosphere for the first time since the creation of the world free from all spiritual refraction? How much humbler and truer to suppose that every century and every generation has its special cloud of illusions through which in due course we must all toil upward, penetrating layer after layer of the illusive mist till we reach at last the summit of the hill of Truth!

I find I have left myself too little time to answer your last two objections as to the "vagueness" of my views and their inability to "commend themselves to the masses." I will try to answer them in my next letter.

XXIX

My dear ――――,

I have been thinking over your objection that my notions are "vague;" feeling that there is some truth in it, but that your words do not quite express your probable meaning. I think you mean, not that the "notions" are vague, but that the proofs are vague. The "notions" are in the Creeds, if you interpret the Creeds spiritually: and I do not think that the Creeds are more "vague" when interpreted spiritually than when interpreted literally. The spiritual Resurrection of Christ, for example—is it more vague than the material Resurrection? If you admit that there is a spirit in man, and that this spirit is made apparently powerless by death, is it "vague" to say that the spirit of Jesus, after passing through this state of death, manifested itself to the disciples in greater power than ever? Even those who maintain the material Resurrection admit that it would be a mere mockery without the spiritual Resurrection, and that the latter is the essence of the act: so that to declare the statement of the spiritual Resurrection of Jesus to be "vague," appears to be equivalent to declaring that *any* statement of the *essential* Resurrection of Jesus is "vague." Again, redemption from sin is a spiritual notion, redemption from the flames of a material hell is a material notion; but is the former more "vague" than the latter? If so, then we are led to this conclusion, that all spiritual notions are more vague than material notions; and the vagueness which you censure is a necessary characteristic of every religion that approaches God as He ought to be approached, I mean, as a Spirit and through the medium of spiritual conceptions. But to my mind you are not justified in thus using the word "vague," which ought rather to be applied to notions wanderingly and shiftingly defined; as for example, if I defined the Resurrection of Jesus as being at one time the rising of His body, at another the rising of His Spirit; or if I spoke of redemption, now as deliverance from sin, and now as deliverance from punishment. Convict me of such inconsistencies, and I will submit to be called "vague;" but at present I plead, "Not guilty."

However I think you meant that the proofs, and not the notions were vague; and here, although you should not have used the word "vague," I will admit that you would have been right if you had said that they were "complex" and "more easy to feel than to define." No doubt the proof of Christ's divinity from the material Resurrection is simple and straightforward enough: "It is impossible that a man's body could have arisen from the grave, and that the man could have afterwards lived with his friends on earth for several days, and then have ascended into heaven, if he had not been under the express protection of God; and such a man we are prepared to believe, if he tells us that he is the Son of God." That certainly would seem to a large number of minds a very plain and straightforward argument —as plain as Paley's *Evidences*. No trust, no faith, no affection, is here requisite: nothing is needed except that rough and ready assumption—in which we are all disposed to acquiesce—that any altogether exceptional and startling power must come from God. It must be admitted that this sort of proof would be cogent as well as direct. Let a man rise from the dead to-morrow, and transport his body through closed doors, and say that he is Christ, and then mount up to the clouds and disappear; and I doubt not

Y

many of those who saw him would cry " This must be the Christ," without so much as enquiring what manner of man he was. But cogent and popular and delightfully simple though it may be, this is not the kind of proof on which Jesus appears to have relied, or by which Jesus has produced a spiritual change in the hearts of mankind. The very fact that no trust or faith or affection is needed in such a demonstration, unfits it for spiritual purposes. In order to believe in the Resurrection of Jesus, a man needs the testimony of all his powers, emotional as well as intellectual, trust and love as well as reason ; and I have endeavoured to shew above that the whole of the training of the human Imagination, and all the mysterious natural provisions which have stimulated the eye of the mind to see what the eye of the body cannot see, have contributed to bring about the faith in the risen Saviour. As we are to love God with our strength and with our mind as well as with our heart and our soul, so are we to believe in Christ with the same collective energy. The proof therefore of Christ's Resurrection and of Christ's divinity is intended to be, in a certain sense, complex, because it is intended to appeal to our every faculty and to be based upon our every experience.

But "this form of Christianity can never commend itself to the masses." Objection in the shape of prophecy is always difficult to meet, and not often worth meeting. However, this prophecy has so specious a sound that it deserves some reply. But first let me ask, Does the present form of Christianity commend itself to the masses? Surely not to the very poor, that is to say, not to the class to whom Christ appears to have specially addressed Himself. And even among the classes which retain the tradition of worshipping Christ, has Christianity been such as would commend itself to Christ? Has not our religion been too often divorced from morality? Has there been

dominant among us that habit of mutual helpfulness—
"comforting one another," as St. Paul calls it—which is
the criterion of a truly Christian nation? Have not the
laws in almost all cases, until the French Revolution, been
made in the interests of the rich, rather than in the interests
of the poor ; and where the poor have been considered,
has not the consideration arisen largely from the fear of
violence and revolution? There has been a certain amount
of alms-giving, or legacy-leaving, on the part of the minority
who have laid themselves out to lead religious lives ; and
there has always been a still more select minority who
have been imbued with a truly Christian enthusiasm for
their fellow-creatures, a passionate desire to do something
for Christ, and to leave the world a little better for their
having lived: but the great unheeding mass of men in
Christian countries has rolled on in its selfish path, less
selfish certainly, less brutishly intent on present pleasure
than the masses of heathendom, and indirectly humanized
and leavened by a thousand Christian influences, but
still not more than superficially Christian. The reason for
this comparative failure has been, in part, that Christ
has not been rightly presented to the hearts of the people.
Too often it has not been Christ at all—it has been
but a lifeless semblance of Christianity—to which they
have given their adhesion. The fear of hell, the hope
of heaven—these have been often the chief motives of
religion ; and alms-giving, church-going, Bible-reading,
and the use of the sacraments, have been the means by
which men have thought they could escape the one and
secure the other. Asking still further the cause for this
perversion, by which Christ has been converted into a
second Law, we find that in some cases, and more
especially in recent times, it appears to have arisen
in part from the miraculous element in our religion.
This has made Christ unreal to some of us by taking

Him out of the reach of our sympathies and affection; this also has artificialized our religious conceptions and divorced our religion from morality by making us think that God will suspend the laws of spiritual nature for us, as He has suspended the laws of material nature for Christ and Christ's Apostles. Hence has arisen too often a pitiable and preposterous reversal of the Pauline theology. We have "died" unto Christ, and "risen again" unto the Law. " Grace " has fled away, and, with it, all natural and harmonious morality; and the whole duty of a Christian man has been degraded to a routine of " works."

It is for this cause that the morality of Agnostics frequently surpasses the morality of professing Christians. The philanthropy of the former, so far as it goes, is at all events perfectly natural. They do not love their brother man in order to obey the Gospel or save their own souls; they love because they must love. Christ's leaven is often in their hearts without any of the corruptions of a conventional Christianity. They do not believe in a capricious Heaven and Hell, but they are drawn towards goodness, kindness, justice and mutual helpfulness, whenever and wherever they see them ; and such worship as they have, they give to these qualities. Hence also in foreign politics the working people and the Agnostics often manifest a much purer and more Christian feeling than church-goers. For the Hyper-orthodox, foreign politics lie outside the Bible ; and whatsoever lies outside the Bible lies, for them, outside morality : but the Agnostic makes no such distinction ; he does not believe that the laws of right and wrong can be miraculously suspended in favour of his own country. The disbelief in a future Heaven makes the poor indisposed to tolerate present remediable miseries in the hope of coming compensation. Hence they shew a much stronger determination not to put up with a state of things in which the happiness and prosperity of a whole nation are purchased by the misery of one class. They are willing enough individually to make sacrifices for one another, and, in bad times the working people have sometimes collectively borne considerable burdens with an admirable patience; but that the unwilling wretchedness of some should form the basis of the prosperity of the rest, and that the rest should be content to have it so—this they cannot endure; and sooner than this, they would prefer to see every class in the nation pulled down two or three degrees in wealth and refinement, if thereby the lowest class could be raised a single degree.

Rich church-goers are far more ready to acquiesce in present inequalities, sometimes consoling themselves with the thought that in heaven all these evils will be redressed, sometimes fortifying their acquiescence in the inevitable with a text of Scripture. But the poor declaim passionately against the Bible, when thus quoted—as being a mere instrument in the hands of the rich, and the priests their accomplices, to keep the miserable in a state of contentment with their misery. It is a pity that the poor should be embittered by misrepresentations against that which is pre-eminently the poor man's Book; for no tribune or democrat more persistently than the Bible takes the side of the oppressed, or more emphatically declares that it is part of God's method to raise up the poor from the dunghill and to fill the hungry with good things, while He casts down the princes and sends the rich empty away. But the fact remains that, even when he raves against his own Book, the poor man is raving in the spirit of the Book. It is not in accordance with the Bible—and still less in accordance with the spirit of the New Testament and of Christ—that any nation should tolerate and perpetuate the misery of a class in order that the whole nation may prosper. Indeed in such a nation permanent prosperity—in any sense, and much more in the Christian sense—is quite impossible. Even though they may suppress rebellion and escape revolution for the time, the governing classes cannot escape the spiritual evils that must ultimately spring from that comfortable acquiescence in the wretchedness of others to which they may give the name of resignation but to which Christ would have given the name of hypocrisy. Material misery *may* imply the immorality of those who are forced to endure it; but it *must* imply the immorality and spiritual degradation of those who acquiesce in it because it does not come nigh them, and because "the Bible says it must be so." Let but such Pharisaism continue for a generation, and it will have gone far to extinguish the purest of religions and to prepare the way for revolutionary strife.

It appears then that what is called "socialism" is really nothing but a narrow and unwise form of Christianity; narrow because it excludes the rich from its sympathies, and unwise because, instead of going to the root of evils, it simply aims at the branches; capable also, of course, (like every other theory) of being made to appear immoral, when adopted for self-interested or vindictive purposes—yet nevertheless containing much more of the Spirit of Christ than that selfish form of Christianity which has for its sole object the salvation of the individual. Socialism owes all that is good in it to Christ.

The gigantic evil of slavery (which is antagonistic to all true socialism) after a contest of eighteen centuries, has succumbed at last in Christian countries to Christ's Spirit and to no other champion. Do you suppose that it perished owing to the "march of intellect," or the discoveries of science, or the general refinement and rise in the standard of comfort and happiness among mankind? There is no reason at all for thinking so. The Law of Moses, as you know, recognized, though it controlled and mitigated, the institution of slavery. The race that gave birth to Socrates, Aristotle, Sophocles, Phidias, Euclid, Archimedes, and Ptolemy, was unable so much as to conceive of a state of society where slavery should not exist: civilization appeared to them to require the servitude of the masses as its necessary foundation. It was not cruelty or callousness that prompted Aristotle to divide "tools" into two classes, "lifeless" and "living" —under which latter head came slaves: it was want of faith in human nature. "Who would do the scullion-work in the great household of humanity if there were no slaves?" Such was the question which perplexed the great philosophers of antiquity and which Christ came to answer by making Himself the slave of mankind and classing Himself among the scullions. How strangely dull and unappreciative do those words of Renan sound, that, if you deduct from what Christ taught, what other people have taught before Him, little will be left that is original! "Taught!" It was not the teaching, it was the doing. Nay, it was not the doing, it was the inbreathing into mankind of a new Spirit, by means of doing, that ultimately destroyed slavery. "Even as the Son of man came not to be ministered unto but to minister and to give his life a ransom for many"—the Spirit that dictated these words, dictated also the death upon the Cross; and this Spirit has destroyed slavery and will establish true socialism upon earth.

"But this Spirit of Christ has never been fully obeyed or even understood by His followers: even St. Paul does not seem to have understood that Christianity was incompatible with slavery." You are quite right. The Spirit of Christ has never yet been fully obeyed, and, when we thus obey it, life will be heaven. Do you not see that your objection ignores the fact that we are not yet in heaven, and that Christianity is to be a gradual growth? Are you not a little like the child who sows his mustard-seed at night and comes down next morning expecting to see the great tree in which the birds of the air ought to have built their nests? The important question is whether the Christian Spirit so far as it has been obeyed, has worked well; so that we may trust it to lead us still further forward into practical ameliorations of our existence, whether individual or national. But to expect it to do everything in eighteen hundred years, is to forget all the teaching of history, astronomy, and geology, three voices that unite in proclaiming that the Hand of God works slowly.

And further, as to your objection that even St. Paul did not realize the incompatibility between Christianity and slavery, what follows from that? Nothing I suppose except a confirmation of the words in the Fourth Gospel, that the followers of Christ must not depend entirely upon St. Paul, but upon that Spirit which shall "guide us into all truth." To my mind it is refreshing and delightful to confess—as I am sure St. Paul himself would have been the first to confess—that he had not fully realized all the consequences to which the Spirit of Christ would lead posterity. I believe that St. Paul wished slaves to take every lawful opportunity of becoming free, but that he would by no means have encouraged slaves to run away or to rise violently against their masters. If he had enencouraged them, and if he had universally succeeded, he would have caused the whole Empire, all civilized society, to collapse at once. Was he wrong in not causing this? I am not prepared to say so. I think he shewed more statesmanlike and Christian intuition in doing nothing of the kind. But he did much. He had no slaves of his own, you may be sure; he worked like a slave all night, that he might preach all day: he bore fetters like a slave, and was proud to call himself a slave for the sake of Christ;

he inveighed against the spirit of slavery, declaring that in Christ " there is neither bond nor free ; " and on the only occasion that we know of, when he had to mediate in a practical way between an angry master and a runaway slave, he sent the man back to his master without conditions or stipulations, but with a letter that was equivalent to an emancipation : "For perhaps he was therefore parted from thee for a season that thou shouldest have him for ever ; no longer as a slave, but more than a slave, a brother beloved, specially to me, but how much rather to thee, both in the flesh and in the Lord. If then thou countest me a partner, receive him as myself." Was not this, practically and morally, more efficacious than if the Apostle had fulminated against the master Philemon fiery utterances about the rights of man and the incompatibility between Christianity and slavery ? Was not Onesimus more sure of being emancipated by the quiet apostolic method ? Was not Philemon likely to feel a quickened sense of new and higher duty when the Spirit of Christ was breathed into his heart by these touching and affectionate words, than if a Pauline edict had confronted him with a "Thou shalt" and "Thou shalt not"? St. Paul's method has been the method of the Spirit of Christ: for eighteen centuries Christ has been saying to men, not "All slavery is unlawful," but to each master about each individual slave, "If then thou countest Me a partner, receive him as Myself." Hence by degrees has been shaped a conviction that slavery in itself is against the will of God.

But the destruction of slavery has not destroyed other problems of life which still await their solution from Christian socialism. When men cease to work from the compulsion of a master, they either give up working, or they work for some other motive—their own subsistence, or their own comfort, luxury, avarice, ambition, the mere pleasure and interest of work, or for the sake of others. Are people to give up working? And, if they work, which of these motives is to take the place of the old bestial coercion which prevailed in the days of slavery? These are the great questions of the present, affecting the happiness, morality, and religion of the whole human race. True Christians and true socialists are here at one. "If a man will not work, neither let him eat" is their answer to the first question; and the more we can combine to make the drone feel that he is out of place in the hive, and that he must either conform to the hive's ways or betake himself elsewhither, the better will it be morally, and therefore ultimately better in all respects, for the inhabitants of the hive. As to the second question, socialists and moralists agree that each must work for the sake of others, and, as far as possible, for all. To my mind, therefore, one of the most hopeful signs of the times is to be discerned in the spread of the higher socialist spirit which protests against making competition the basis of national prosperity. Disguise it as you may, competition contains an ugly element which was clearly brought out by its first eulogist, the practical agricultural Hesiod, who tells us that there are two kinds of strife, namely, war and competition. The latter, he says, is good; for it rouses even the sluggard to action, when he sees his neighbour hastening to wealth:

"— this strife is good for mortals,
And potter *envieth* potter and carpenter carpenter."

This is the plain truth. Competition is always in danger of producing "envy," and, when it is carried consistently to its extreme—as where a large manufacturer undersells and ruins small manufacturers that he may secure a monopoly—it verges on that other kind of strife which Hesiod has himself described as "blameful;" it becomes a kind of war, and is manifestly unchristian. Christianity might have been therefore expected to protest against it; but it has not done so: that task has been reserved for the informal kind of Christianity called socialism. But very much more than protest is needed. The problem of competition and how to dispense with it—or how to restrain it while remedying its evils—is far more complex than that of slavery. Some people regard it as an inherent law of human society, a natural and continuous development of the law of the struggle for existence which we have inherited from our remotest ancestry. Others, while admitting this primæval origin, hope that, as progressive man has worked out from his nature much else of the baser element, so he may in time eliminate this also. But, if any success is to be attained, all sorts of experiments will have to be tried; all sorts of failures will have to be encountered; and it may be that in the end the Pauline method of dealing with slavery may be found the best means of dealing with competition—not so much protesting and fulminating, but the earnest, informal action of individual enthusiasm. Action like St. Paul's may prepare the way for legislation; but, without change of temper, mere legislation cannot permanently help a people to deal with a great social difficulty.

In the solution of the complicated problems presented by competition, socialism, when severed from Christianity, labours (1885) under most serious disadvantages. Ignoring Christ, it reads amiss the whole of the history of the past and is in danger of making terrible mistakes in the future. Even where it avoids revolutionary extravagances, it is tempted to trust far too much to force, moral if not physical coercion, legislative enactments, and other shapes of what St. Paul would call " Law." Looking up to no Leader in heaven, it does not feel sufficiently sure of ultimate success. " He that believeth," says the prophet, "shall not make haste:" now socialism has no firm basis of belief and therefore is disposed to "make haste," not always the haste of energy, sometimes the spasmodic haste of self-distrust and error, followed perhaps by dejection or inaction. Its neglect of the true religion leads it into political as well as religious mistakes. Taking too little account of sentiments, imaginations, and associations, it aims at a merely material prosperity which, if attained, would leave the minds of men still vacant and craving more ; and besides, it proceeds by methods which excite alarm and distrust in many well-wishers. The most serious evil of all is that the leaders of the socialist movement, if they themselves see no Leader above them, are actuated by no sense of loyalty and affection such as Christians should feel for Christ, and consequently are far more exposed to the dangers arising from their own individual weaknesses and shortcomings. Their mainspring of action is a passionate enthusiasm for poor toiling humanity : but how if humanity shews itself to them at times in its basest aspects, ungrateful, suspicious, mean and shabby, timorous and traitorous, quite unworthy of their devotion ? Are they to serve such a god as this ? And it is a perishable god too ; for must not all things perish, and the earth itself become ultimately as vacant as the moon ? For so vile a master as this, then, are they to endure to be humiliated and attacked by the rich and powerful, envied and slandered by rival leaders, occasionally suspected even by the very poor to whom they are giving their lives ? In moments of depression, when thoughts like these occur—as occur they must—it is hard indeed for a leaderless leader of men to refrain from flinging up his task, or from continuing to pursue it out of mere shame of inconsistency, or mere love of occupation, excitement, and power. When that change comes over the tribune of the poor, all is over with him. His work is done, though he may have done nothing. Outwardly such a man's conduct may be little changed, but inwardly his spirit is dead within him. His religion—for it was a religion to him—is now dead ; and sooner or later his changed influence must make itself felt in an infection of deadness spreading through the whole of the multitudes whom he once inspired.

It is for these reasons that I look to a simpler form of Christianity as the future religion of the masses ; first because I see that the most active religious forces of the present day are already unconsciously following on the lines traced by Christ's spirit ; and secondly, because these movements already exhibit a deficiency which the worship of Christ alone can fill up.

The worship of Christ as the type and King of men helps to solve the problems of the individual as well as those of the nation. As long as human nature is what it is, as long as friends and families are parted by death, as long as the mind is liable to be weighed down by depression, and the body to be racked by physical pain, so long will there be hours when we shall all look upward and demand some other consolation than the commonplace ; " These misfortunes are common to all." Stripped of all myth and miracle, the life and death and triumph of Christ convey to the simplest heart the simplest answer that can be given to the irrepressible question, " Whence comes this misery ? " From the cross of Christ there is sent back to each of us this answer, " We know not fully ; but our Leader bore it, and good came of it in the end." And when we stand at the brink of the grave and ask, " What is death ? " again the answer comes back from the same source, " We know not fully ; but He passed through it and He still lives and reigns."

But besides the powerful influence of religion in the critical and exceptional moments of our lives, the influence of Christ would come full of strength and blessing to the working men of England even if they acknowledged Him, at first, in the most inarticulate of creeds, as the man whom they admired most: "We used to think that Christ was a fiction of the priests; at all events not a man like us in any way; a different sort of being altogether; one who could do what he liked—so people said—and turn the world upside down if he pleased: and then we could not make him out at all. Why, thought we, did he not turn the world upside down and make it better, if he could? It was all a mystery to us. But now we find he was a man after all, like us; a poor working man, who had a heart for the poor, and wanted to turn the world upside down, but could not do it at once; and he went a strange way, and a long way round, to do it; but he has come nearer doing it, spite of his enemies, than any man we know; and now that we understand this, we say—though we don't understand it all or anything like it—'He is the man for us.'" I say that even if this rudimentary feeling of gratitude and admiration for their great Leader could possess the hearts of English working men—and this is surely not too much to expect—much would come from even this inadequate worship. And, for myself, I unhesitatingly declare that I would sooner be in the position of a working man who doubts about Heaven and Hell and even about God, but can say of Christ, "He is the man for me," than I would be in the position of the well-to-do manufacturer who is persuaded of the reality of Heaven and Hell and of the truth of all the theology of the Church of England, but can reconcile his religion with the deliberate establishment of a colossal fortune on the ruin of his fellow creatures.

But I do not believe that the feeling of the working man for Jesus of Nazareth could long confine itself to admiration. It is not so easy to make a happy nation or a happy world as the working man thinks: and this he will soon find out. When sanitation, education, culture, science, political rearrangements, enlargements for the poor, and restrictions for the rich, have all done their best and failed—as they necessarily must fail, unless helped by something more—then the working man will find what that "something more" is, without which nothing effectual can be done. Then he will perceive that, after all, unless there is a spirit of mutual concession in classes and individuals, no Acts of Parliament can ever be devised to secure lasting prosperity and concord. Then he will awaken to the fact that Jesus of Nazareth revealed and exemplified that spirit of concession or self-sacrifice, and that it was by this means that He went as far as He did toward "turning the world upside down;" and so he will be gradually led still further to see that the way which He went was after all not such a very "long way round," but a divine way, a way truly worthy of the Son of God. I believe that the recognition of this single fact would go further than even the recognition of the marvellous phenomena which manifested the Resurrection of Christ, to convince working men that the man who possessed this sublime intuition into spiritual truth, and the perfect unselfishness and self-control needful to give effect to his plans for the raising up of mankind, must be no other than the Son of God. The rest would follow. They would find they had been all their lives on a wrong track in their search after the divine reality; worshipping brute force while protesting against it; bowing in their hearts to pomp, and wealth, and high birth, even while they professed to deride them; despising things familiar and near; gaping in stupid servile admiration at things far and unknown; yet all the time God was near them, among them, in them; the Spirit of God was none other than the spirit of true socialism; the Son of God was none other than the poor and lowly Workman of Nazareth.

APPENDIX

APPENDIX

XXX

My Dear ———,

Excuse my delay in answering your letter of last month. The fact is I have not so much leisure as I had. I was glad indeed to hear from you (last Christmas, I think) that you could not so lightly put away the worship and service of Christ as you had felt disposed, or compelled to do, some eighteen months before ; that the question appeared to you now a deeper one than you had then supposed, not to be decided by mere historical evidence but, to some extent, by the experience of life ; and that you were inclined at least so far to take my advice as to wait a while, to stand in the old ways, and to adhere—so far as you honestly could—to old religious habits, including the habit of prayer and attendance at public worship. This was as much as I could reasonably hope. I could not expect that a few letters from one who is quite conscious that he does not possess the strange and sometimes instantaneous influence exerted by a strong religious character, would do all that will, I trust, be done for you by patience, by a prayerful and laborious life devoted to good objects, and by cherishing habits of reverence for the good, and of thoughtfulness for all. I had been in the habit of regularly giving my Sundays, and occasionally some hours on week days, to our theological correspondence: but when I received that announcement from you, I felt that my time might now be devoted to other objects, and I made arrangements accordingly. Hence, when your recent letter reached me, I was not quite at leisure to reply to it immediately. But you pressed me to answer " one last question," which I should rather call two questions (for they are quite distinct, although you combine them so closely as to leave me uncertain whether you recognize the wide difference between them): "Can a man who rejects the miraculous element in the Bible remain a member or a minister in the Church of England?"

Your first question I should answer with an unhesitating affirmative. The Church of England does not require from its lay members any signature of the Articles or any test but a profession of belief in the Creed at the time of baptism, renewed in the Catechism and Confirmation service; and I cannot think that any sincere worshipper of Christ ought so far to take offence at one or two expressions in the Creed—which may be interpreted by him metaphorically, though by others literally—as to separate himself on that account from the national church. Grant that his interpretation may be a little strained, nay, grant even that he is obliged to say "I cannot believe this;" yet I should doubt the necessity, or even wisdom and rightness, of cutting himself off from the Church of England because of one or two clauses in the Creed, as long as he feels himself in general harmony with the Church doctrine and services. There would be no end to schisms, and no possibility of combining for worship, if everyone separated himself from every congregational utterance with which he could not heartily agree in every particular. On this point I find myself obliged to remember for my own sake, and to apply to myself, the advice I once gave a very little child many years ago. We were singing a hymn, and had come to the words :

> "Ah me, ah me, that I
> In Kedar's tents here stay :
> No place like that on high,
> Lord, thither guide my way."

" I suppose," said the child (who was young but somewhat old-fashioned in thought and expression), " that these words mean that you want to die, if they mean anything. But I don't want to die. So I don't think I ought to say them." In my own mind I sympathized very much with the objector ; but I endeavoured to meet the objection. " Hymns," I said, " are written not for single persons but for congregations. In a whole churchful you will find all sorts of people of different ages and ways of thinking. Some are glad and strong, others sad and weak. Some rejoice in life and look forward eagerly to labour. These are mostly the young ; but the older sort are sometimes tired of life and longing for rest. Now when we are singing a hymn we must all do our best, young and old, happy and sad, to enter into one another's feelings, and we must not expect that every word in every hymn will precisely represent our own particular feelings at the moment : the time will perhaps come when the words that now seem meaningless to us will exactly represent our deepest feelings, and we shall wonder how we could have ever failed to feel them ; but for the present we must not be disposed always to be asking, ' Do I agree with this? Do I exactly feel that ? ' Of course if it occurs to you that these or those words are so opposite to what you think, that you would be telling a lie to God in uttering them, why then you must not utter them : but you ought not to suppose that in a church service God exacts from you a rigid account for every word of the congregational utterances in which you take part : if you can heartily join in the greater part of the service, do not be afraid; He accepts your prayers and praises." Many years have passed away since I spoke thus: and, since then, I have found myself often obliged to repeat to myself, for my own guidance, the advice which I then gave to guide another. In a public service one must give and take, and I see no reason at all why a believer in non-miraculous Christianity should not find himself in harmony with the services of the Church of England. His interpretation both of the Bible and of the Prayer-book will be different from that of most of the congregation; but he will accept both the Bible and the Prayer-book as the best books that could be used for their several purposes, and would be sorry to see them replaced by anything that could be devised by himself or by those who think as he does.

So far I can speak confidently; but I am more doubtful as to the answer that should be given to your second question, "Can a believer in non-miraculous Christianity remain a minister in the Church of England?" Looking at the Articles, if I were forced to assume that every one of them is binding on a Church of England minister, I should say that a belief in the miraculous is necessary for every one who can honestly sign an assent to the Article on Christ's Resurrection, which asserts that, "Christ did truly rise again from death, and took again His body with flesh, bones, and all things appertaining to the perfection of man's nature, wherewith He ascended into heaven." These words distinctly declare the Resurrection of Christ's material body; and as I do not believe in the fact, I cannot assent to the words, nor do I see how any believer in non-miraculous Christianity can assent to them.

Perhaps you may think, in your innocence, that this disposes of the question, arguing logically thus: "The

Church of England appoints certain Articles as tests of belief for her ministers; A cannot assent to one of these Articles; therefore A has no right to remain a minister: there is no loophole out of this logical statement of the case." There is not: and if the Church of England were governed in accordance with logic, I (and a good many others) ought to have left the ranks of her ministers as soon as we found that we had been forced to reject a single clause of a single Article. But the Church has not been for several generations governed in this logical way. Besides practically and generally allowing among its members a great degree of freedom and latitude, it has enlarged that latitude during the last generation by a specific and authoritative alteration of the terms of subscription to the Articles. When I signed them—which I did, with perfect honesty and sincerity, some three or four and twenty years ago—we were obliged to "assent and consent" to "each and every" Article in each particular: I forget the exact terms, but I know they were as stringent as they well could be. But in 1865 the Clerical Subscription Act introduced a new form:—" I assent to the Thirty-nine Articles of Religion and to the Book of Common Prayer. . . . I believe the doctrine of the Church of England as therein set forth to be agreeable to the Word of God." Now if "therein" meant "in each and every clause of each and every Article," that would have been tantamount to a mere repetition of the old requirement. Obviously therefore this alteration implies an obligation of the subscriber to assent, no longer to "each and every Article" in particular, but to the Articles as a whole, regarded as an expression of Anglican doctrine. Consequently, at present, the necessity of subscription need not repel any one unless he finds himself unable to accept "the doctrine of the Church of England as set forth," not in detail, but generally, in the Articles and the

Prayer-book; and I need not say that a believer in non-miraculous Christianity by no means occupies a position of such dissent as this.

The only obstacle therefore for a scrupulous minister will be in the services of the Church and in the reading of the Bible: and here I admit that there is a very considerable obstacle, though it appears to me to be less than it was a dozen years ago, and each year lessens it still further. The difficulty lies, not in the scepticism of the minister (who may be a more faithful worshipper of Christ than any one in his flock) nor in any congregational suspicion or alarm (for his advanced views lie quite beyond the horizon of the thoughts of any country congregation, and any but an exceptional congregation elsewhere) but almost entirely in the minister's own uneasy sense of a difference between himself and his people; in his fear that he may be acting hypocritically; in his consequent loss of self-respect; and in a resulting demoralization affecting all his work.

Clearly this is a difficulty which would be diminished, if not altogether removed, by publicity; but as long as it is not publicly recognized that widely different interpretations of the Scripture are possible and compatible with the worship of Christ, the difficulty is a very serious one. Whenever such a man reads the Bible in the discharge of his public duty, he is liable to be haunted with the consciousness that he is two-faced. He conveys to his congregation an obvious meaning and they assume that he accepts that meaning himself; but he does not. Suppose, for example, he reads the story of the battle of Beth-horon: his congregation believes that it is listening to the most stupendous miracle that the world has witnessed; the minister believes that he is reading an account of one of the twenty, or more, decisive battles of history. Similarly, in the New Testament, if he reads the narrative of the feeding of the 4,000 or 5,000, he reads it as a religious legend, curiously preserving a deep spiritual truth, but of no value except for its emblematic meaning ; but his congregation listens to him as if he were reciting one of the most important proofs that Jesus was no mere man, but truly the Son of God. I do not wish to exaggerate the difference between the rationalizing minister and the literalizing congregation. Both he and they believe that in the battle of Beth-horon God was working out the destiny of Israel and preparing for Himself a chosen people ; both he and they believe that Jesus Christ was the true Bread of Life ; and similarly, as regards many other miraculous narratives of the Scriptures, the congregation and the minister, though divided as to the acceptance of the historical fact, will be united in accepting the spiritual interpretation which is the essence of the narrative. Moreover, every year is probably increasing the number of the laity who take the same esoteric view as the minister takes about many of the miracles. In any educated congregation there must be a large number of men, and there will soon be a large number of women, who do not believe in the literal stories of Balaam's ass, Elisha's floating axe-head, and Samson's exploit with the jaw-bone. Unless educated people are kept out of our churches, or separate themselves from the Church, this number must soon increase. Thus the gulf between the rationalizing minister and the congregation tends yearly to diminish through the action of the congregation ; and if only both the esoteric and the exoteric interpretation of the Scripture were generally recognized as being compatible with the faithful worship of Christ, I do not see why the minister should not claim for himself, without any sense of constraint or insincerity, the same freedom of interpreting the Bible which is accorded to the laity.

There still remains however the clause in the Creed stating the Miraculous Conception, which to me appears the greatest difficulty of all. It is one thing, in my judgment, to repeat the prayers of the Church and to read passages from the sacred books of the Church, as the mouthpiece of the congregation, and rather a different thing to stand up and say—not only as the mouthpiece of the congregation, but in your individual character, as a Christian, and as a priest as well—" I believe this, or that," and to take money for so saying ; while all the time you are saying under your breath, " But I only believe it metaphorically." Here, again, my scruples would be removed, if it were only generally understood that the metaphorical interpretation was possible and permissible. As regards the Athanasian Creed, for example, I should have no scruples at all. For the tone and spirit, as well as for the phraseology, of that Creed, I feel the strongest aversion. Yet I should repeat it as the mouthpiece of the congregation without any hesitation, because they would all know that the Church of England, so far as it can speak through the archbishops and bishops, has signified that the repulsive clauses in the Creed may all be so explained as practically to be explained away. I do not in the least believe that this mild interpretation of the damnatory clauses explains their original meaning ; but that matters little or nothing. Provided there be no suspicion of insincerity, I am willing to make considerable sacrifices of personal convictions in so complex a rite as congregational worship. The clergyman whom I most respect has not read the Athanasian Creed for thirty years: for my own sake, as a participator in the worship of his church, I rejoice ; but all my respect for him did not prevent me from doubting sometimes whether he was right in this matter, until I found that his action had been prompted by an expression of feeling on the part of some representative members of his congregation. For if one clergyman is justified in omitting the Athanasian Creed whenever he likes, I do not see why another is not justified in reading it whenever he likes: the liberty of the clergy might easily become the slavery of the laity. I should therefore be ready to read the repugnant Athanasian Creed because every member of my congregation would know (and I should feel justified in letting them know from the pulpit) that I read it in obedience to the law and in spite of my convictions. But I am not so ready, at present, to read the Apostles' Creed or Nicene Creed, although I cordially accept them except so far as concerns the one word which expresses the Miraculous Conception. My reason is, that I should not like to leave my congregation under the impression that I accepted that dogma, and on the other hand I should not feel justified in using a pulpit of the National Church to explain why I rejected it.

Here again, as in the previous instance, I feel that times are rapidly changing, and the freedom of ministers in the Church of England is rapidly increasing. For scruples as to the use of the Creeds, no less than for scruples as to the reading of the Scriptures, publicity is the chief remedy wanting to dissipate scruples; and time is on the side of freedom. Belief in miracles now rests on an inclined plane; friction is daily lessening, the downward motion is rapidly increasing; in a few more years the authorities of the Church of England may recognize, not with reluctance but with delight, that there are some young men who know enough of Greek, and of history, and of evidence, to be convinced that the miracles are unhistorical, and who, nevertheless, are worshippers of Christ on conviction, with a faith not to be shaken by anything that science or criticism can discover, and with a readiness to serve Christ, as ministers in the English Church, if they can do so without sacrifice of their opinions and without suspicion of insincerity.

Personally, I have not felt these scruples very acutely. Circumstances have placed me where nothing has been required of me which might not have been done as well by a Nonconformist as by a member of the Church of England. To help a friend, or do occasional work in an unofficial way, has never caused me the least misgiving; for I have always remained in cordial accord with the forms of worship current in the Church of England. The only difference that my views have made in my clerical action has been this, that I have preferred for a time not to place myself in any position where ministerial work might officially be required of me. Yet even these scruples have been doubtfully entertained, and would vanish altogether if ever I were to publish a volume of such letters as I am now writing to you, so that I could be sure that my opinions were no secret from my Bishop and from such members of my congregation as were likely to understand them.

The advice which I have given to myself, I should also be inclined to give to others who are already ministers in the Church of England, and who have scruples of conscience in consequence of some divergence from orthodox views: "Stay where you are, as long as you feel that you can sincerely worship Christ as the Eternal Son of God, and as long as you can preach a gospel of faith and strength, not only from the pulpit but also by the bedside of the dying. If you can do this, you may stay, though you are obliged to interpret metaphorically some expressions in the Creed. If you cannot do this, go at once, even though you can accept every syllable in all the Creeds in the most literal sense."

To young men who have not yet been ordained and who incline to "rational" views of Christianity, I have been disposed hitherto to give different advice: "Wait a while. The fashion of men's opinion is rapidly changing; the excessive fear of science on the part of the Clergy—many of whom come from Public Schools where they have received no training in the rudiments of science or mathematics—is, strange to say, predisposing all but extreme High Churchmen to welcome the adhesion of any who are firm believers in Christ, even though they may doubt or reject the miracles. It would be a miserable thing to be ordained, and to undertake the task of preaching a doctrine implying the highest conceivable morality, and presently to find yourself condemned by those to whom you should be an example as well as an instructor, for what appears to them patent insincerity—condemned by others, and perhaps not wholly acquitted by yourself. In a few years you may perhaps find it possible to be ordained not upon tolerance but with a hearty reception, and then there need be no concealment of your opinions."

Such is the language that I have hitherto used on the very few occasions when I have been consulted, generally advising delay. But now I am inclined to think that the time has come when young men with these opinions ought not to wait, but ought at least to set their case before the Bishops, leaving it to them to accept or refuse them as candidates for ordination. Schisms and prosecutions are very objectionable things, but there are worse evils even than these. There is the danger of hypocrisy, spreading, like an infection, from oneself to others. The hour has perhaps come for authorizing or condemning the extreme freedom of opinion which some of the Broad Churchmen have assumed. Proverbs and texts might be quoted in equal abundance to justify action or inaction in the abstract; but two important practical considerations appear to me to dictate some kind of action without delay.

On the one hand, we hear the complaint that the ablest

and most conscientious men are deterred by scruples from entering the ministry in the Church of England, even when they feel a strong bent for clerical work. If this scarcity of able candidates for ordination continues for many more years, we shall have bad times in store for us. Already I think I have noted, among some ministers who are conscious of but little intellectual and not much more spiritual power, a disposition unduly to magnify their office, the ritual, the mechanical use of the sacraments, parochial machinery, processions, sensational hymns, church salvation-armies, and church-routine generally, because they feel they have no evangelic message of their own, no individual inspiration. In some degree, such a subordination of self is good and may argue modesty; but in many cases it is not good, when it leads young men to materialize and sensualize religion, to suppose that the preaching of Christ's Gospel and the elevation of the souls of men can be effected by ecclesiastical battalion drill; to dispense with study, thought, and observation; to acquiesce in the letter of the collected dogmas of the past, and to hope for no new spiritual truth from the progress of the ages controlled by the ever fresh revelations of the Spirit of God.

On the other hand, there is the opposite evil, on which I have already touched—I mean the danger that some of the more intellectual among the clergy, those who do not sympathize with sacerdotalism and are popularly reckoned among the "Broad Church," may not only be suspected of insincerity in professing to believe what they, as a fact, disbelieve, but may also become actually demoralized by self-suspicions and hence indirectly demoralize their congregations. I confess my sympathies are very much with a man in that position. He has been sometimes the victim of cruel circumstances. In his youth, the religious problems of the present day lay all in the background. Before he was ordained, he may very well have discerned no difficulties at all in the career before him, nothing but the prospect of a noble work, to which he felt himself called. His life was probably spent in a public boarding-school, where he scarcely ever had a minute to himself for thought and meditation; it being the ideal of the educator so to engross the time and energy of each pupil in studies or in games that the average youth might be kept out of moral mischief and the clever youth might get a scholarship at Oxford or Cambridge. When he came to the University he found himself expected to devote himself to "reading for a degree," and there was little or no time for 'theology; after taking his degree he found himself under the necessity of earning his living, and if he was intending to become a clergyman he naturally desired to be ordained as soon as possible. If he was very fortunate, he may have contrived (as I did) to get a year's reading at theology while he supported himself by taking pupils; but that was probably the utmost of his preparation. Soon after reaching his twenty-third year he was ordained. And now, for the first time, leaving school and college, he begins to realize what life means, and to think for himself. Can we wonder that this "thinking for himself" produces considerable changes of thought? If he is healthy, and active in his parish, and has not much time for reflection and reading, the changes will be long deferred, and he will be scarcely conscious of them: but if he has any mind at all in him, and gives it the least exercise, it is hardly possible that an able and honest student of the Bible at the age of forty-six, when he comes to compare the opinions of his manhood with those of his youth, will not find that he has ceased to believe, or at all events to be certain of, the historical accuracy of a good deal which he accepted with unquestioning confidence at the age of twenty-three.

Changes of this kind are inevitable, and they ought not to be feared. Yet perhaps the fear of them deters some of the more thoughtful young men from presenting themselves for ordination. They know that they believe in such and such facts now, but, say they, "Many sincere and thoughtful persons dispute the truth of these facts; and what will be my position some ten years hence if I find that I am driven to deny what I now affirm?" What one would like to be able to reply, in answer to such an appeal, would be, that the worship of Christ does not depend upon the truth of a few isolated and disputable pieces of evidence, but upon the testimony of the conscience based upon indisputable (though complex) evidence; so that, if the man's conscience remains the same, he need not fear lest the fundamental principles of his faith will be shaken by any historical or scientific criticism. From the terrestrial point of view, Christ is human nature at its divinest. Whoever therefore in the highest degree loves and trusts and reveres human nature at its divinest, he naturally worships a representation of Christ, even though he may never have heard of the name. Now life will bring a young man many disappointments and disillusions and paradoxes: but no one, who has once worshipped Christ in this natural way, need fear (or hope?) that life will ever bring him anything more worthy of representing human nature at its divinest, anything therefore more worthy of worship, than Jesus of Nazareth. The only danger is, that one may cease to be able to love and trust and revere the objects that deserve these feelings. There is indeed that danger, just as there is the danger that one may cease to be able to be honest. But what young man, in mapping out his future, would make insurance against such a moral paralysis? A man ought no more—a man ought still less—to contemplate the possibility of becoming unable to worship Christ, than the possibility of becoming unable to revere a kind father or love affectionate children. If then our candidate for ordination regards Christ in this spirit, one would like to encourage him to present himself for ordination even though he may already doubt the Biblical narrative on some points, and though he may be pretty certain that he will change his mind on many others by the time he is twice as old as he is now. However it rests very much with Bishops to settle this question; and the question as to what the Bishops might do is so important as to demand a separate letter.

P.S. Since writing the above remarks about the reluctance of the ablest men at the Universities to be ordained, I have been told that the state of things is even worse than I had conceived at Cambridge. There, at the two largest colleges, Trinity and St. John's, I am told that of the Fellows who took their degrees between 1873-9 only eight, out of sixty or thereabouts, took holy orders; and of those who took degrees between 1880-6, only three out of sixty. Trinity is conspicuous; of the sixty Fellows who took degrees from 1873-86 only two have been ordained.

XXXI

My dear ——,

I reminded you in my last letter that ordination or non-ordination must largely depend upon the judgment of the Bishops. This, I suppose, must have always been the case to some extent: but there are reasons why it may well be so now to a greater extent than before. The important change made in the form of subscription to the Thirty-nine Articles has supplied a solid and definite ground upon which the Bishops may fairly claim to ascertain from candidates for ordination some details about their religious opinions. In the times when candidates had to assent to every point in every Article, no further examination was necessary: but now that the candidate is allowed (by implication) to dissent from some things in the Articles, the Bishop may surely, without any inquisitorial oppression, say: "Before I ordain you, I should like to know, in a general way, how far your dissent from the Articles extends." Some Bishops may be inclined to shrink from such an interrogation, as though it implied doubt of the candidate's sincerity: and of course such an examination might be abused in a narrow or bigoted or even tyrannical manner. But on the whole, I think, it might be even more useful as a protection and help to the young candidate than to the Bishop. Here and there, perhaps, a young man might be advised to give up, or defer, the prospect of ordination; but others (who would have otherwise been deterred by scruples) might be encouraged to be ordained in spite of some intellectual difficulties ; and this fatherly encouragement from a man of authority and experience would be a great help and comfort, strengthening the young man in the conviction that mere intellectual difficulties could not interfere with his faith in Christ. Still more valuable would be the young man's consciousness that he could not be called insincere or hypocritical, since he had concealed nothing from the Bishop, who, after hearing all, had decided that there was nothing to exclude him from ordination.

I would therefore advise any man who desired to be ordained but was deterred by present scruples or the fear of future scruples, to write at an early period to the Bishop at whose hands he would be likely to seek ordination, stating his difficulties frankly and fully, and asking whether they would be considered an impediment. If he felt any touch of doubt on the subject of the miracles, I would have him make them the subject of a special question. In some dioceses I should expect the answer to be unfavourable. From others perhaps the answer would come that the Bishop was " unwilling to undertake so heavy a responsibility; each man must decide for himself whether he can honestly read the services of the Church and the lessons from the Scriptures without believing in miracles." That answer would be, in my judgment, regrettable, though not unnatural or indefensible. But even that answer would be of value, as it would be a record that, at all events, the Bishop had not been kept in ignorance of anything that the candidate ought to have revealed to him : and this in itself would be of great value in lightening for a scrupulous and self-introspective young man the burden of the questions which might sometimes arise in his mind as he read aloud in the congregation the words of the Bible or the

Prayer-book. Moreover, I should anticipate that every year would see an increase in the number of those dioceses from which a still more favourable answer might be returned: "If with all your heart you worship Christ as the Eternal Son of God, if you can honestly and sincerely accept the Church services as excellent (though imperfect) expressions of congregational worship; and the Scriptures as super-excellent (though imperfect) expressions of spiritual fact; if you feel that you have a message of good news for the poor and simple as well as for the rich and educated, and that you can preach the spiritual truths which you and all of us recognize to be the essence of the Gospel, without attacking those material shapes in which, for many generations to come, all spiritual truths must find expression for the vast majority of Christians, then I can encourage you to come to the ministry of Christ. I myself am of the old school and believe in the miracles, or if not in all, at all events in most; but I recognize that this belief—though to me it seems safer and desirable—is not essential: come therefore to the ministry, with the miracles if you can, without them if you cannot."

Here indeed is a reasonable criterion of fitness for ordination: and if a man cannot satisfy this, I do not see how he can complain of being excluded. But no other criterion seems likely to be permanently tenable. For imagine yourself to be a Bishop, trying to lay down some short, precise, and convenient test, as regards the belief in the miraculous: where are you to draw the line? A young man, eminently fit in all respects for ministerial work, comes to you and says that he accepts all the miracles but one; he cannot bring himself to believe that Joshua stopped the movement of the sun (or earth). What are you to do? Reject him? Surely not: not even though you were Canon Liddon, raised (as I hope he will be raised) to the episcopal bench. The Universities would join in protest against your bigotry; the whole of educated society would secede from the Church on such conditions: the masses of non-Christian and semi-Christian working men would cry out that such a rejection was a portent of tyranny, and that the men who could accept admission to the priesthood on such terms as these were no better than superstitious dolts and slaves, creatures to be suppressed in a free country! Well, then, you admit him: will you reject his younger brother next year, who finds that he cannot accept the miracle of Balaam's ass speaking with a human voice? Certainly you will admit him too. And now where are you to stop? If you admit a man who denies two miracles, will you accept a man who denies a third, say, the miracle of Elisha's floating axe-head? And if three, why not four? why not five? and so on to the end of the list?

Again, a man comes to you and says that he feels obliged to reject as an interpolation—although willing to read them as part of an erroneous but long cherished tradition—the well-known words at the end of the Lord's Prayer, "for thine is the kingdom, the power and the glory, for ever and ever:" what will you do to him? Refuse him? Surely not. The Revisers of the New Testament have themselves rejected the addition, and I am quite sure no scholar who valued God's Word, and certainly no Bishop, would wish to reject a man for preferring the New Version of the Bible to the Old. But, if you admit him, what are you to say to his companion, who rejects also the last twelve verses of St. Mark's Gospel? In my opinion, a man must be, Hellenistically speaking, an "idiot,"—a Greek "idiot," what the Greeks call *idiotès*—to believe in their genuineness. But even though you, being a busy Bishop, may have forgotten a good deal of Greek, you cannot forget the decision of the Revisers. For here again the Revisers are on the young man's side. They have printed this passage as a kind of Appendix, placing an interval between it and the Gospel, and appending this note: "The two oldest Greek MSS. and some older authorities, omit from verse 9 to the end. Some other authorities have a different ending to the Gospel." Now if you admit the rejecter of these two passages, will you refuse his companion, who tells you he is compelled to agree with the Revisers also as to a third passage, John vii. 53—viii. 11, where the Revised Version brackets several verses, adding this note, "Most of the ancient authorities omit John vii. 53—viii. 11. Those which contain it vary much from each other"? You must certainly accept him. But if you accept him, what are you to say to young men who go further and reject whole books of the New Testament, for example, the Second Epistle of St. Peter; the genuineness of which has been impeached by a great consent of authorities, and concerning which Canon Westcott says that it is the "one exception" to the statement that the combined canons of the Eastern and Western Churches would produce "a perfect New Testament"? And if we let him pass, under Canon Westcott's wing, how shall we deal with the next candidate, who reminds us that Luther rejected the Apocalypse and the Epistle of St. James, and declares that he cannot help agreeing with Luther? What lastly is to be the fate of those who avow that they cannot shut their eyes to the traces, even in the Synoptic Gospels, of considerable interpolations or late traditions, especially in those portions which contain miraculous narrative? Perhaps we might feel inclined to say, "We will take our stand on Westcott and Hort's text, or on the text of the Revised Version, and will refuse any candidate who rejects a word of the New Testament that is contained in either of these texts; the line must be drawn somewhere, and we will draw it there."

What! Shall we reject a candidate for ordination because he does not accept the Gospel according to Westcott and Hort, or the Gospel according to an unauthorized though scholarly knot of men called the Revisers? Impossible! all Christendom would cry shame upon us. On the whole, we seem driven to the conclusion that no candidate for Anglican ordination can be reasonably rejected for believing that parts of the Bible are spurious or un-historical, provided that he is willing to read in the presence of the congregation the portions of Scripture appointed by the Church.

If the test of miracles fails, and if the test of an infallible book fails, so too does failure await the test of an infallible Creed. It would be, at all events, departing strangely from the spirit of the Reformers and from the spirit of the Articles, to allow men laxity as regards the interpretation of the Scriptures, which are regarded as specially inspired, and yet to pin them to the letter of the Creeds, which are regarded as being authoritative because they are based on the Scriptures. If a candidate were to tell you, his Bishop, that " he accepted the Resurrection of Christ, and even of Christ's body, but that he could not honestly say that Christ rose on the third day; for Christ was buried on the evening of Friday, and rose early on the morning of Sunday, that is to say, on the second day," you would perhaps reason with him, and say that it was the Jewish way of reckoning; and if he were then to reply to you that to the greater part of the congregation this way of reckoning was unknown, and that the phrase might therefore convey a false impression—what would you say to this ultra-conscientious young man? This probably: that "the Creeds of Christendom could not be disturbed on account of the eccentricities of well-meaning individuals; that, if this was his only obstacle, you, his Bishop, could take upon yourself to justify him in repeating these words as the mouthpiece of the congregation; that it was quite open to him to explain the true meaning of the words from the pulpit; and that little misunderstandings of this kind, if indeed there was danger of any, were insignificant as compared with belief in the essential fact that Jesus rose from the dead."

When the young man goes out—probably satisfied, unless he is very obstinate, and you a little impatient—let us suppose that another man comes in, with a different objection to the same clause. He accepts the essential fact that Jesus rose from the dead, and he does not object to the words, "the third day," but he does not believe that the material body of Jesus rose from the tomb. He believes that Jesus Himself, that is to say, His spirit, rose from the dead, and that He manifested Himself to His disciples in a spiritual body, which, in accordance with some law of our human spiritual nature, was manifested to those, and only to those, who loved Him or believed in Him.[1] This is a more serious objection by far: for you have to consider, first, whether the young man is likely to hold fast his belief in the spiritual Resurrection of Jesus, when based on such evidence as this; and secondly whether he can preach the Gospel of the risen Saviour without raising all sorts of questions and difficulties in minds unprepared to grapple with them. At this point, then, I cannot blame your episcopal judgment if you take time to decide, and if, before deciding, you do your best to ascertain what manner of man you have to deal with, and, in particular, whether his stability is equal to his ability. "Doubts and difficulties" may sometimes betoken, not so much a mind that thinks for itself, as a disposition to affect singularity and to strain after constant novelty. But if you are satisfied on this point, I think you would do well to admit him to ordina-

---

[1] For the apparent exception of St. Paul, see above, p. 244.

tion. I would not exclude from the ministry any one who can conscientiously worship Christ in accordance with the services of the Church of England, and preach the Gospel without shaking the faith of the masses.

Perhaps I shall seem to you (not now in the temporary episcopal capacity which you have occupied during the last few paragraphs, but as plain ———) very illiberal in excluding from the broad boundaries of the National Church those who are unable to worship Christ. But I am not prepared to alter the Nicene Creed or the Church Services; and if I could not worship Christ, I cannot think that I myself should desire to be included in the Church of England, as long as that Creed and the Church Services remained in use. For how could I offer prayer to Jesus? or say, in any sense, "I believe in Jesus Christ, God of God, Light of Light, very God of very God"? No plea of metaphor would ever enable me to repeat these words with any honesty, as long as I found myself unable to worship Christ. I confess to a secret feeling that many of those who at the present time think they do not worship Christ, do in reality worship Him; and I have good hopes that some of them may, in time, when they search out their deepest feelings, find out that they have long been unconsciously worshipping Him, and that they can accept, with a spiritual interpretation, some things that have hitherto appeared to them inadmissible.[1] But to demand that the Creeds and Church Services may be remoulded, is a very different thing from asking to be allowed to put a metaphorical interpretation on one or

[1] You should look at a most interesting and instructive article by Dr. Martineau in the *Christian Reformer* (vol. i. p. 78), in which he points out that, in a certain sense, the faith professed by Trinitarians "in the Son, is so far from being an idolatry, that it is identical, under change of name, with the Unitarian worship of Him who dwelt in Christ. He who is the Son in one creed is the Father in the other; and the two are agreed, not indeed by any means *throughout*, but in that which constitutes the pith and kernel of both faiths."

two phrases in them. When Parochial Councils are established, it may be found ultimately possible to give some larger latitude in the modification or multiplication of Services so as to make them more inclusive: but, after all, congregations meet for worship, not for the sake of being liberal and inclusive; and the inclusion of non-worshippers of Christ can hardly be demanded from a Church that worships Christ. Nor must the inclusion of "advanced thinkers" be carried to such an extent as to exclude the great mass of ordinary believers.

I myself, deeply though I sympathize in all essential matters with the Church of England, should nevertheless be willing not only to be excluded from it, but also to see excluded all who may take the same views as I take, rather than that the simple faith in Christ entertained by the great body of Christians should be injured by the premature disruption of those material beliefs and integumentary illusions with which, at present, their spiritual beliefs are inseparably connected. And this brings me to another side of the question. If I were publishing an appeal to the Bishops, I should certainly add an appeal to the younger Broad Church clergy. It ought not to be asking too much from a young preacher who is an "advanced thinker," to remember that some reverence is due to the simpler members of his flock. Many of those whom he authoritatively instructs are older, wiser at present, of larger experience in life, some of them perhaps more spiritually minded, than he is. What if their deepest and most cherished religious convictions, right in the main, are tied to certain expressions and narratives that may not be historically accurate? Does it follow that their feelings are to be outraged at any moment by assaults upon the ancient forms and expressions of their belief from the lips of a young man who professes to accept these forms, and takes the money of the Church for accepting them? Such attacks upon the forms are at present worse than useless, because they are sure to be construed into attacks upon the spirit. In time a change will come, and even now a minister may do something to prepare the way for the change. He may institute Bible lectures to which he may invite the attendance of those alone who wish to study the Bible critically, and those whose reading and attainments qualify them to criticize, or to follow criticism. But, from the pulpit, matter of this kind should be altogether excluded.

Nor need the preacher fear lest such restriction should shackle his liberty and take the life out of his sermons. In almost every case one invariable rule can be laid down which will give ample scope to him and no offence to his hearers: "Always preach what you believe to be true, and never go out of your way in order to attack what you believe to be untrue." For example, your flock believes that Christ's body (the tangible body) was raised from the grave; you do not. Well then, do not attack their material belief; but preach your spiritual belief. Teach them that Christ's Resurrection implies a real though invisible triumph over the invisible enemy death; a real, though invisible, sitting at the right hand of God; a real, though invisible, presence in the heart of every one who loves and trusts Him. Thus you may teach the habit of reverence, simultaneously with the habit of inquiry; a love of the old forms, combined with a still deeper love of the new truths that may be discovered beneath them; thus you will not shake the faith of a single child; you will be impressing upon all alike unadulterated, precious truth without sacrificing a tittle of your own convictions; and at the same time you will be insensibly preparing the younger portion of your flock to detach the material part of their belief from the spiritual, and to retain the latter when the time may come that shall force them to give up the former. In a similar spirit you should deal with the Ascension and the Incarnation, not pointing out the difficulties involved in the material belief of those dogmas, nor saying a word to disparage those who believe in them, but doing your utmost to bring out the spiritual truths and invisible processes which are represented by those dogmas. Surely such a self-restraint as this is not more than may fairly be demanded from any honourable man, I will not say from a Christian, but from a gentleman. Your congregation are in their own parish church; they are bound by conventional respect and by deeply-rooted reverence for tradition and for the House of God, not to manifest any such open disapprobation of your teaching as would be freely permissible at a public meeting; you are their servant, and the servant, the paid servant, of the National Church; and yet you have them at your mercy while you stand in the pulpit. Profound consideration may fairly be expected from you for their prejudices, as you may please to call them; and all the more because they are, as it were, in possession of the church, while you are an innovator, holding what must—at all events for some time to come—appear to the multitude an entirely new doctrine: they "stand on the old ways."

If the teachers of natural or non-miraculous Christianity could be trusted to preach in this spirit, they might, I think, do a good work as ministers in the Church of England, without injury to themselves, and with much advantage to the nation. If not, they must come out of the Church for the purposes of teaching; and that, I fear, would result in mischief both for the Church and for the State. I believe that not a few of the educated clergy are either suspending their belief about miracles, or have decided against them;

and if these were suddenly to be banished, or gradually to drop out of the clerical ranks without receiving any successors of their way of thinking, the gulf would be widened between the clergy and the educated laity. The men who might discover new religious truth and prepare the way for new religious development, having henceforth to earn their living in other ways, would find little leisure for critical study. The end would be that the nation would be for a time divided between superstition and agnosticism ; and sober religion would go to the wall.

Not indeed that the destinies of the Gospel of Christ are to be supposed to be permanently determinable by the fate of a fraction of the Broad Church section of the English clergy ! The attraction of the natural worship of Christ—strange, nay, impossible though it may seem when first presented to the miracle-craving mind—is far too great to admit the possibility of its ultimate failure. But first there must come a vast and depressing defection on the part of those nominal Christians who have hitherto worshipped Christ on the basis of an infallible Church, or on the basis of an infallible Book, or on the basis of indisputable Miracles. Perhaps this collapse will be precipitated by the discovery of a copy of some Gospel of the first century, turned up when Constantinople is evacuated by the Turks. You cannot have forgotten how this year (1885) the educated religious world in England held its breath in horrible suspense when the correspondent of the *Times* telegraphed that among the Egyptian manuscripts recently purchased by an Austrian arch-duke, there had been disinterred a fragment belonging to a Gospel preceding, and differing from, any now extant. From this terrible discovery orthodoxy was delivered, for this once, by the learning of Professor Hort : but who shall guarantee that a Professor Hort shall be able, or even willing, to deny the proto-evangelic claims of the next-discovered manuscript from the East? And then, what will become of some of us!

In any case, with or without such discoveries, the present word-faith, and book-faith, and authority-faith in the Lord Jesus, must sooner or later collapse; and people must be driven to the conclusion that the Lord Jesus Himself must somehow be worshipped through Himself—Jesus through the Spirit of Jesus, that Spirit which is apparent in families and nations and Churches as well as in the New Testament, the Spirit of Love whence springs that mutual helpfulness which in the New Testament we call "fellowship" and in the newspapers "socialism." This and this alone will help us to apply our science to settle land questions, Church questions, and war questions, policy domestic and foreign, and to establish concord in the world, the nation, and the human heart. I do not say that a time will ever come when there will be no obstacles to faith in Christ. Moral obstacles will still exist to make faith difficult: but some at least of the intellectual difficulties by which we now shut ourselves out from Christian hope will then be dissipated. *Odium theologicum* will become meaningless. There will have arrived at last that blessed time, predicted (1603) by Francis Bacon (shall we say just three hundred years too soon?), bringing with it "the consumption of all that can ever be said in controversies of religion;" and henceforth there will be no "controversies," only discussions and discoveries.

Then, with its mind freed from superstitious terrors and full of an unquenchable hope, the human race, owning its allegiance to the Eternal Goodness, and accepting as its captain the Working Man of Nazareth, will address itself steadily to the work of Christian socialism, honouring and encouraging labour without unwise and spasmodic pampering of it, dishonouring and discouraging idleness without unwise and direct recourse to forcible suppression of it; remembering always that, as the ideal Working Man was subject to law, so must they be subject to law, and as He bore suffering for the good of others, so must they be prepared to suffer as well as to work. This is true socialism and this is true Christianity. Do you deny it, and say, "This is not the Christianity that has been current for eighteen centuries"? I reply, Perhaps not; and, if it is not, we can call it by some other name. You remember the saying of Lessing, that after eighteen centuries of Christianity, it was high time to try Christ. Let us then amend our phrase and say that true socialism will not be "the Christian religion" but something better. It will be the Christian Spirit.

We are taught by our Scriptures that it has been sometimes God's method to teach the wise in this world by means of those whom the world calls foolish, and the strong and the rich in this world by those whom the world calls weak and poor. If history is thus to repeat itself, it may be reserved for the semi-Christian or non-Christian working man, for the heretic or agnostic socialist, to guide orthodox and religious England into a higher and purer and more spiritual form of Christianity. Yet on the other hand, since intellectual movements come often from above, though moral movements come from below, I cannot give up the hope that it may be reserved for the clergy of the Church of England to do something towards the removal of those merely intellectual difficulties which are at present keeping multitudes of the workers, and not a few of the thinkers, in our country, from recognizing their true Deliverer.

DEFINITIONS

i. Reality

1. *Absolute reality cannot be comprehended by men, and can only be apprehended as God or in God by a combination of Desire and Imagination, to which we give the name of Faith.*
2. *Among objects of sensation those are (relatively) real which present similar sensations in similar circumstances.*

ii. Force

"Imagined" is inserted, throughout these Definitions, as a reminder that the existence of all these objects of definition, however real, is suggested to us by the Imagination.

Force is that which is imagined to immediately produce, or tend to produce, motion.

Why "immediately"? Because a particle of "matter" —attracting, as it does, every other particle of "matter"— may be said to "tend to produce motion." Yet "matter" is not said to *be* force, but to "*exert*" force. "Matter" is imagined to attract "matter" through the medium of force, or "mediately." But force is imagined to act "immediately." Hence the insertion of the word.

B B

iii. Cause and Effect

When one thing is imagined to produce, or tend to produce, a second, the first is called the Cause of the second, and the second the Effect of the first.

iv. Spirit

Spirit, i.e. Breath or Wind, is a metaphorical name—implying subtleness, invisibility, ubiquitousness and life-giving power—given to the ultimate Cause of Force; and hence sometimes to the Cause of beneficent Force in the Universe, i.e. God; sometimes to the Cause of Force in the human individual; more rarely to the Cause or Causes of maleficent Forces in the Universe.

v. Matter

The existence of Matter has never been proved; and it is nothing but a hypothesis. All the phenomena called "material" might be explained, without Matter, by the hypothesis of a number of centres of force. The *raison d'être* of Matter is the notion of tangibility. But scientific men now tell us that no atom ever touches another. If this be so, scientific tangibility disappears and the *raison d'être* of Matter disappears, with it. But it is so natural a figment that we shall all probably talk about it, and most of us probably will believe in it, until human nature is very much changed.

Matter cannot be defined positively except by repeating, in some disguise, the word to be defined, as thus:—

Material, or Matter, is a name given to an unascertained and hypothetical "material," "matter, "*substance,*" or "*fundamental stuff,*" of which we commonly imagine all objects of sensation to be composed.

vi. Nature

1. *Nature means sometimes the* (1) *ordinary, or* (2) *orderly course of things apart from the present and direct intervention of human Will; sometimes the* (3) *ordinary or* (4) *orderly course of humanity; sometimes the* (5) *ordinary or* (6) *orderly course of all things.*
2. *Law of Nature is a metaphorical name for a frequently observed sequence of phenomena* (*apart from human Will*), *implying, to some minds, regularity; to others, absolute invariability.*
3. *Miracle means a supposed suspension of a Sequence, or Law, of Nature; Marvel, or Mighty Work, means a rare Sequence of Nature, in which great Effects are produced by Causes seemingly, but not really, inadequate.*
4. "*Supernatural*" *is the name given, in these letters, to the existence of a God; and to His creation and continuous development of all things: the divine action being regarded, not as contrary to Nature, but as above Nature; not as suspending the sequences of Nature, but as originating and supporting them.*

vii. Will

The Will is the power of giving to some one of our desires, or to some one group of compatible desires, permanent predominance over the rest.

An addition might be suggested: "the power of controlling our desires." But we appear never to control our desires except by enthroning some one desire (or group of desires)—whether it be the desire to gain power, to ruin an enemy, to do right, or to serve God.

viii. Attention

Attention is the power by which we impress upon our mind that which is present.

ix. Memory

Memory is the power by which we retain or recall to our mind that which is past.

x. Imagination

Imagination is the power by which we combine or vary the mental images retained by Memory, often with a view to finding some unity in them; and by which we are enabled to image forth the future through anticipating its harmony with the past and present.

xi. Reason

Reason (or, as some prefer to call it in this limited sense, Understanding) is the power by which we compare, and, from our comparisons, draw inferences or conclusions. By means of it we compare the suggestions of the Imagination with the suggestions of Experience, and accept or reject the former in accordance with the result of our comparison.

xii. Hope

Hope is desire, of which we imagine the fulfilment, while recognizing the presence of doubt.

xiii. Faith

The following Definition appears to me to be the basis of all theology. It is no more than an emphatic restatement of the old saying, " Faith is the *assurance of* (or *giving substance to*) things *hoped for."* Since *hope* is but a weaker and more hesitant form of *desire*, the *imaging forth of* (or *giving substance to*) things earnestly *hoped for* must imply the vivid *imagination* of the fulfilment of things *desired*.

Faith (when not loosely used for Belief) is desire (approved by the Conscience) of which we imagine the fulfilment, while putting doubt at a distance.

" *Faith* in a friend " means a *desire*—as well as a belief —that he will do what you think he ought to do. " Faith " should never be used to express a belief that something undesirable or wrong will happen, *e.g.* " I have great *faith* that the boy will go wrong." " Faith " in the uniformity of Nature implies a desire that Nature should be uniform, and a feeling that it is God's will. In moments when we dread the uniformity of Nature we should say that we have a " conviction " or " expectation " of it, not that we have " faith " in it.

" Putting doubt at a distance is intended to include the different degrees of faith: in the highest faith, the " distance " is infinite.

"When "faith" is said to be "shaken," we may mean that, though the desire may remain, doubt is not "put at a distance;" or that the Conscience no longer approves of the desire; or that the desire itself is weakened.

xiv. Belief

Belief (when it is not used for Faith) means a sense, mixed with doubt, that the affirmations of our mind will harmonize with Experience.[1]

xv. Certainty, or Conviction

Certainty, or Conviction, is a sense, unmixed with doubt, that the affirmations of our mind will harmonize with Experience.

xvi. Knowledge

1. *Absolute knowledge, which is possessed by no man, would be an identity between our mental affirmations and those of the Creator; who knows all things in their Essence and Causes.*
2. *Knowledge (relative and ordinary) is (very often) a name loosely given to a harmony between our mental affirmations and the affirmations of the vast majority of those who have (or are thought by the majority to have) the best opportunities for observation and judgment.*

   It might be more usefully defined as those mental

---

[1] Some might prefer "harmonize with experience *or with fact.*" But "harmony with *fact*" can *never* be proved: you can only prove harmony with your experience, or with the general experience, of the fact; or with experience of what others say about the fact.

affirmations which harmonize with our nature and environment, i.e. with our spiritual and material experience.

xvii. Illusions and Delusions

Illusions are mental affirmations not harmonizing with immediate experience, but preparatory for absolute knowledge. Delusions are mental affirmations not harmonizing with experience, nor preparatory for absolute knowledge

THE END

www.ingramcontent.com/pod-product-compliance
Lightning Source LLC
Chambersburg PA
CBHW030341230426
43664CB00007BA/489